IMAGES
of America

MORRISVILLE

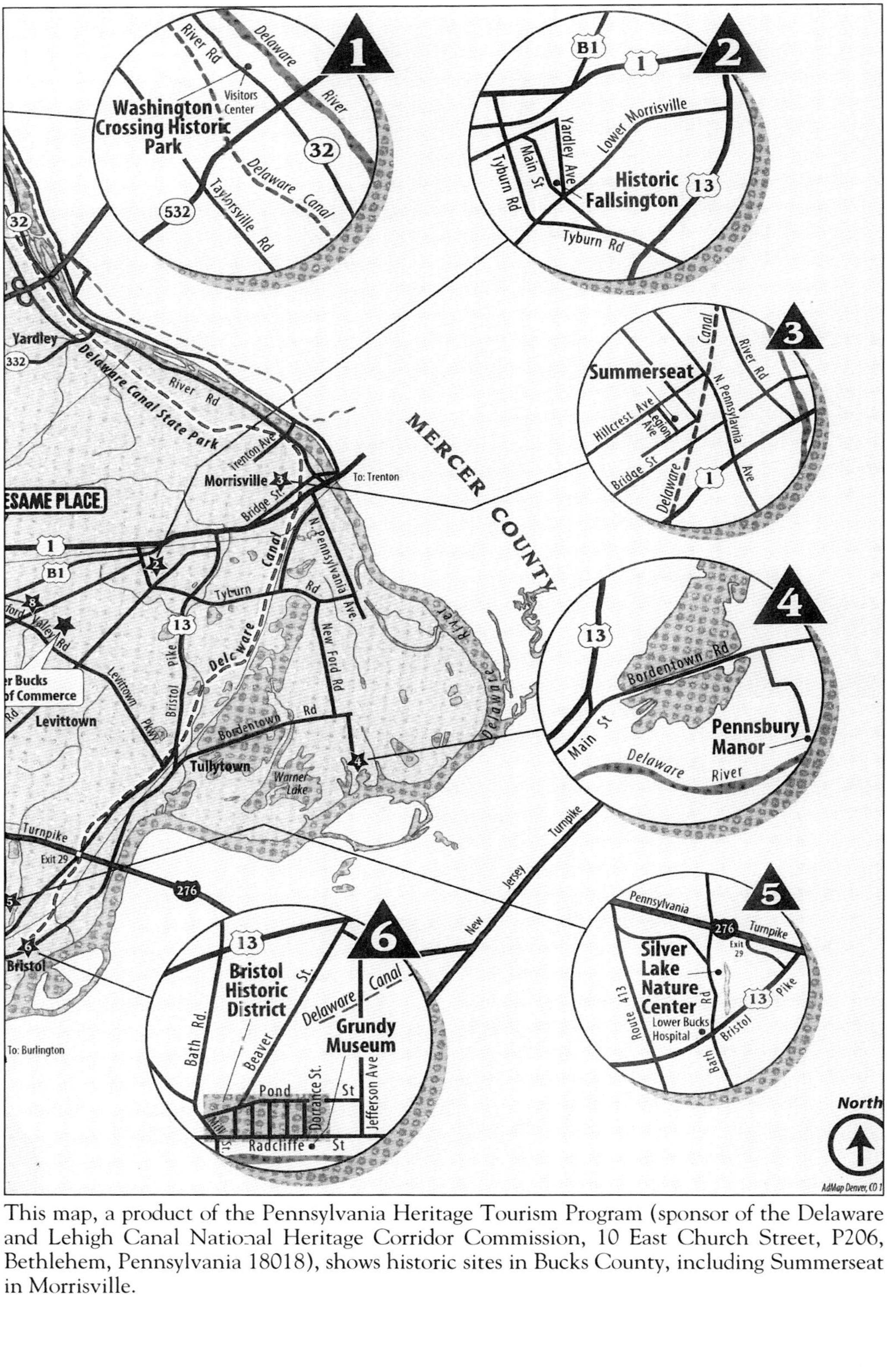

This map, a product of the Pennsylvania Heritage Tourism Program (sponsor of the Delaware and Lehigh Canal National Heritage Corridor Commission, 10 East Church Street, P206, Bethlehem, Pennsylvania 18018), shows historic sites in Bucks County, including Summerseat in Morrisville.

IMAGES
of America

MORRISVILLE

James A. Murray Jr.

ARCADIA
PUBLISHING

ISBN 978-0-7385-9020-2

Published by Arcadia Publishing
Charleston, South Carolina

Printed in the United States of America

For all general information contact Arcadia Publishing at:
Telephone 843-853-2070
Fax 843-853-0044
E-mail sales@arcadiapublishing.com
For customer service and orders:
Toll-Free 1-888-313-2665

Visit us on the Internet at www.arcadiapublishing.com

Contents

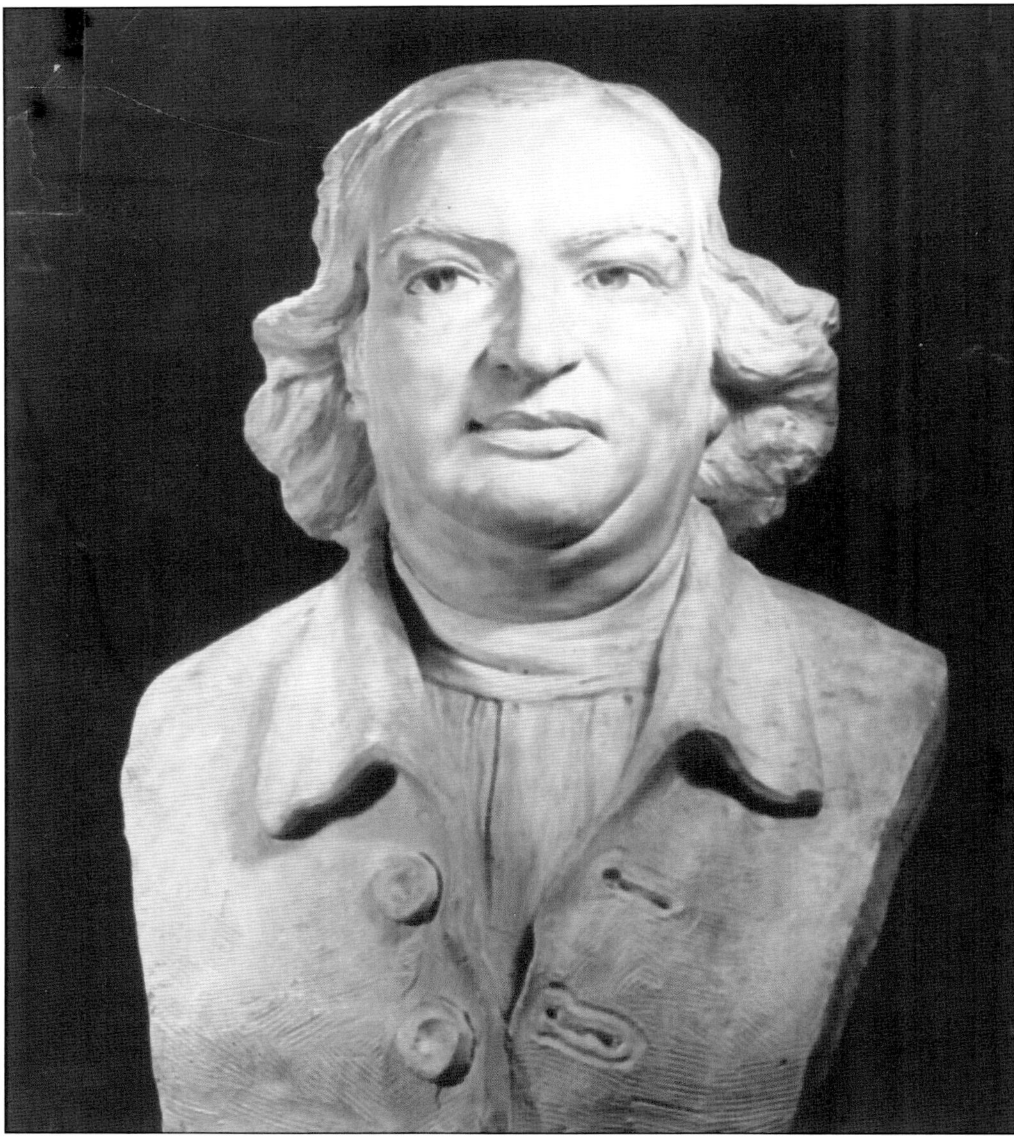

This bust of Robert Morris, from whom Morrisville takes its name, was made by H.C. Mueller of the National Tile Company, who presented it to the borough during its centennial celebration in 1904. Morris played a major role in the War for Independence by cosigning for the government when the nation's credit was nonexistent. For example, responding to George Washington's appeal for financial help, Morris obtained $50,000 with his personal guarantee and enabled the general to keep his army together and cross the Delaware to campaign successfully in New Jersey in 1776 and 1777.

Introduction

"The Falls of the Delaware"—Almost the Capital of the U.S.

Before it was Crewcorne, Colvin's Ferry, or Morrisville, the area at the falls of the Delaware River in Bucks County, Pennsylvania, became the starting point for land measurement in the Keystone State. An outcropping of massive gray boulders is marked by a monument and bronze tablet stating that "Near this spot stood the white oak tree that marked the starting point of the survey of the first tract of land purchased of the Indians by William Penn July 15, 1682, on land in the Tenure of John Wood and by him called Graystones over against the Falls of the Delaware . . ." Earlier still the falls had been a strategic location for camps by the Lenni Lenape Indians and, in 1624, a settlement for a small group of trappers.

A major flood in 1687 added to the strategic advantage of the site by carving out a creek that left an island completely separated from the Pennsylvania mainland. Because it was at the fall line, the fast-flowing stream dropped 8 feet from where it left the river to its return into the Delaware, providing a source of waterpower to turn water wheels and grindstones in mills. A Philadelphia merchant, Adam Hoops, established a gristmill in the mid-1700s. Subsequently a sawmill, snuff factory, splitting mill, sheet-rolling mill, button factory, and a hat factory were added to what was to be known as the "Delaware Works." This was part of the property that Robert Morris acquired in 1791. He placed his son in charge of the businesses.

Hoops acquired the land at the Falls of the Delaware from Josiah Wood, who owned several hundred acres and a one-mile frontage of the river. In addition to the mill, Hoops constructed (or perhaps added to) a home on high ground about a half-mile from the river. This home, which came to be called "Summerseat," was to be a significant focal point in early American history.

Summerseat had three prominent figures as owners in the 1700s, and one especially famous temporary resident. Thomas Barclay, Hoops' son-in-law, became owner of Summerseat in 1773. Barclay was the owner when George Washington established his headquarters at Summerseat on December 8, 1776. Washington had just completed a retreat across New Jersey with Sir William Howe, commander of a large force of British soldiers and Hessian mercenaries, in somewhat leisurely pursuit. Nevertheless, when Washington commandeered all the boats for miles along the river to ferry his troops across—keeping the boats on the Pennsylvania side to prevent the British from following—Howe's army was close behind. The British arrived in Trenton, New Jersey, the afternoon of December 8, just after the last of Washington's ragged army had completed the crossing. Washington remained at Summerseat in what was then called Colvin's Ferry—now Morrisville—until December 14, when Howe returned to winter quarters in New York with most of his troops. It is almost certain that Washington began planning his historic attack on Trenton, guarded by fifteen hundred Hessians under Colonel Johann Rall, while still at Summerseat. Historic Morrisville Society holds annual reenactments of Washington's arrival at Summerseat on the first Saturday of December.

The two other prominent early owners of Summerseat were Robert Morris and George Clymer. Both had been signers of the Declaration of Independence and the Constitution, and Summerseat is probably unique in having had two signers of both documents as owners.

Morris acquired Summerseat and surrounding acreage with the idea that the "Falls of the Delaware" would make an ideal site for the nation's capital, being about halfway between the two major cities of the time, Philadelphia and New York. It was also ideally situated to be reached by water, since boats could proceed up the Delaware as far as the fall line, and the stage line between Philadelphia and New York passed through the town to the ferry that crossed the river.

Morris nearly succeeded in having Morrisville selected as the capital site, but lacked support from his fellow Pennsylvania senator, William Maclay, who wanted it farther inland, along the Susquehanna River. Nevertheless, Congress twice voted to begin surveys to locate a capitol building—probably about where Morris's Summerseat still stands today—but lack of funds prevented anything further being done. When the decision to select a capital site was finally made, southern representatives reached an agreement with Alexander Hamilton: if New York would support the plan to locate the capital along the Potomac River, the southerners would support his plan for stabilizing the country's credit and currency. The Potomac site prevailed over Morrisville by two votes. Incidentally, Morris also favored Hamilton's financial plan, which he helped develop. In fact, in reviewing *The Papers of Robert Morris* (published by the University of Pittsburgh Press), the *Journal of American History* commented that "It is not too much to say that when this [documentary] record is fully disclosed Alexander Hamilton will be seen standing in the long shadow cast by Robert Morris."

In more recent years the major north-south rail line and the Route 1 highway were routed through Morrisville and industry thrived, the town becoming a rubber, plastics, and tile manufacturing center. But these businesses began to decline slowly after the 1960s. When they finally closed in 1980 and 1982, the town lacked a significant industrial base.

This book will not attempt to present a detailed history of Morrisville, but will cover some highlights over two centuries from colonial times to the 1960s. The pictures are largely from the collection of photographs in Historic Morrisville Society's files at Summerseat, but a number were kindly provided by individuals (see Acknowledgments). They are not a complete pictorial history but are intended to provide a flavor of what the town was like in years past. The town has not had another Morris or Clymer in that approximately two hundred-year span, but its citizens have done some impressive things and a few of them will be chronicled in words and pictures in the following pages. For example, a diminutive attorney from Morrisville defeated James Michener in a congressional election despite the famous author's name recognition; father-and-son football players became a successful sculptor (the father) and a tenor with an operatic quality voice (the son); and the first woman painter to support herself in Bucks County solely as an artist lives in Morrisville. But mostly this is a book about a small town in America, a town with a rich early history but one that is otherwise typical of the first half of the twentieth century.

One

The Early Years

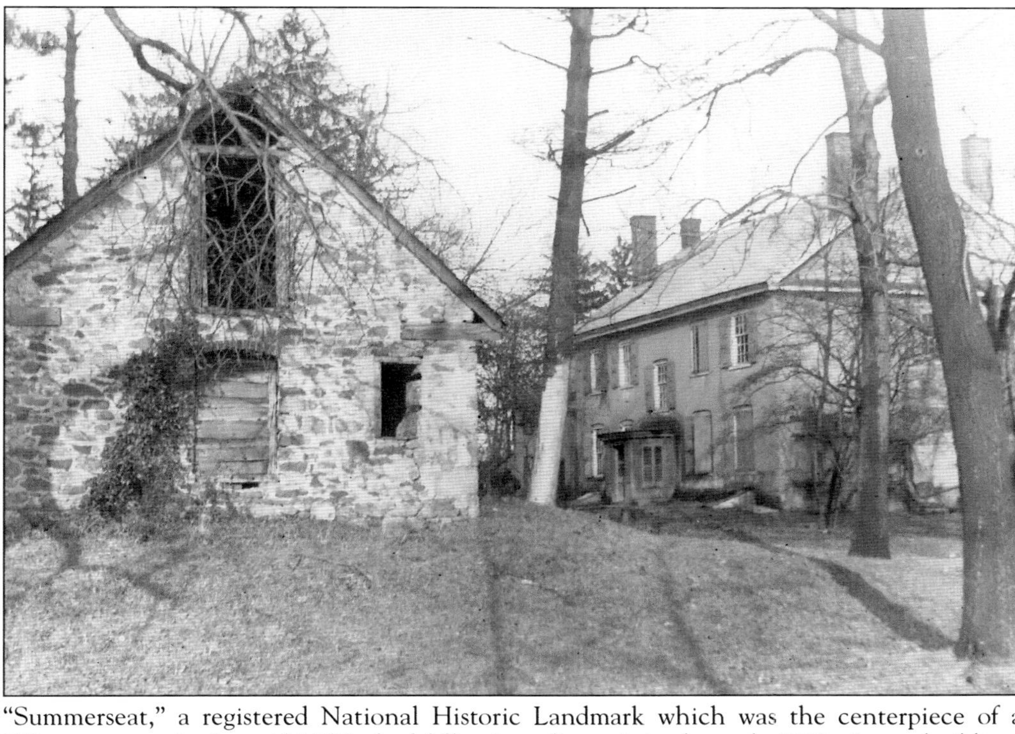

"Summerseat," a registered National Historic Landmark which was the centerpiece of a 221-acre estate in the mid-1700s, had fallen into disrepair in the early 1900s. Its outbuildings were deteriorating and eventually the stones from which they were constructed were removed and used to restore other historic buildings in the area. The home, when owned by Thomas Barclay in 1776, had been Washington's headquarters from December 8 to 14. Later it was owned by two signers of the Constitution and Declaration of Independence, Robert Morris and George Clymer.

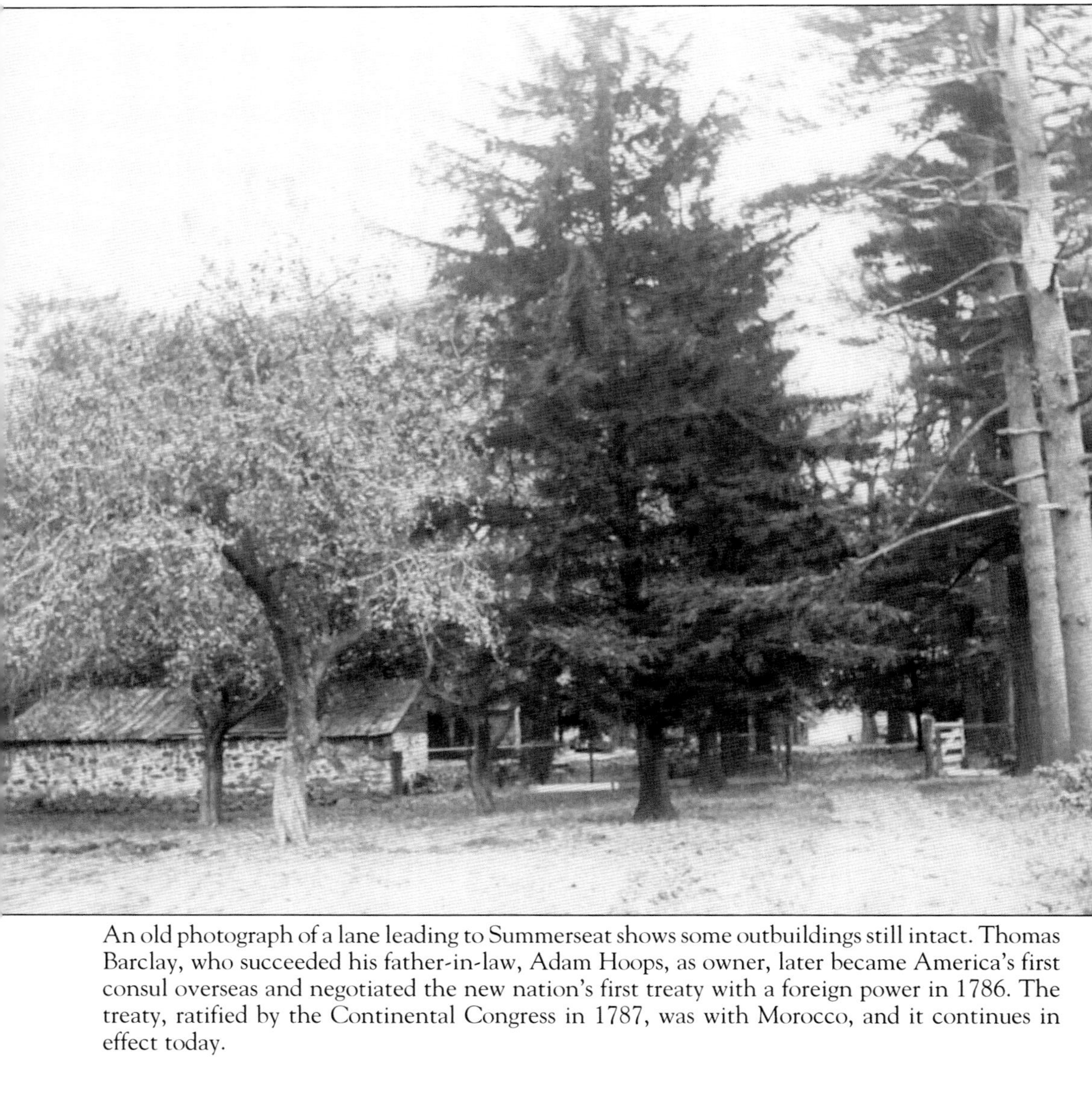

An old photograph of a lane leading to Summerseat shows some outbuildings still intact. Thomas Barclay, who succeeded his father-in-law, Adam Hoops, as owner, later became America's first consul overseas and negotiated the new nation's first treaty with a foreign power in 1786. The treaty, ratified by the Continental Congress in 1787, was with Morocco, and it continues in effect today.

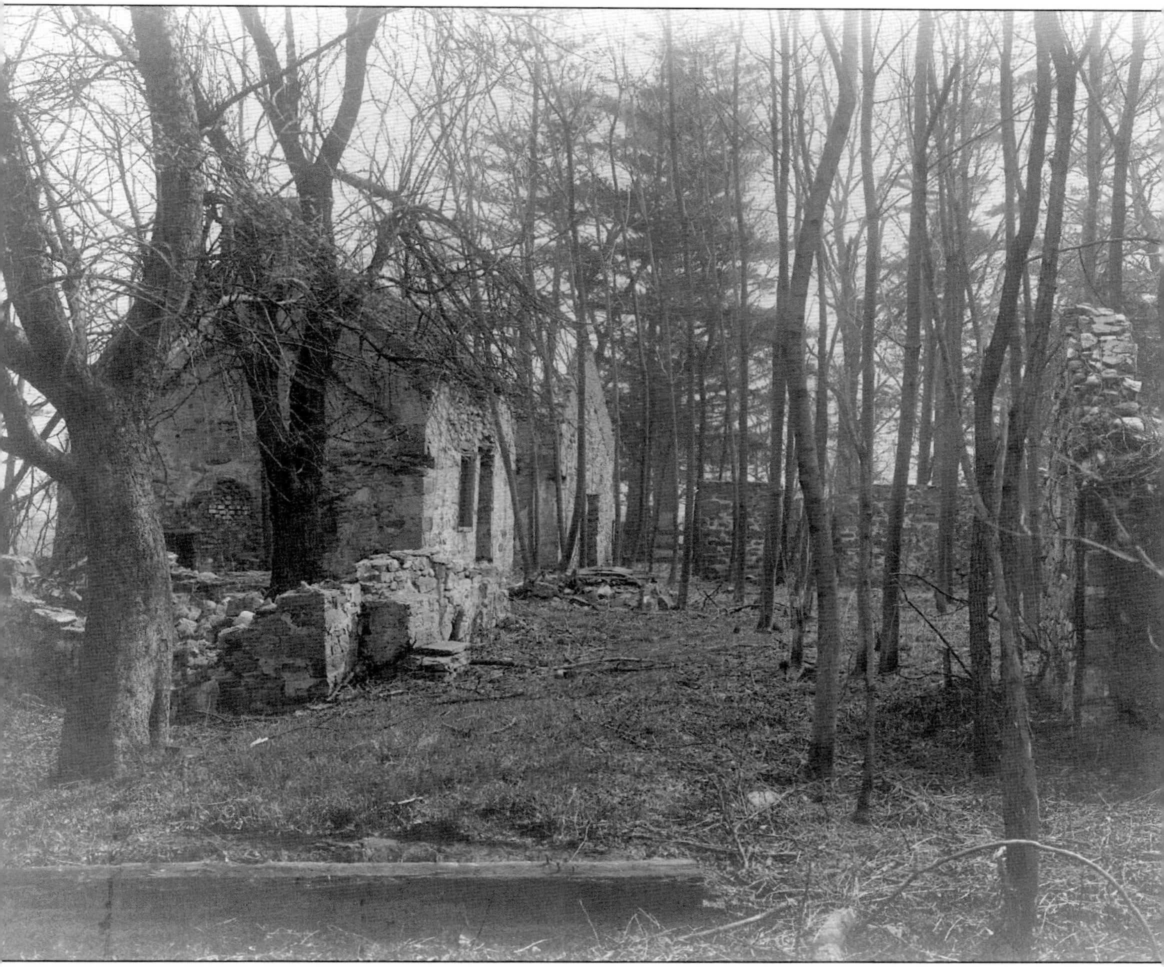

There were a number of outbuildings on the Summerseat property. This building is believed to have been slave quarters in the 1700s, but this has not been confirmed. The stones were salvaged and used in construction elsewhere. When George Clymer acquired the property from Robert Morris it included 2,500 acres that were divided into fourteen farms. Summerseat had a stone barn, stables, and coach house among its outbuildings. Clymer and Thomas Fitzsimmons bought this land, plus several homes and the mills of the "Delaware Works," for $41,000 plus an assumption of $100,666.67 in mortgages!

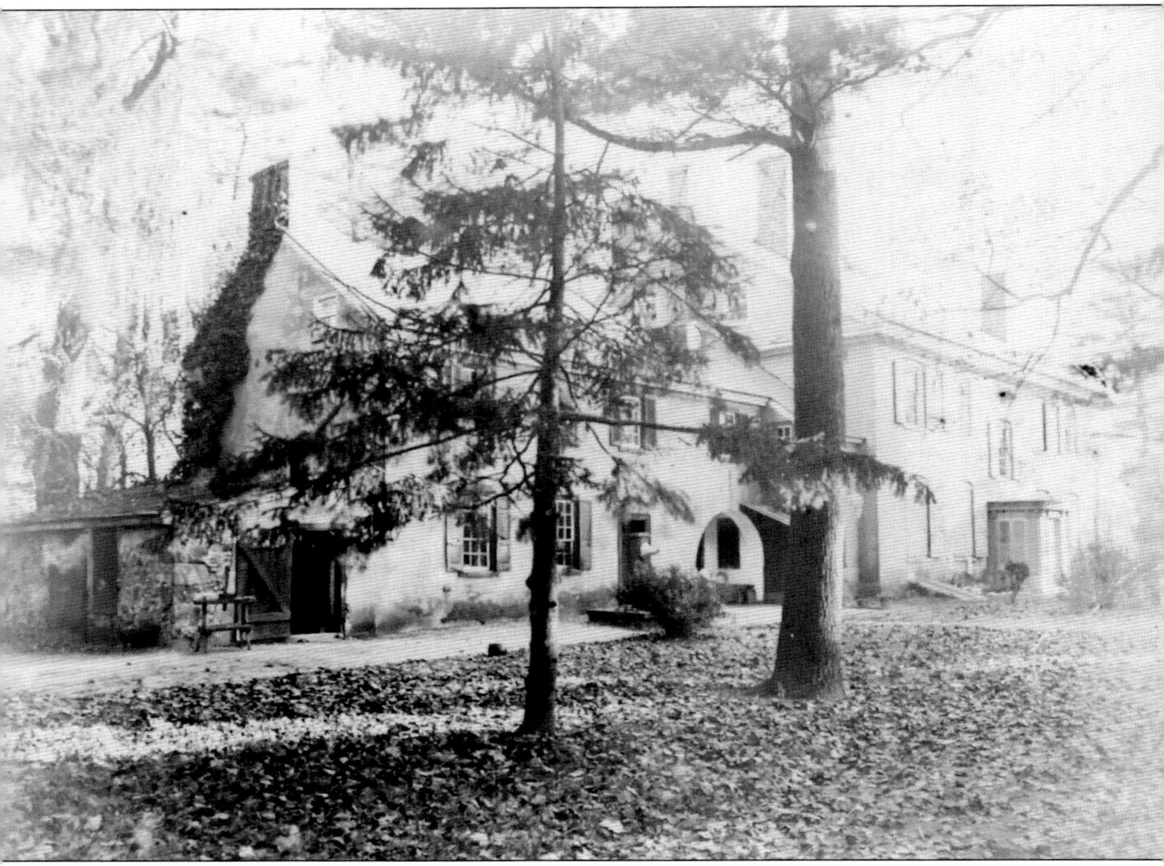

A large "kitchen wing," since removed from Summerseat, contained several rooms and a walk-in fireplace. An archway is visible showing the passageway between the main house and the portion containing the kitchen. The kitchen included a large brick oven for baking.

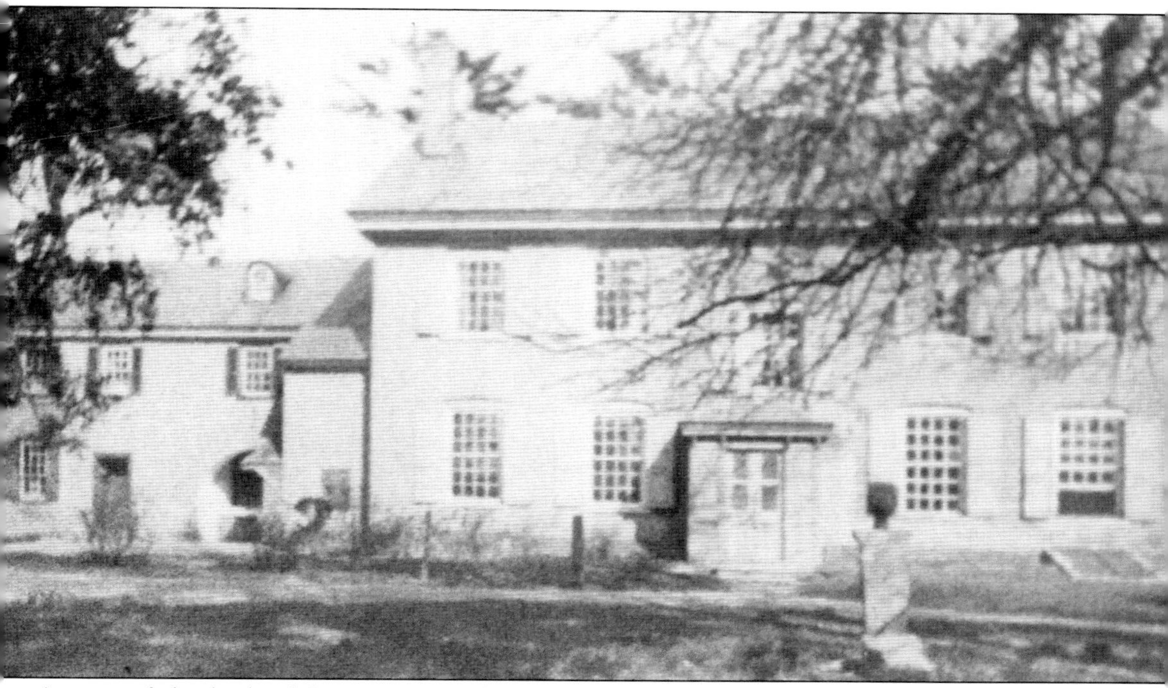

A view of the back of Summerseat with the "kitchen wing" intact. Not only did George Washington use Summerseat as a headquarters, but so did General John Sullivan. Another American general, Anthony ("Mad Anthony") Wayne, conducted a court martial of two captured British spies at Summerseat and allowed the unfortunate pair to read Thomas Barclay's Bible for consolation the night before they were hanged in January 1781.

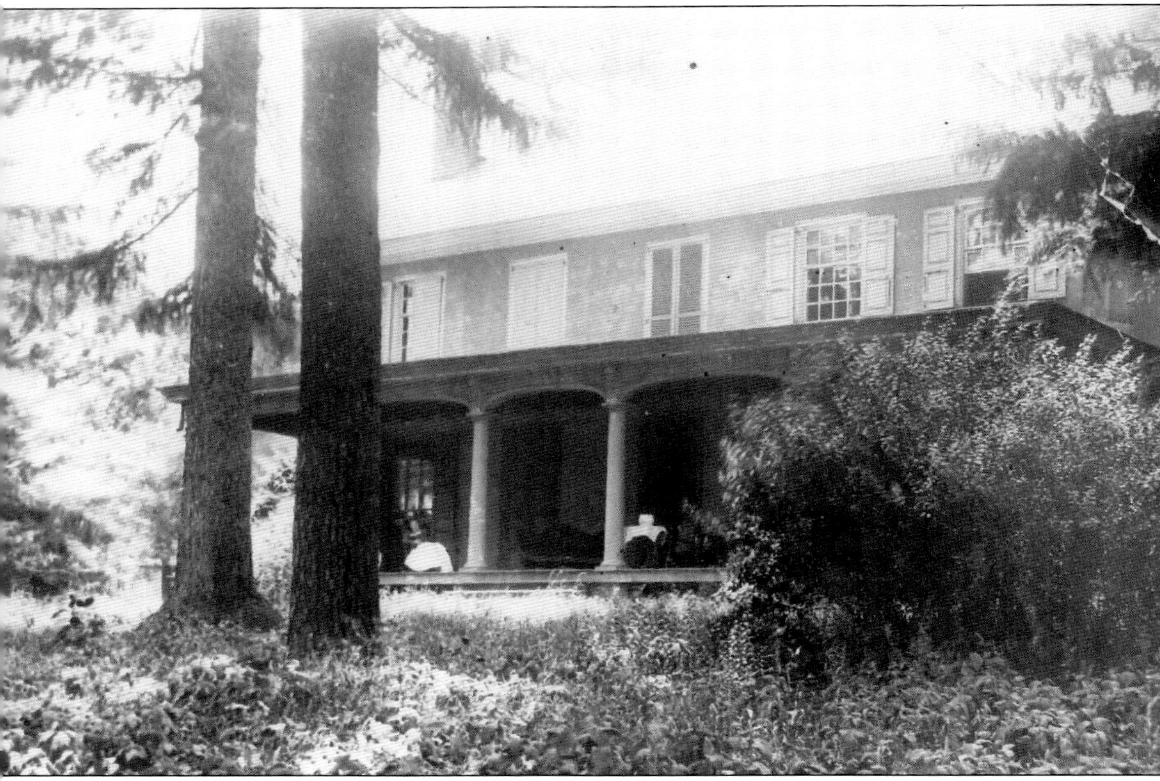

In Victorian times, a front porch was added to Summerseat and the windows were extended to the porch floor. Later it was returned to its original conformation, thanks to the careful restoration planned by Thomas Stockham, a civic leader.

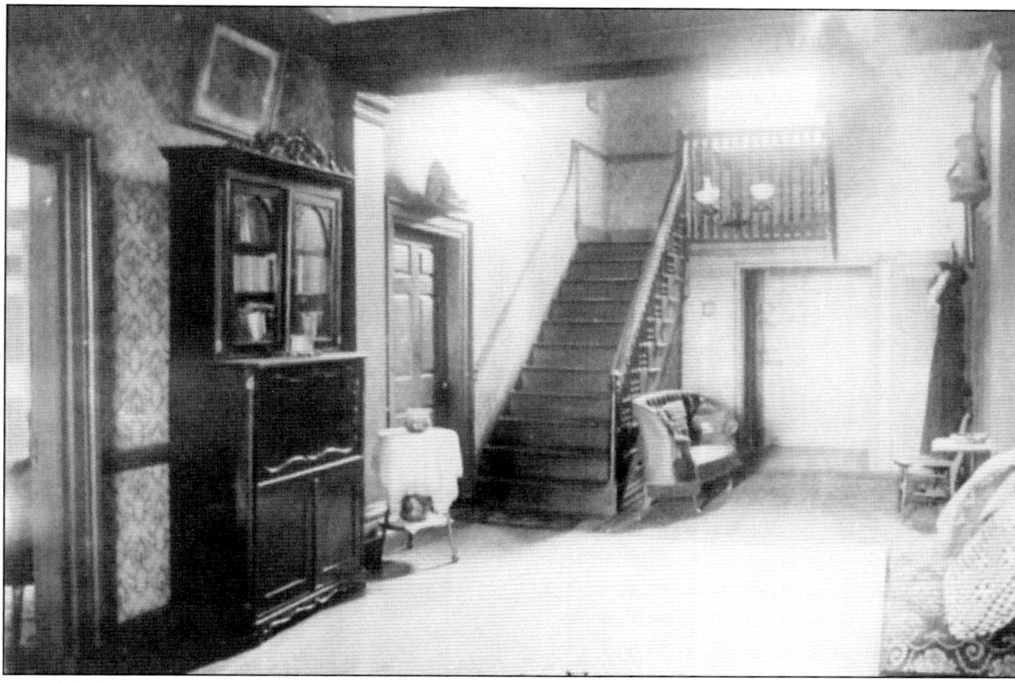

An old photograph of the front hall in Summerseat shows how it looked in the 1800s.

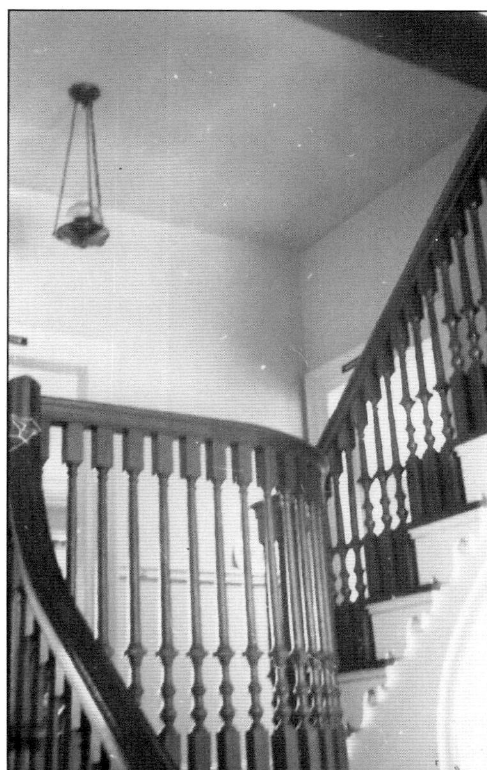

Looking upstairs from a landing, Summerseat appears much the same today as it did in the past. When Thomas Stockham planned its restoration he took pains with details, such as requiring that a few missing spindles be replaced with exact reproductions of those that had remained intact.

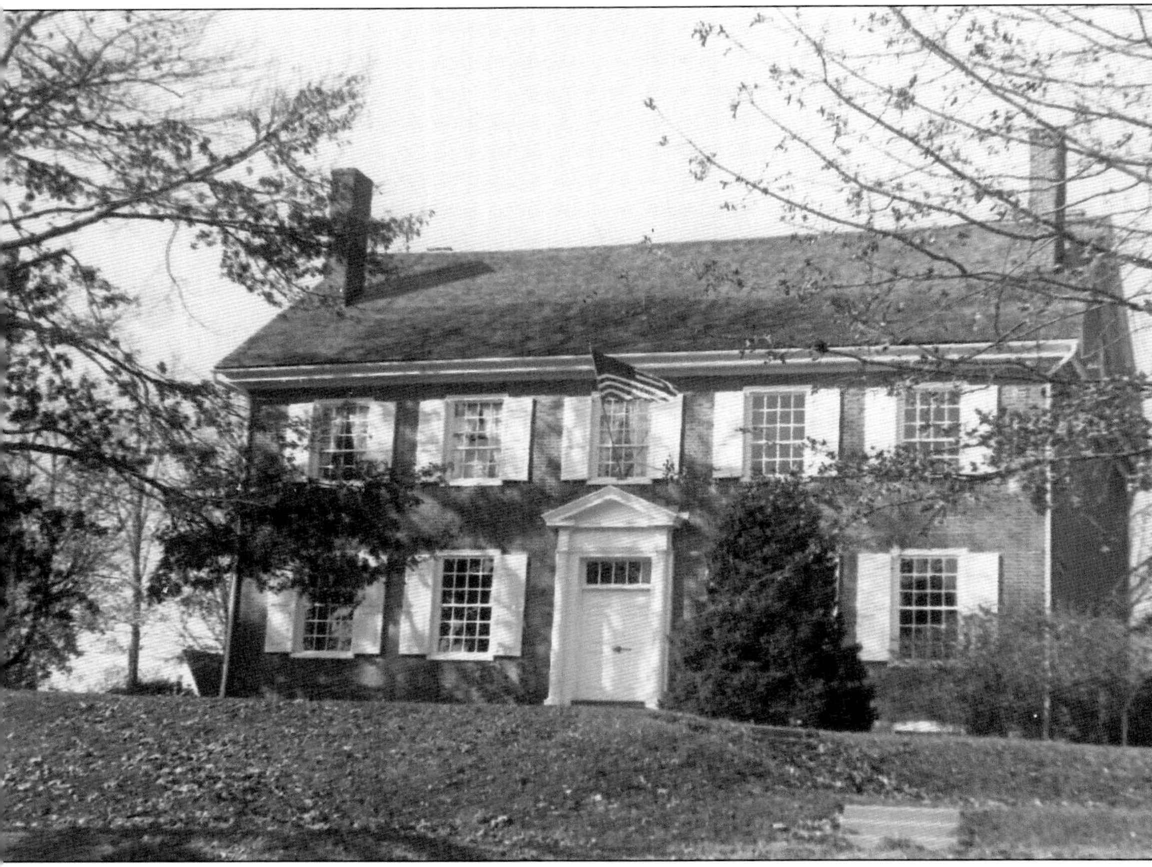

Summerseat is maintained by Historic Morrisville Society, a non-profit organization of volunteers who open the building to visitors on the first Saturday of each month. On the first Saturday in December the society conducts a reenactment of Washington's 1776 arrival, with the help of the Third Pennsylvania Light Infantry as portrayed by members of Historical Military Impressions. This picture shows the front of Summerseat as the building looks today.

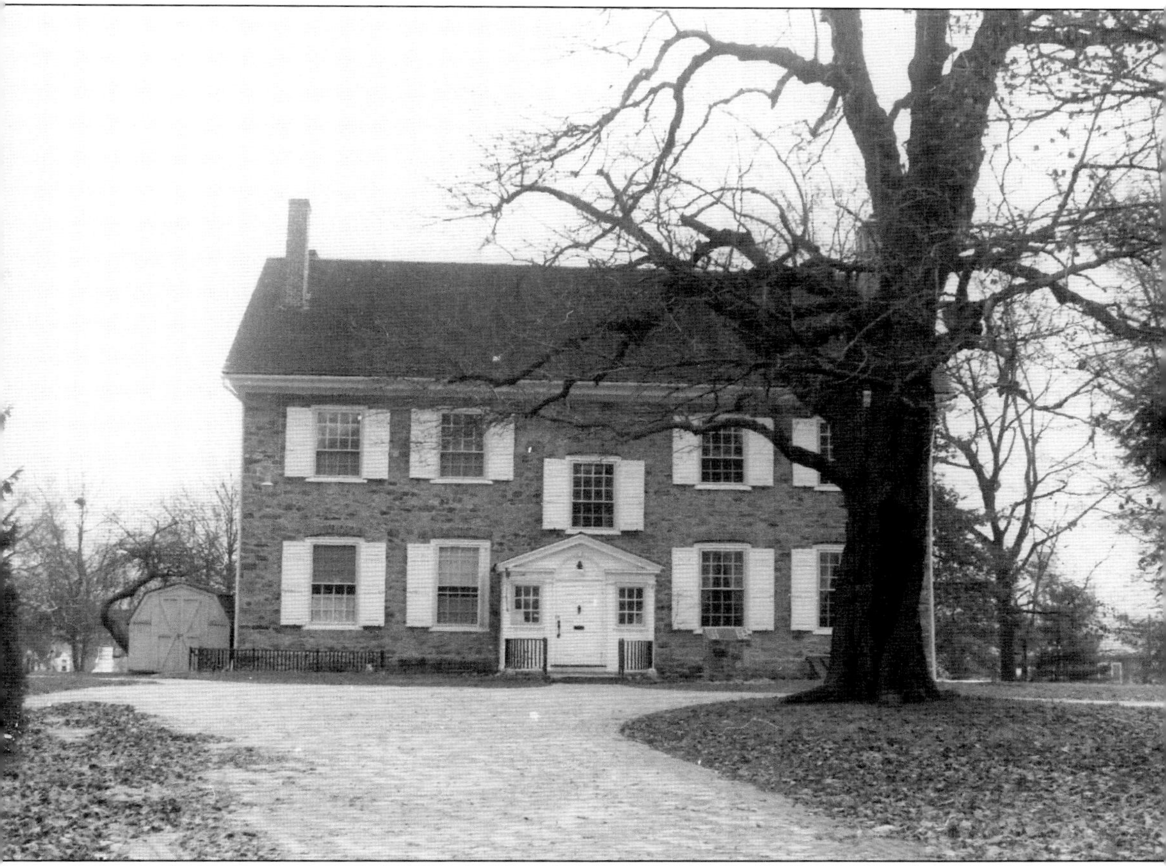

Most visitors think the back door of Summerseat is the front entrance, because this is the door that is always open when Historic Morrisville Society holds open house or special events.

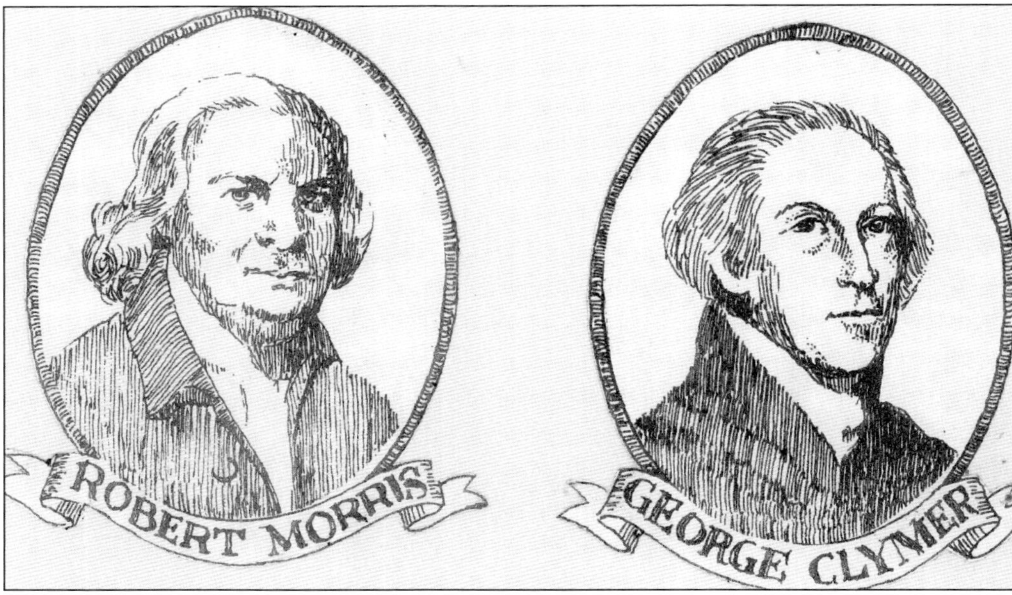

Robert Morris owned Summerseat and about 2,500 surrounding acres from 1791 to 1798, and George Clymer was the owner from 1798 to 1805, making Summerseat probably the only home in America to have been owned by two signers of the Declaration of Independence and the Constitution.

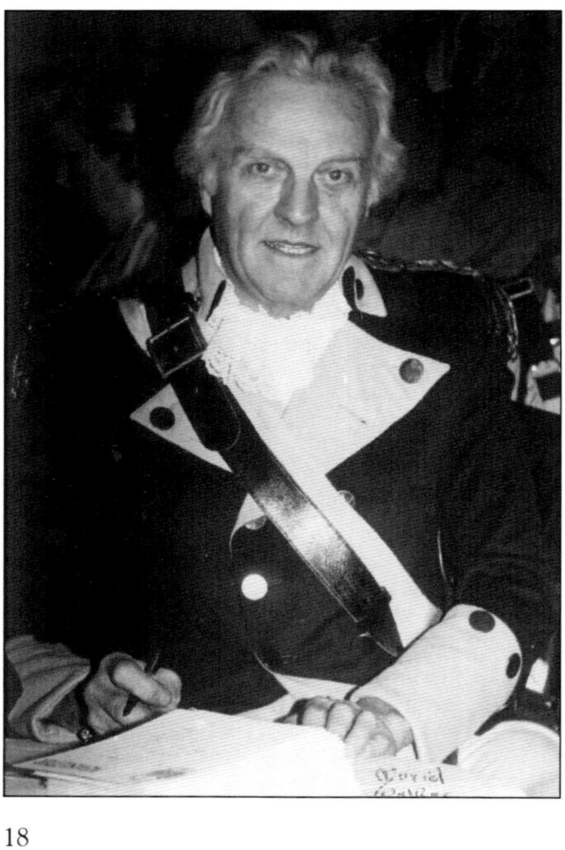

There have been several reincarnations of George Washington at Summerseat, reenacting his arrival in 1776. The first was actor/producer St. John Terrell, who also began the reenactments of Washington crossing the Delaware at Washington Crossing, Pennsylvania. Terrell, who was the radio voice of Jack Armstrong ("The All-American Boy") in 1933, was active in founding the Bucks County Playhouse in New Hope, Pennsylvania, and was the founder of the Lambertville, New Jersey, Music Circus.

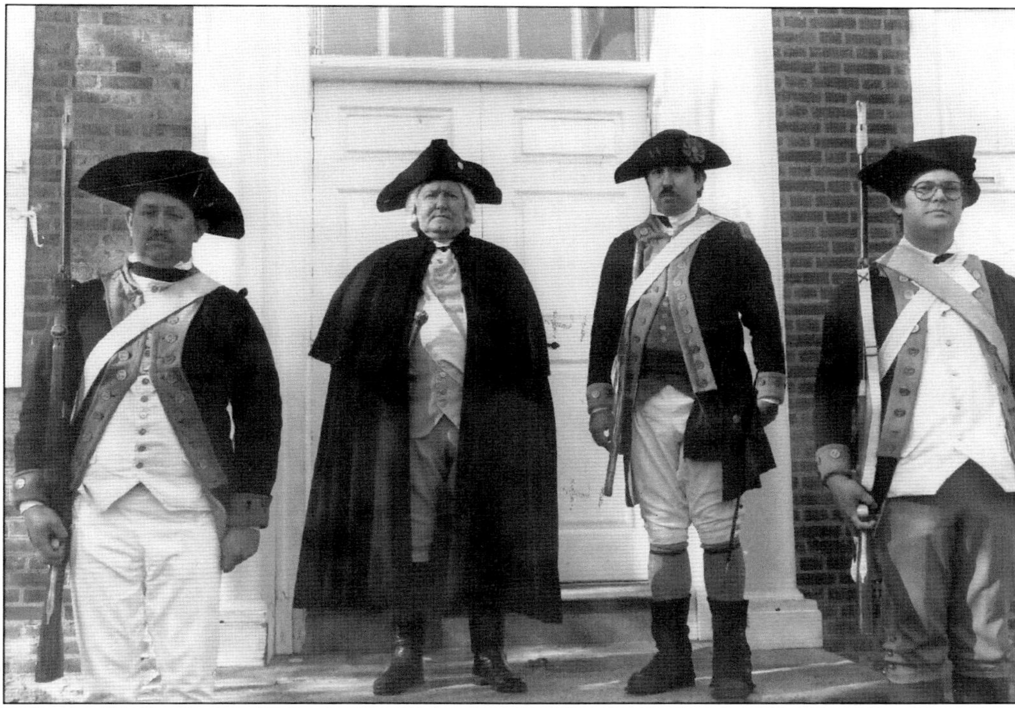

Another reenactor who portrayed Washington at Summerseat was Lee Reed, an executive at the Reedman Auto Sales Center. He is shown outside the front door of Summerseat flanked by members of the Egg Harbor Guard reenactors group.

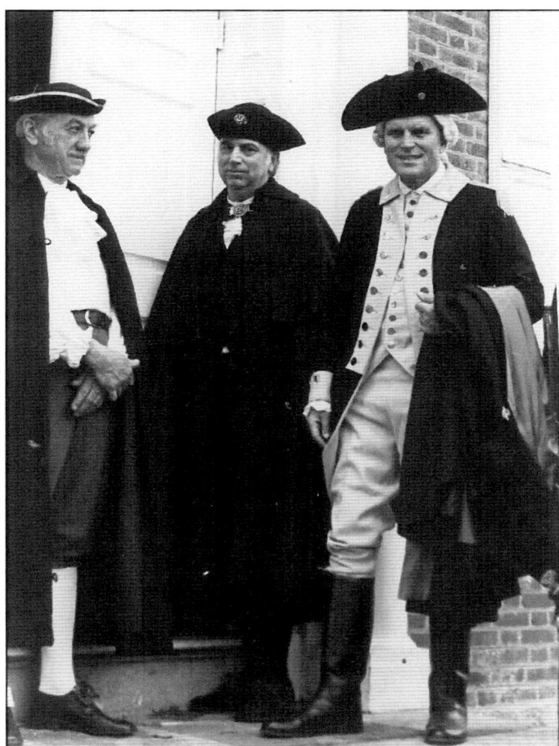

A well-known Washington was Jack Kelly (right), a medalist in the Pan American Games and Olympics as an oarsman. He was the brother of Princess Grace of Monaco, and is shown here at Summerseat with John Warenda Sr. (left) and Marvin Bennett.

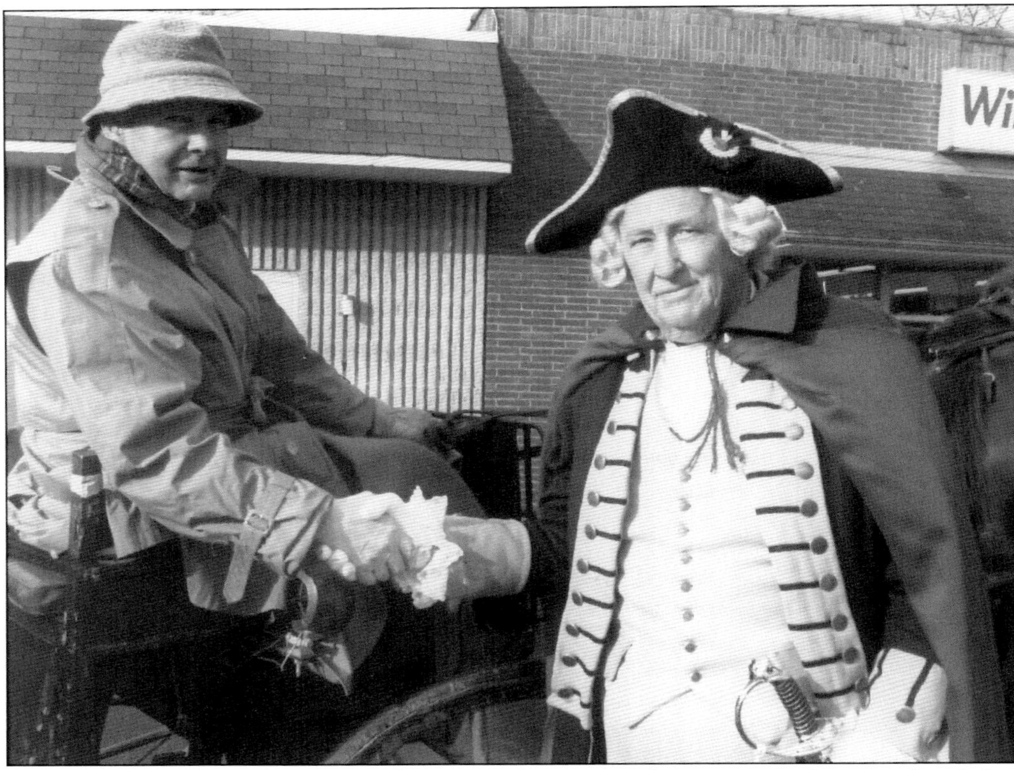

No one portrayed Washington with more enthusiasm and attention to historic detail than James Gallagher (right), pictured with Sam Snipes, Esquire, Yardley attorney and Falls Township historian.

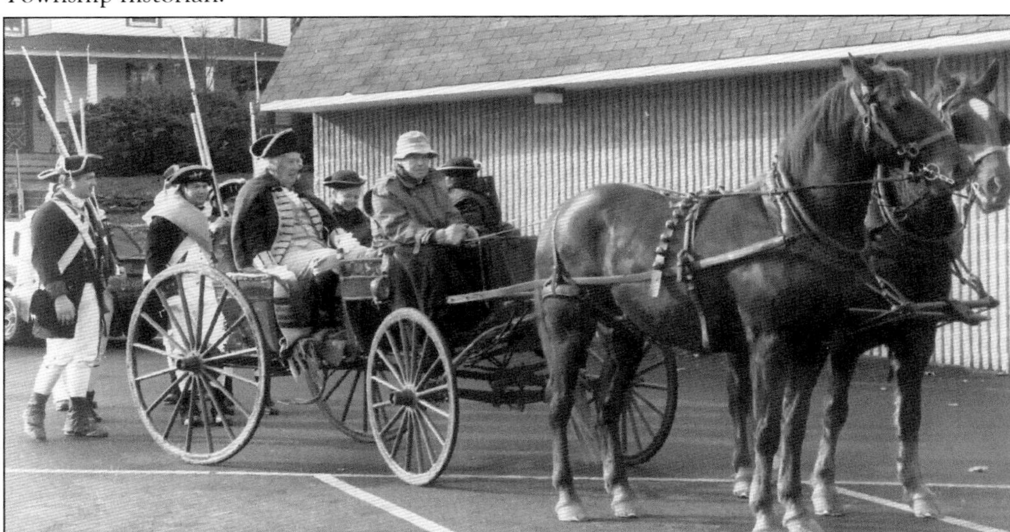

Reenactments of Washington's arrival often took the form of a mini-parade from the Morrisville Shopping Center down Pennsylvania Avenue and up Hillcrest to Summerseat. Sam Snipes volunteered to drive Jim Gallagher as Washington in his carriage, escorted by members of Historical Military Impressions as colonial soldiers.

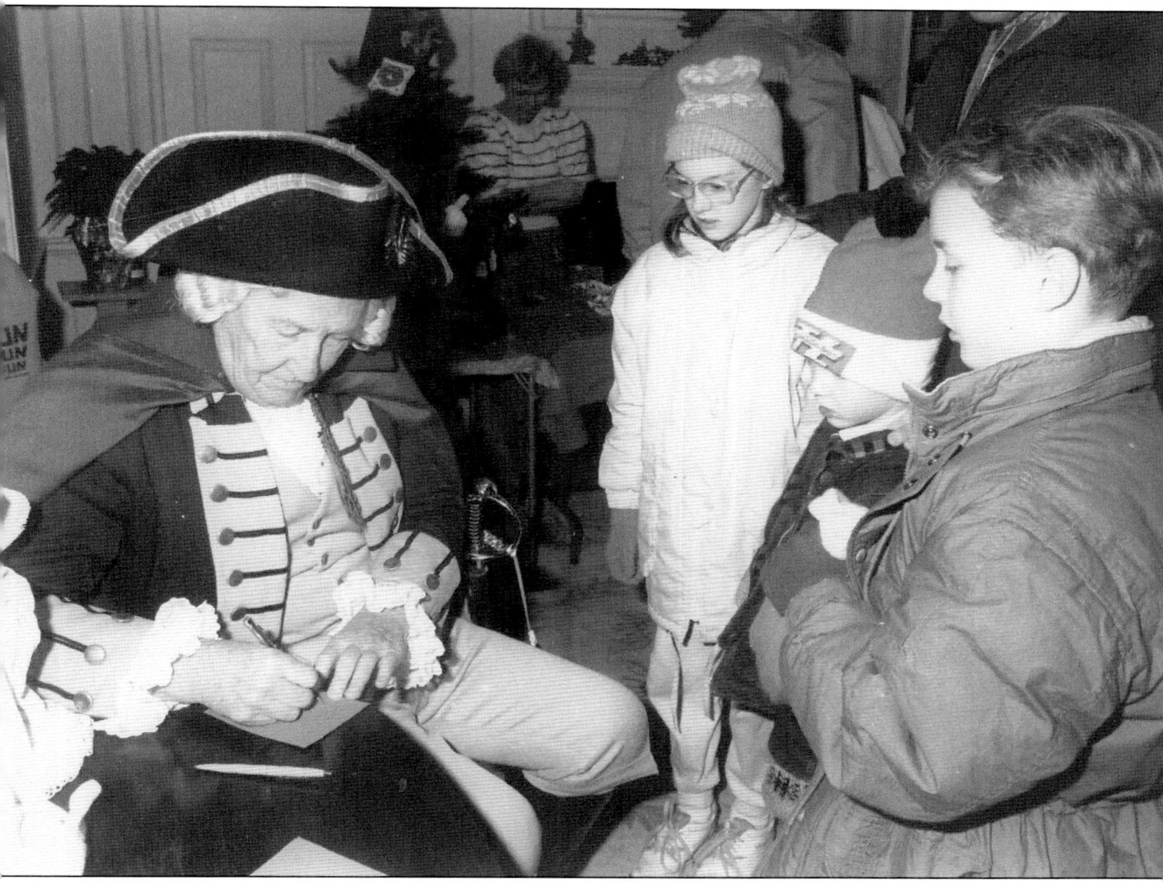

Jim Gallagher's representation of Washington extended to the ability to replicate the general's signature with remarkable accuracy. This *Yardley News* photograph by George Robinson shows Gallagher signing "G. Washington" autographs for youngsters at Summerseat. When Washington was at Summerseat in 1776 he wrote many letters of instruction to his officers at locations up and down the Delaware River. For example, on December 11 he wrote that he believed it "highly necessary that the post at Dunk's Ferry should be guarded." Dunk's Ferry was located in what is now Neshaminy State Park, Bensalem Township.

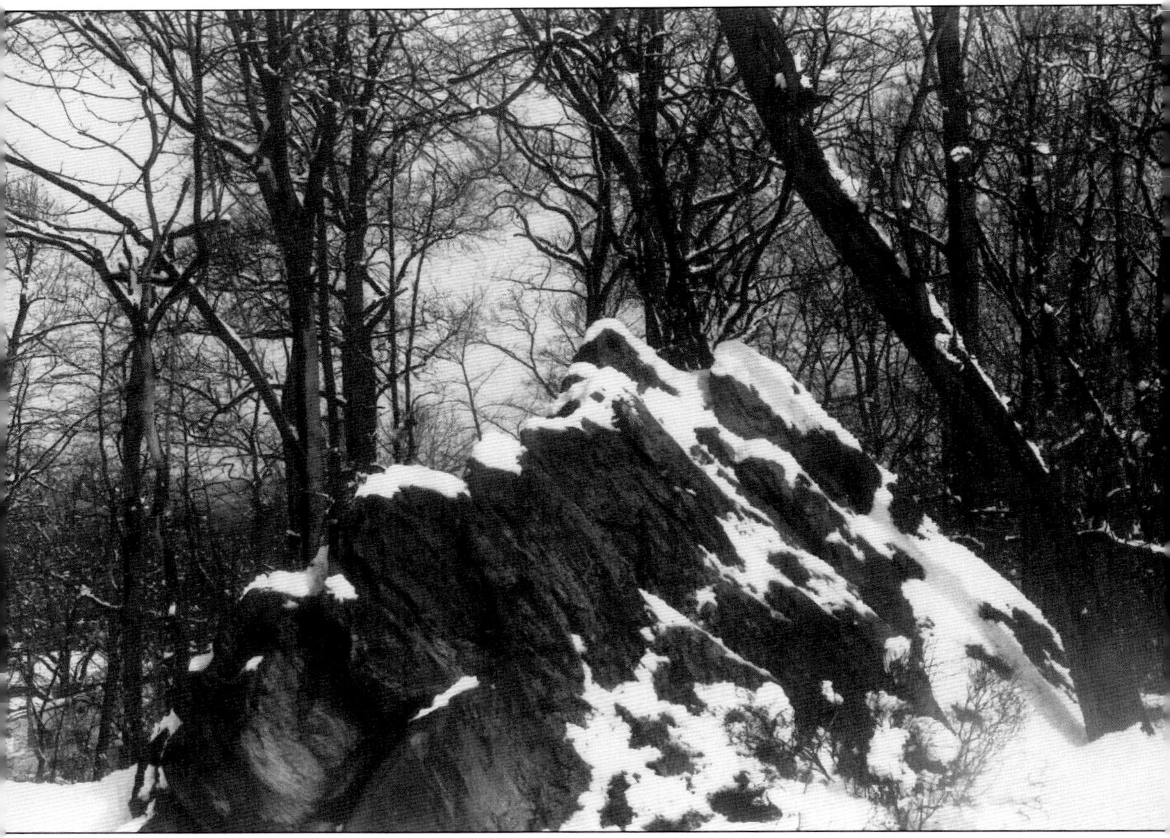

In addition to the historic significance of Summerseat, Morrisville is the location of William Penn's first land purchase from the Lenni Lenape Indians, which took place on July 15, 1682. The site where the purchase agreement was reached is marked by a massive gray boulder on the edge of an ancient forest, with three hundred-year-old trees.

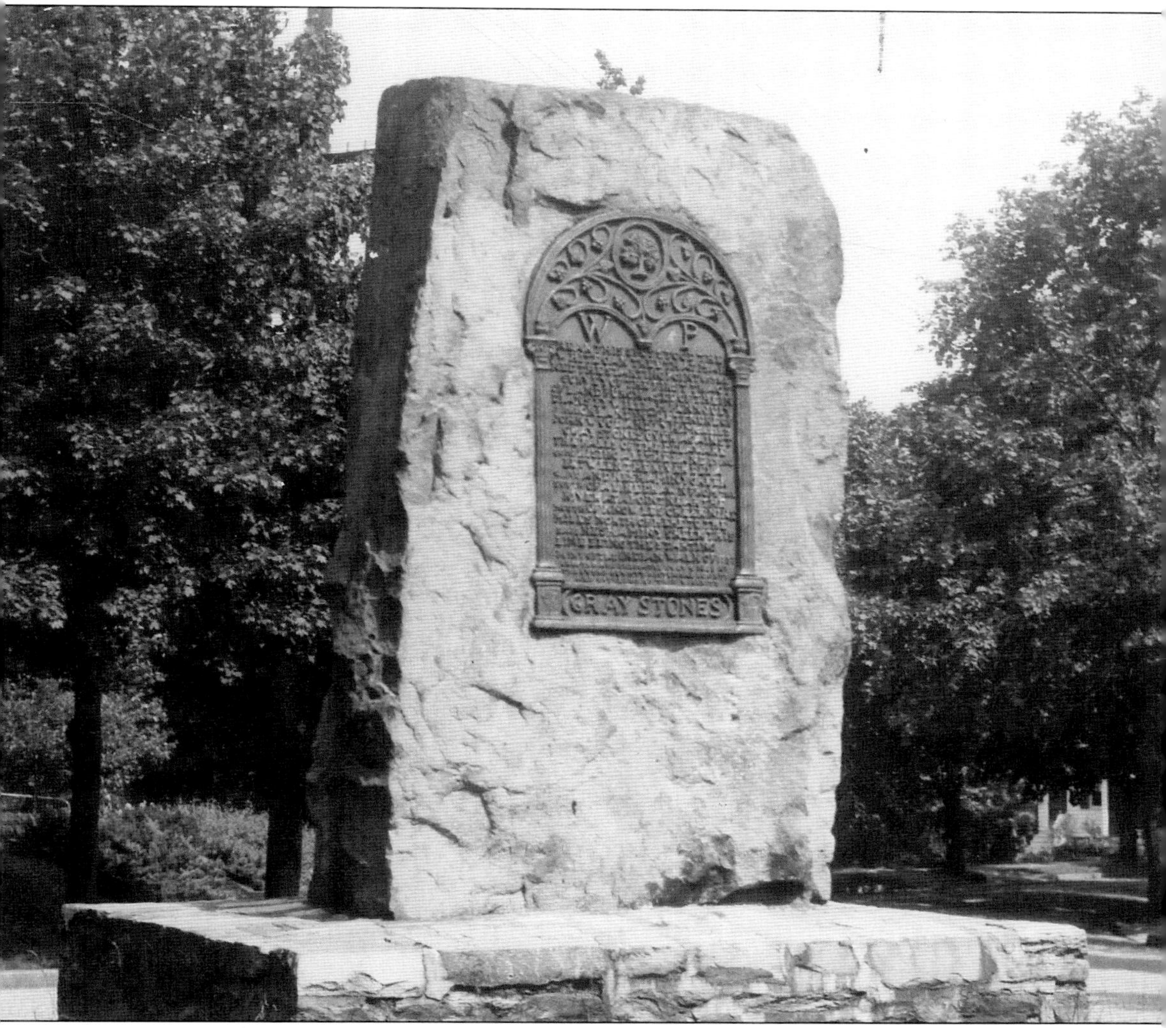

At the intersection of Crown Street and Highland Avenue, near the gray boulder, a monument stands with a plaque that identifies "Gray Stones" as the site that, according to Falls Township historian Sam Snipes, became the beginning point of all land surveys in Pennsylvania.

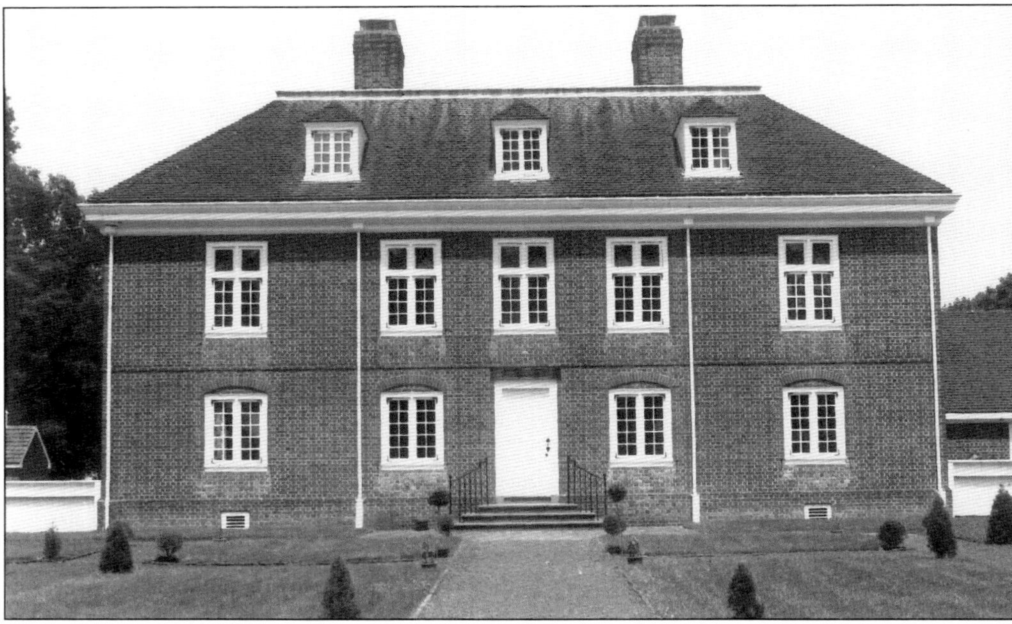

Closely associated with Morrisville, having the same mailing address though not actually in the borough, is Pennsbury Manor, a reconstruction of the manor house and outbuildings as they were when William Penn lived there in 1684. Pennsbury Manor, which is supported by the state and private fund-raising , has a full-time staff and is open to the public.

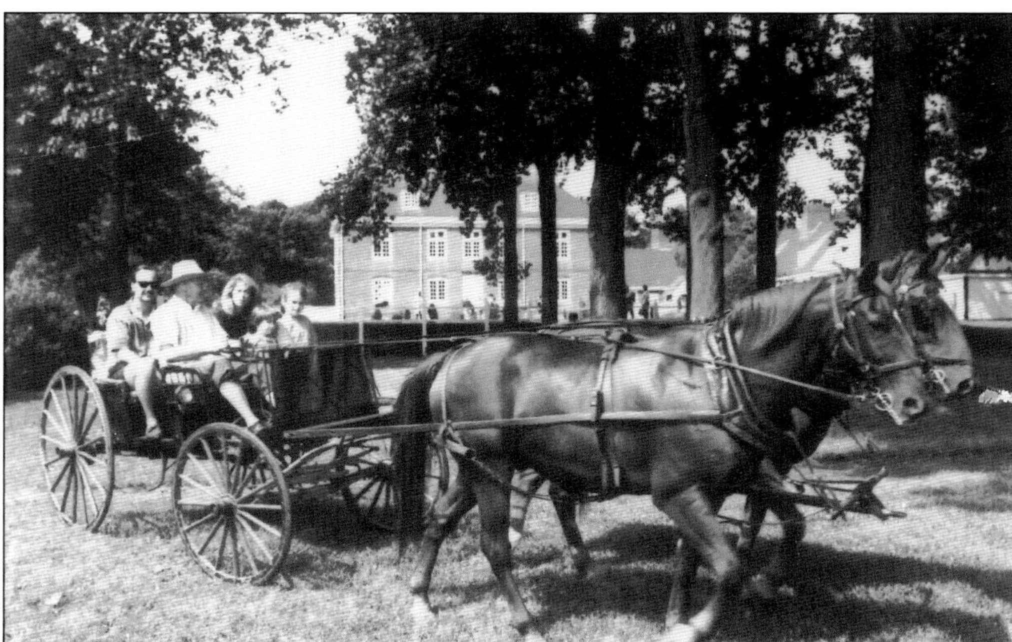

Carriage rides are among the many family activities at Pennsbury's seventeenth-century manor fair.

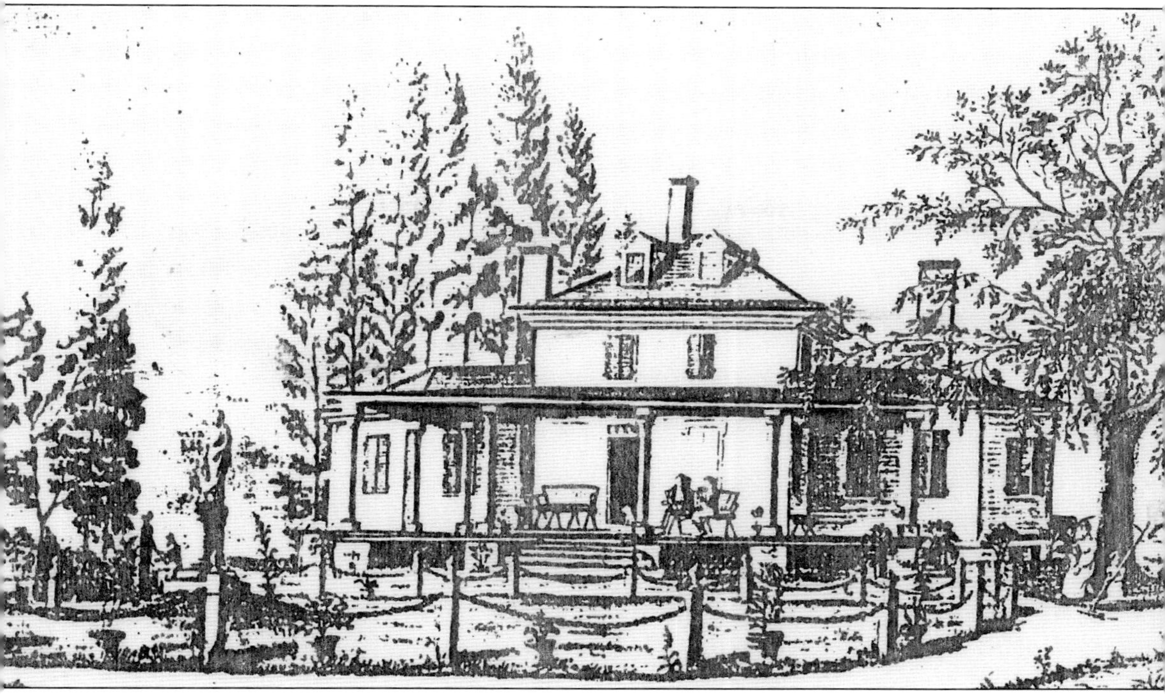

There was a second home owned by the Morris family in Morrisville, purchased by French General Jean Victor Moreau in 1804. Moreau, who had been a rising star in the French army, had a falling out with Napoleon Bonaparte, who had him exiled. Moreau lived in Morrisville until Christmas 1811, when the house burned to the ground. A marker on Bank Street, on the site of the Bridge Commission parking lot, shows the location.

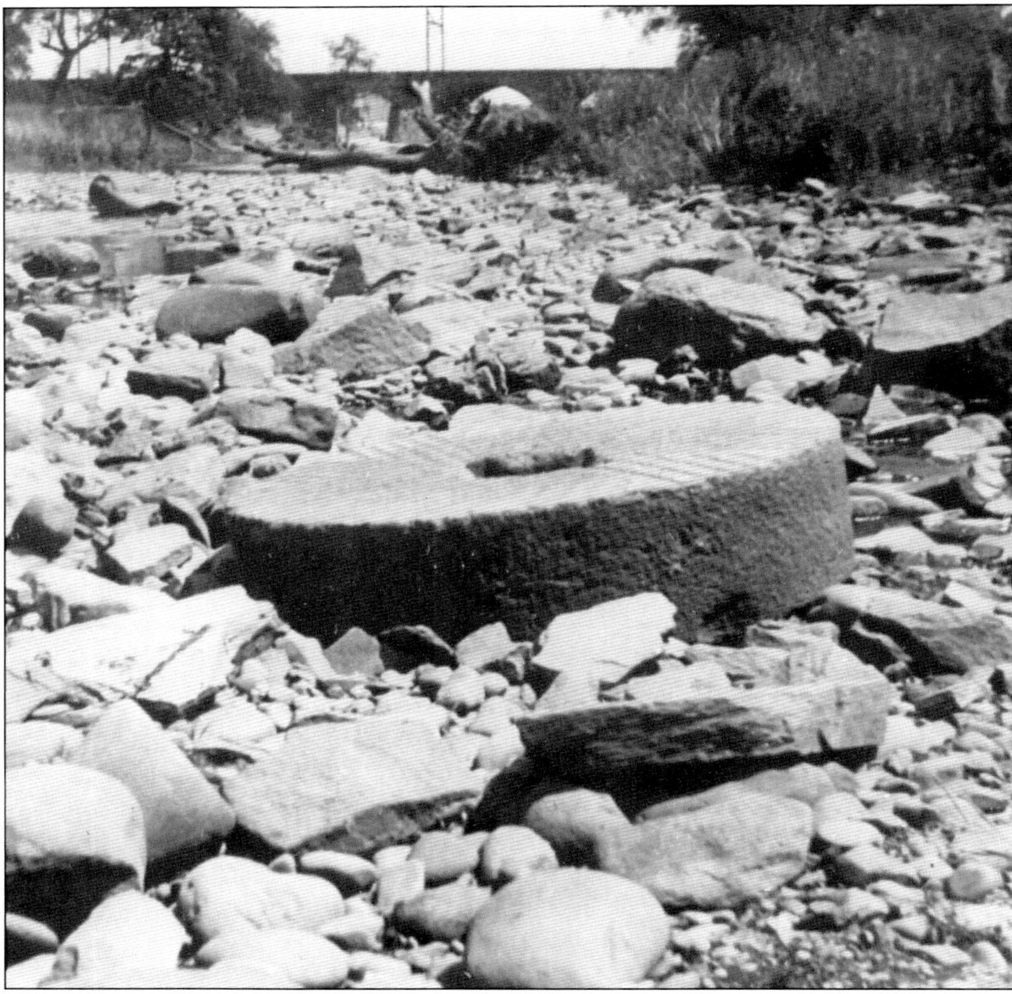

A flood in 1687 carved out a fast-flowing creek at Morrisville and Adam Hoops used the water to power a mill. Over the years, milling and manufacturing moved inland, but when the creek was dammed in 1938 a large millstone was found in the dry creek bed. The stone disappeared for several years, but was tracked down by James Wood, Morrisville historian, and returned to serve as a monument at Bridge Street, near the "Trenton Makes" bridge across the Delaware. In 1797 Robert Morris' "Delaware Works" included a gristmill, a slitting mill (for slitting iron into nails), a rolling mill (for rolling bar iron into sheets and hoops), a mill for rolling ship bolts, a shop for drawing wire, a mill for grinding plaster of paris, and a sawmill.

Two

Business and Industry

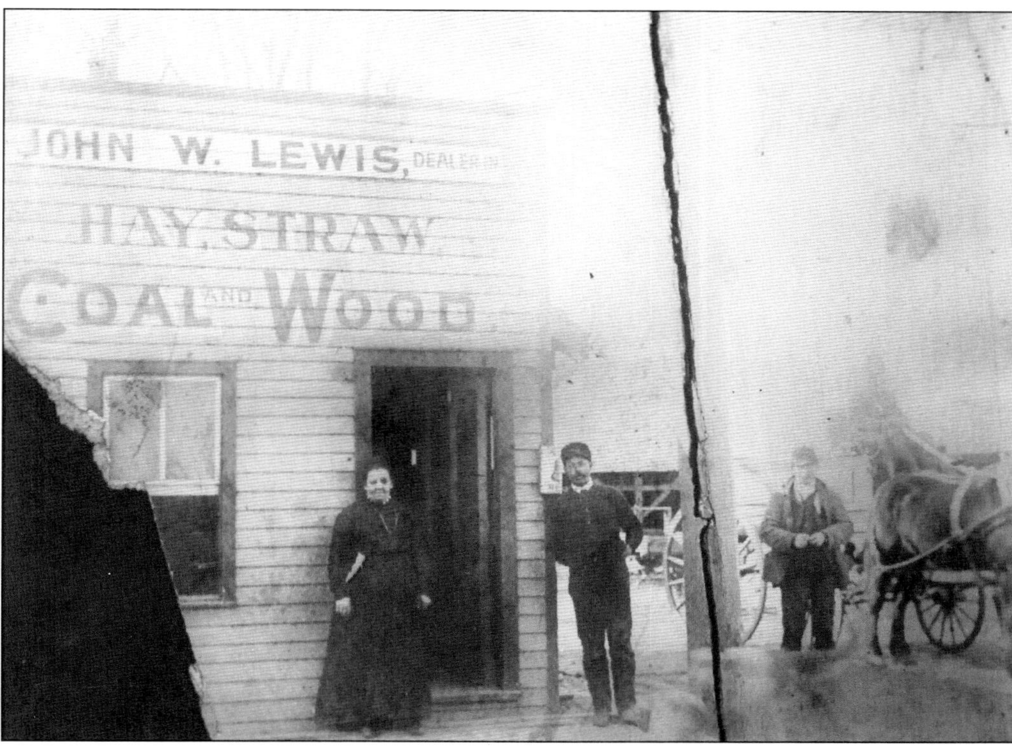

One of Morrisville's early businesses was John Lewis's dealership in hay, straw, coal, and wood. His horse-drawn delivery wagon can be seen at the right, though the driver is indistinct in this old photograph.

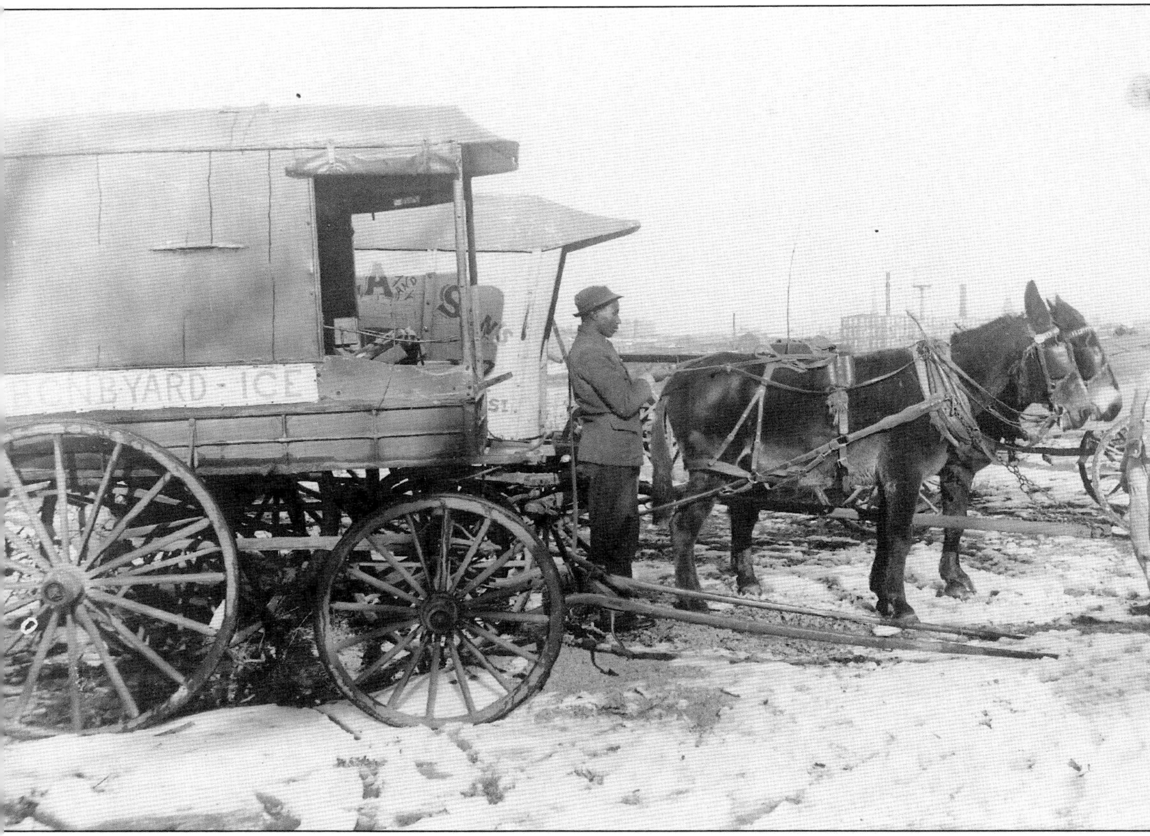

Another early business was the BCNB Yard ice delivery service. The mule-drawn ice wagon was photographed in 1910 at the ice yard's location near the river in the lower part of Morrisville.

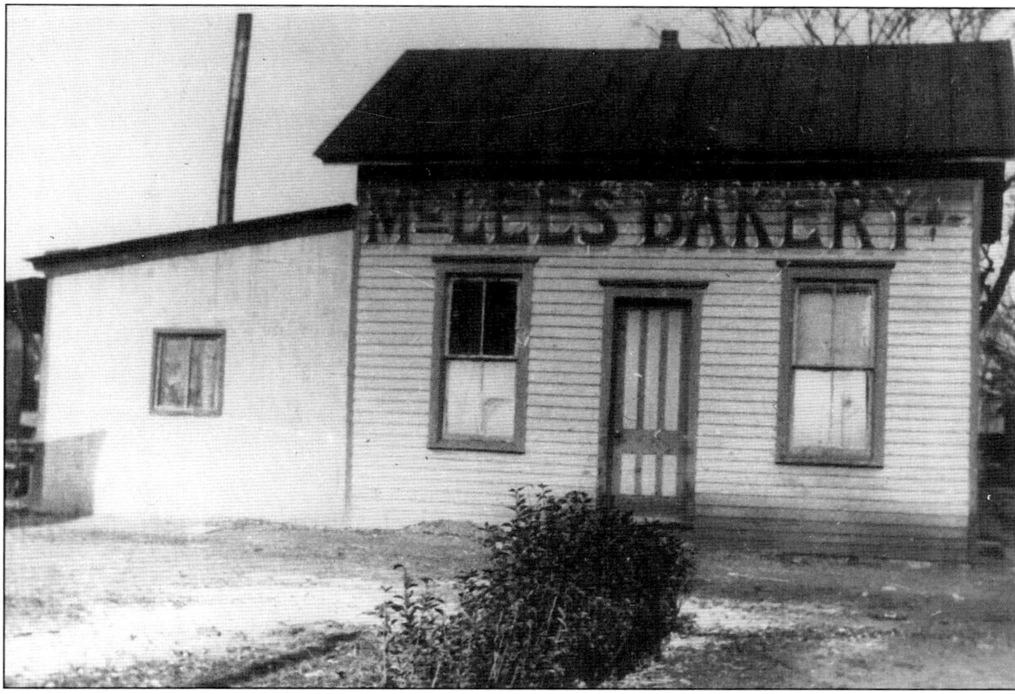

McLee's Bakery is no more, but it is memorialized by "McLee's Alley," off Bridge Street between Washington Street and Delmorr Avenue.

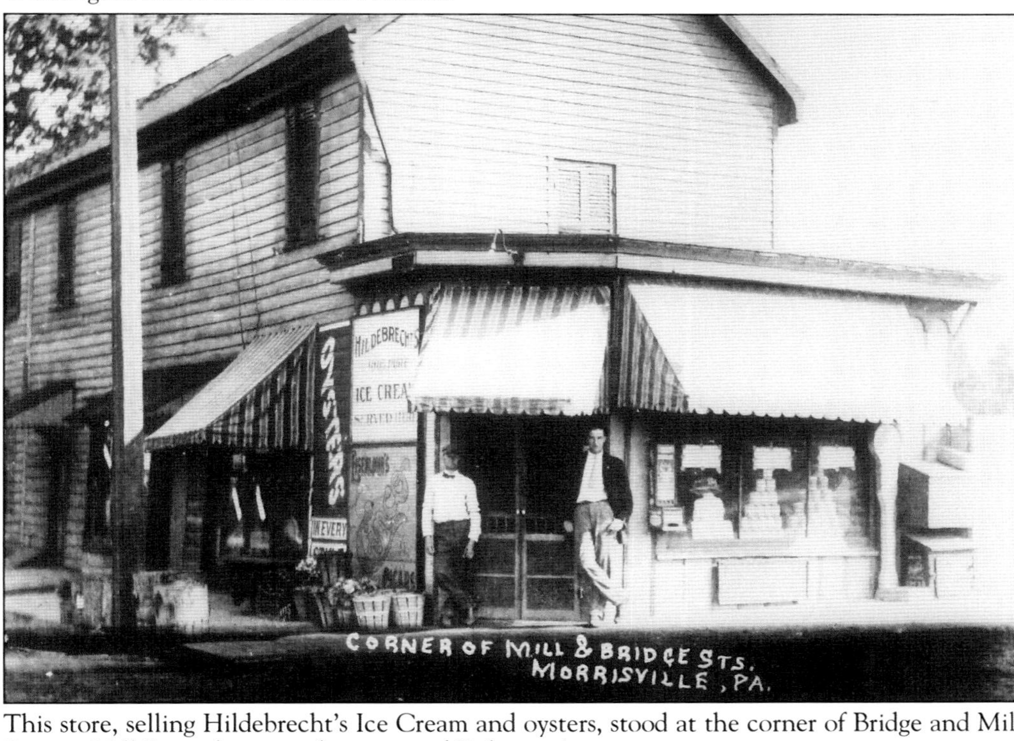

This store, selling Hildebrecht's Ice Cream and oysters, stood at the corner of Bridge and Mill Streets. Mill Street has since been named Delmorr Avenue.

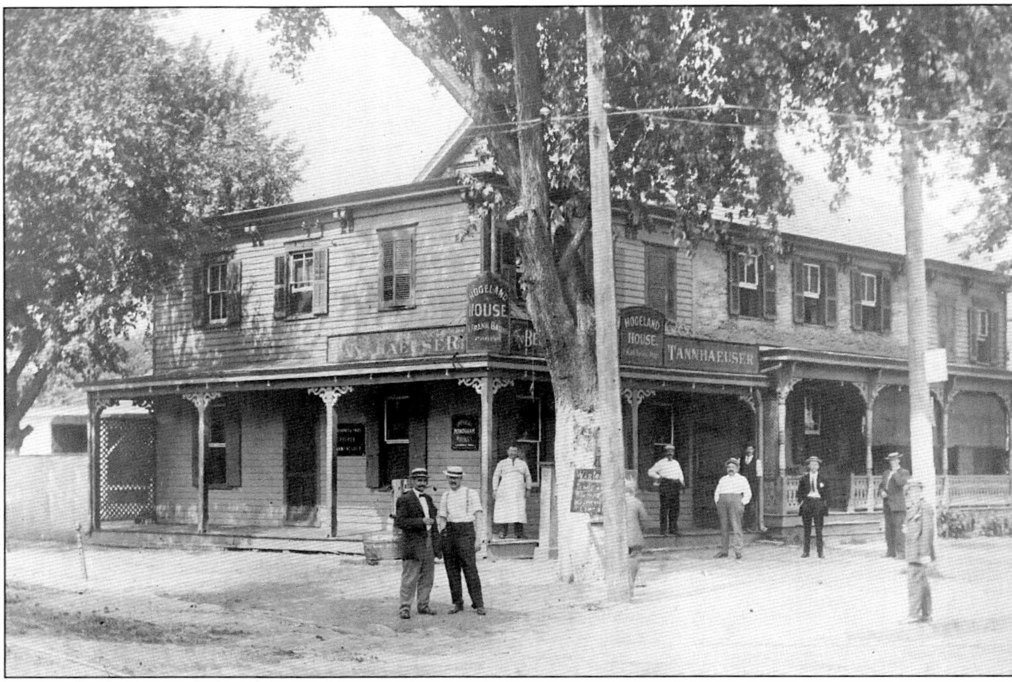

The Hogeland House Hotel stood at the intersection of Bridge Street and Pennsylvania Avenue, the present location of CoreStates Bank.

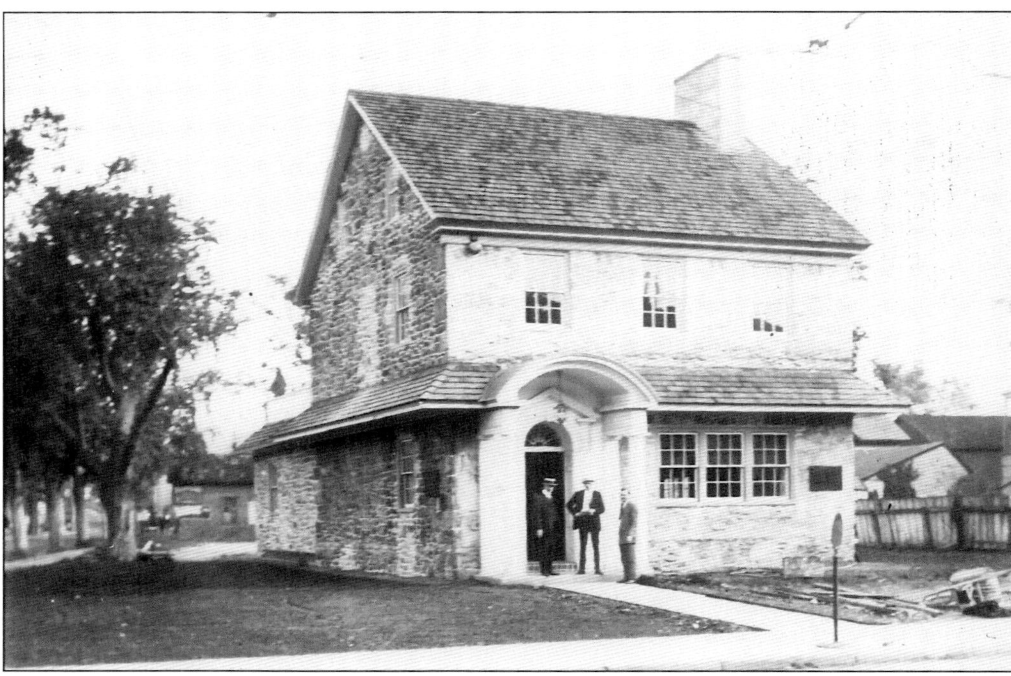

An early version of the Morrisville Bank, at Bridge Street and Pennsylvania Avenue, replaced the Hogeland House. The bank has undergone several enlargements and passed through a number of ownerships to the present CoreStates Bank.

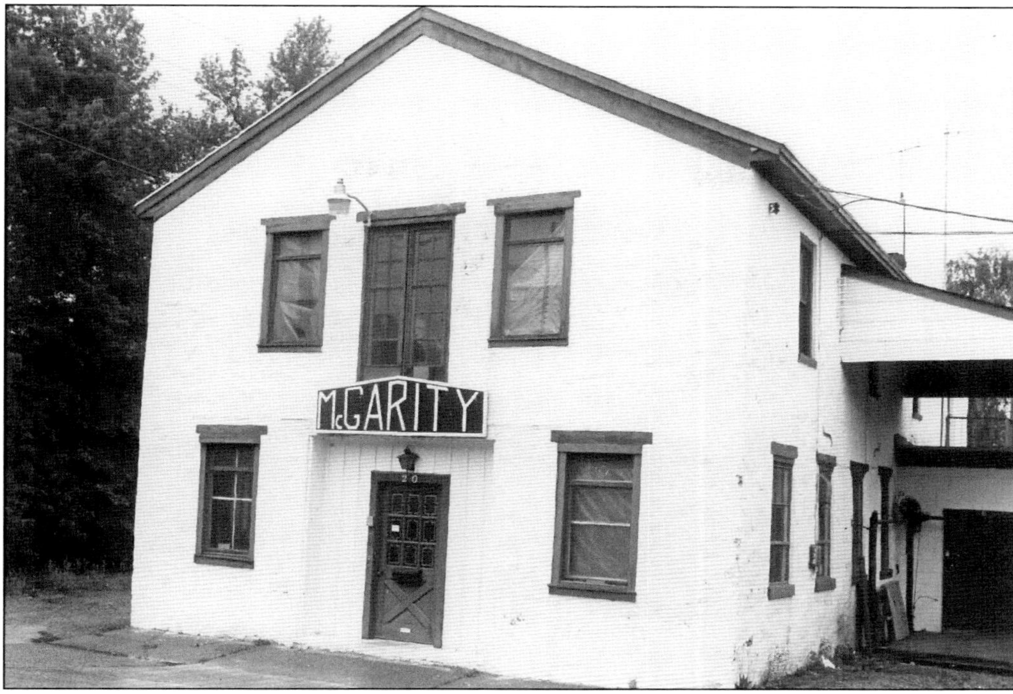

McGarity's Bindery has long been a Morrisville landmark, next to the canal and towpath, facing Union Street. But before it was a bindery it was a paper mill, a morgue, and also served for a time as the First Presbyterian Church.

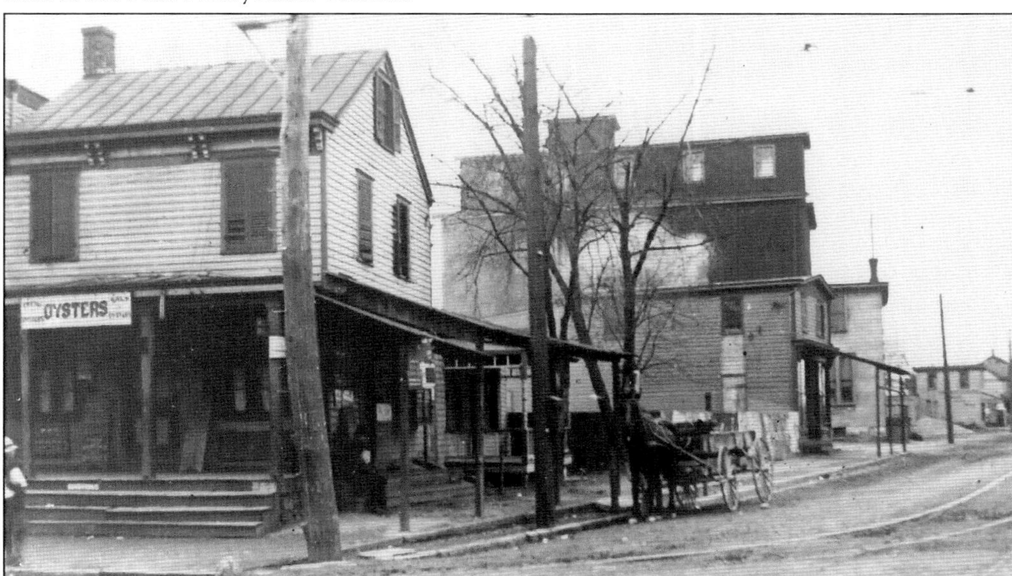

Looking south on Pennsylvania Avenue where it intersects with Bridge Street, the Howell and Johnson feed mill is visible in the background while at the corner is Lewis Burns' oyster emporium. Judging by the many establishments that sold them, oysters must have been popular with Morrisville's residents at the turn of the century. Lewis Burns was a Civil War veteran and his picture appears with two other veterans in Chapter Four.

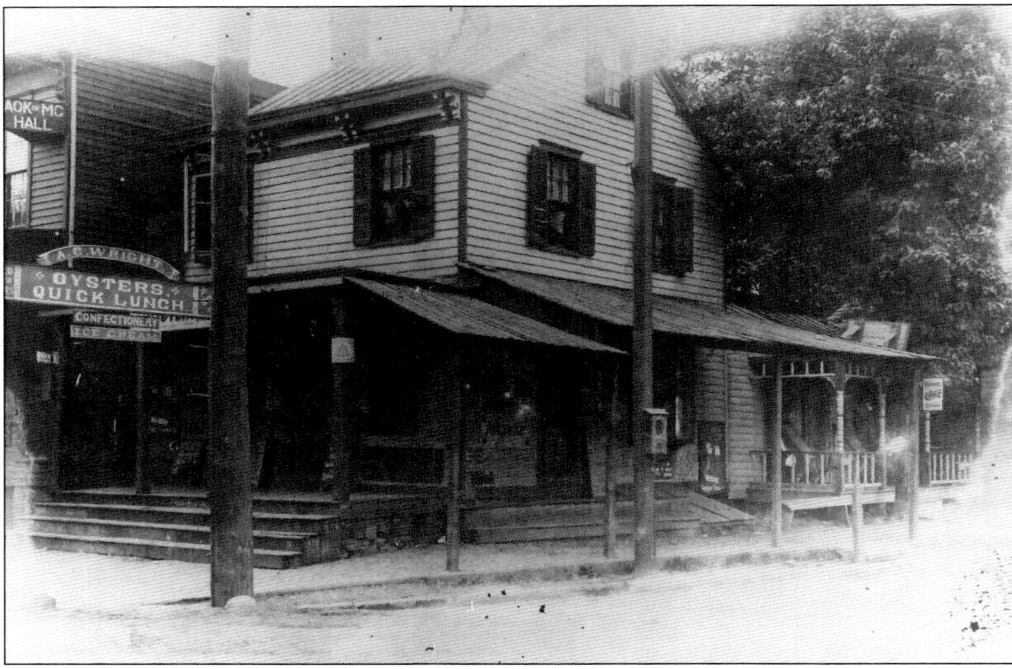

Attesting to the continuing popularity of oysters, Burns' store was replaced by A.G. Wright's Quick Lunch—featuring oysters. At left a sign is visible on the "AOK and MC Hall." Historian George Lebegern explains that the letters stand for "Ancient order, Knights of the Mystic Chain." This fraternal organization was founded in the late 1800s to provide its members with access to life insurance as well as social and civic activities.

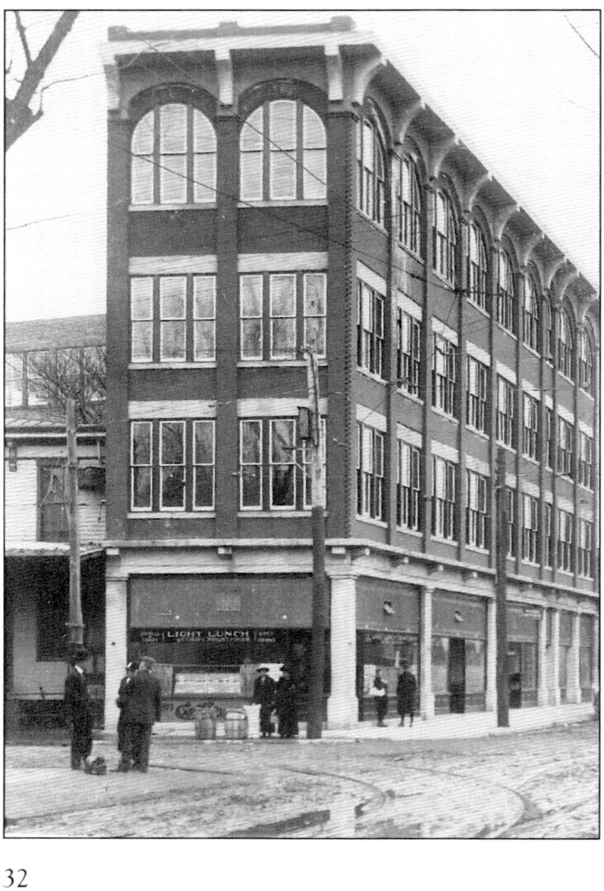

The Stockham Building, which was considered a skyscraper in its day, replaced Wright's Quick Lunch at the corner of Pennsylvania Avenue and Bridge Street. There is no record of oysters being sold in this building.

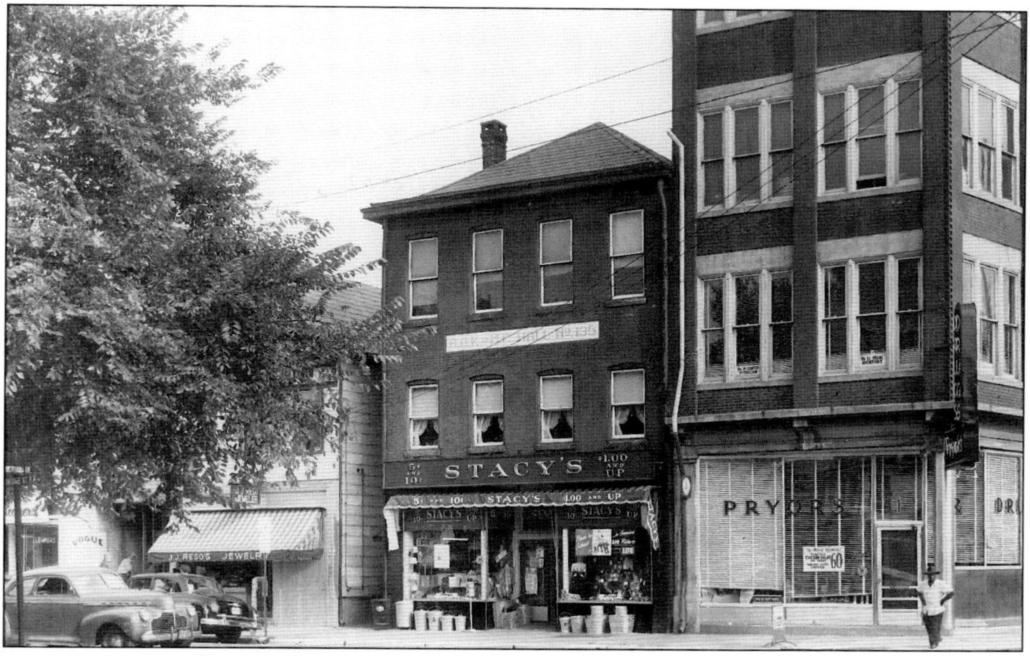

A more recent photograph shows the business district at Pennsylvania and Bridge as it looked during the 1940s. Pryor's Drugstore in the Stockham Building was flanked by Stacy's 5-and-10- cent store, with Reso's Jewelry next along Bridge Street. The "AOK of MC" sign is still in place in the 1990s, though the businesses are long gone.

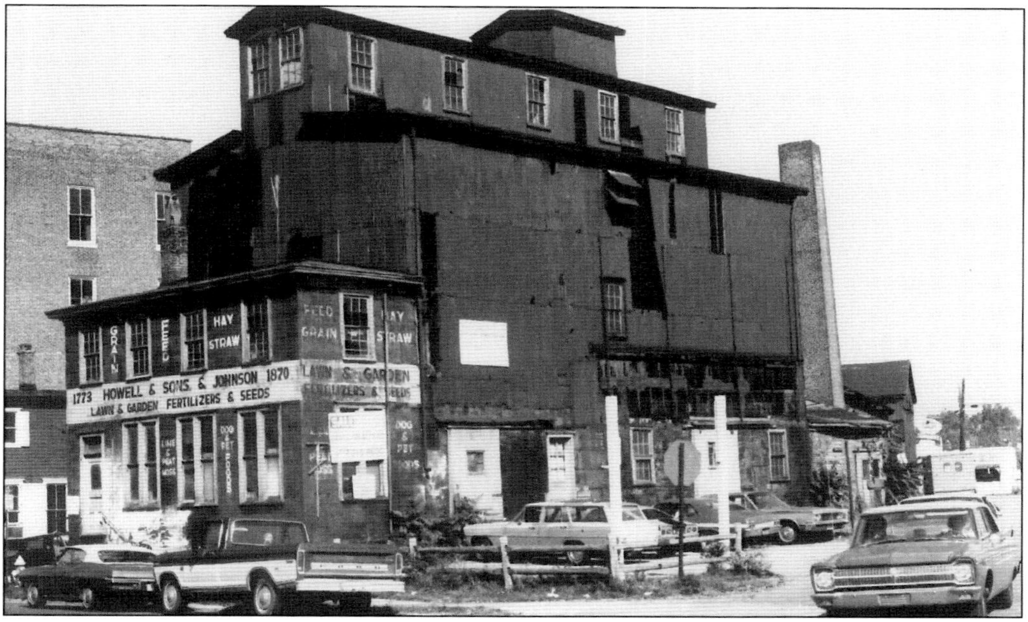

The Howell & Sons & Johnson mill, on Pennsylvania Avenue, though not on the riverside location of early gristmills, was a direct descendant of those businesses. The sign recognizes the mill's antecedents by including the dates 1773 and 1870, and advertises that seeds, lawn and garden fertilizers, grain, feed hay, and straw were available for purchase.

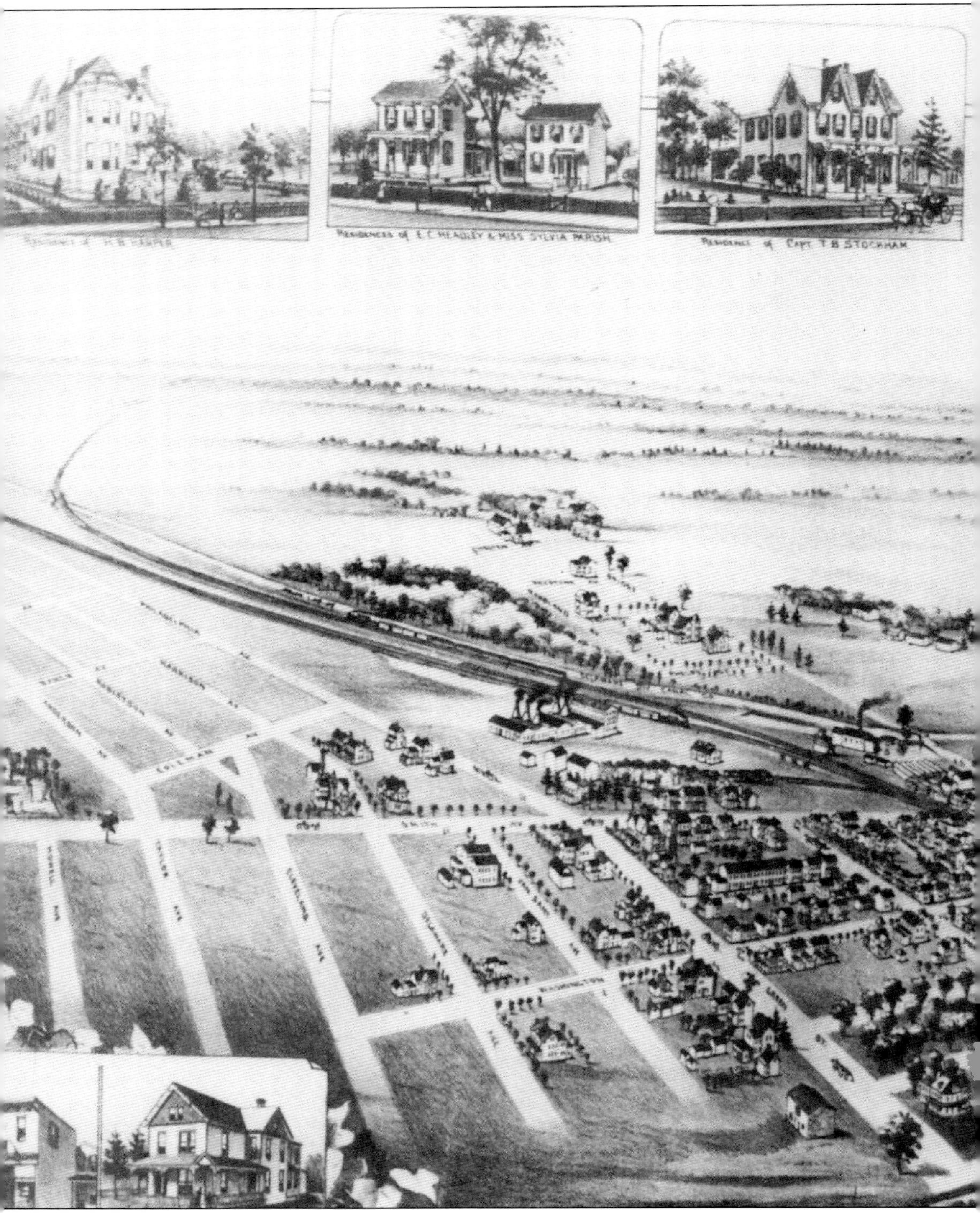

A map of Morrisville in 1893, by T.M. Fowler shows the single bridge that accommodated railroad, horse-drawn buggy, and pedestrian travel, and the fast-flowing stream that cut a true

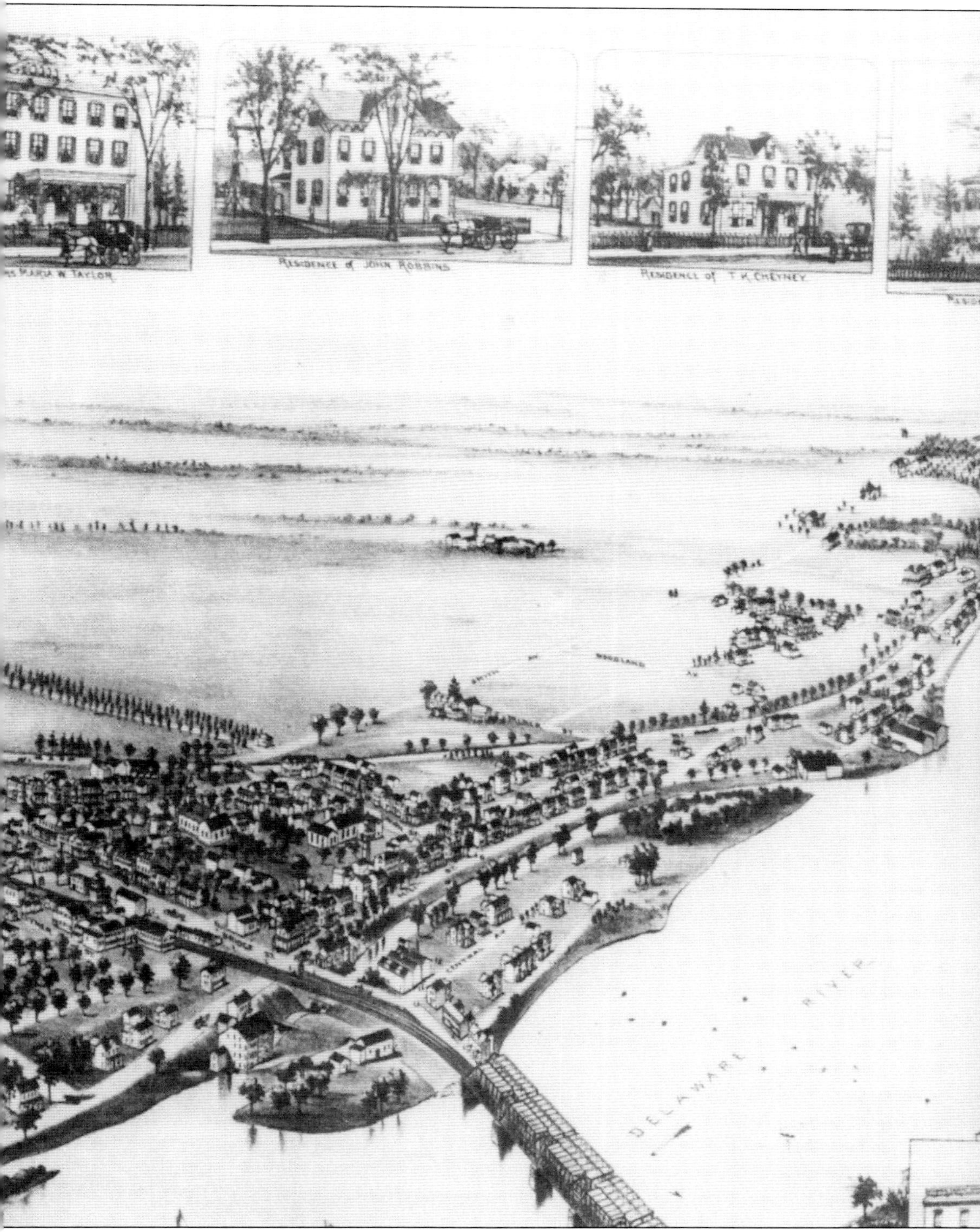

island off from the borough and provided power for the old mills. Summerseat can be seen at the end of a long row of trees in the upper center of the illustration.

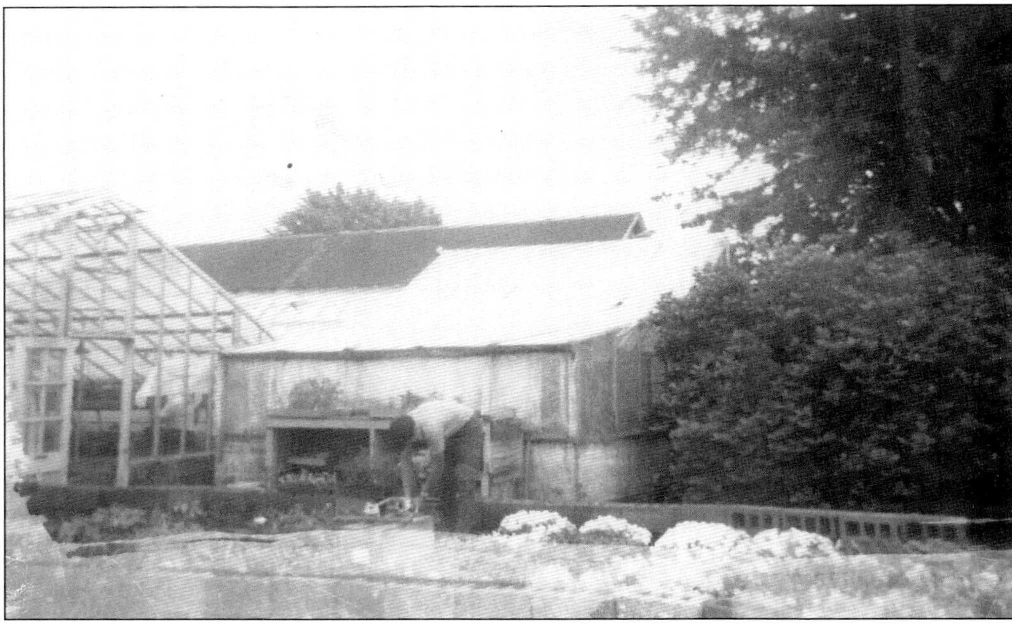

The Marrazzo family proved to be an entrepreneurial force in Morrisville and bordering Lower Makefield Township, starting from this modest greenhouse in Manor Park. Dan Marrazzo moved from this location to establish Marrazzo's Manor Lane Florist and Garden Center on Yardley Road. Norm Marrazzo established Centre Fruit, a gourmet food store, at Marrazzo's Big Oak Shopping Center on West Trenton Avenue.

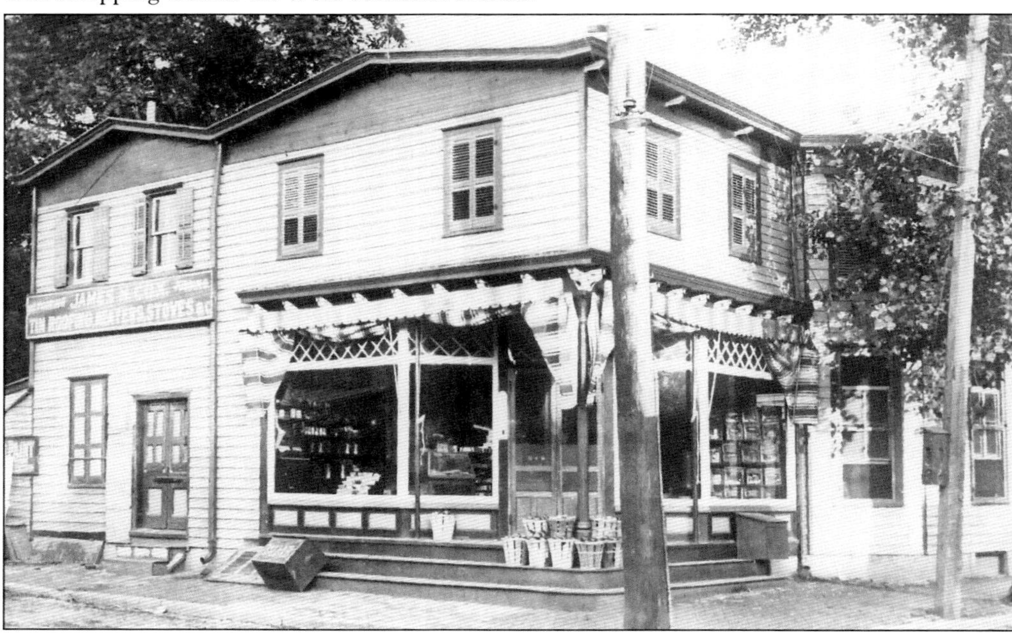

Looking north on Pennsylvania Avenue, diagonally across from the Stockham Building, there was a general store, which later became part of the American Stores chain. James Cox's business was located next to the store, fronting on Bridge Street. It sold a variety of wares, including tin roofing, heaters, and stoves, and advertised "repairing" and "jobbing."

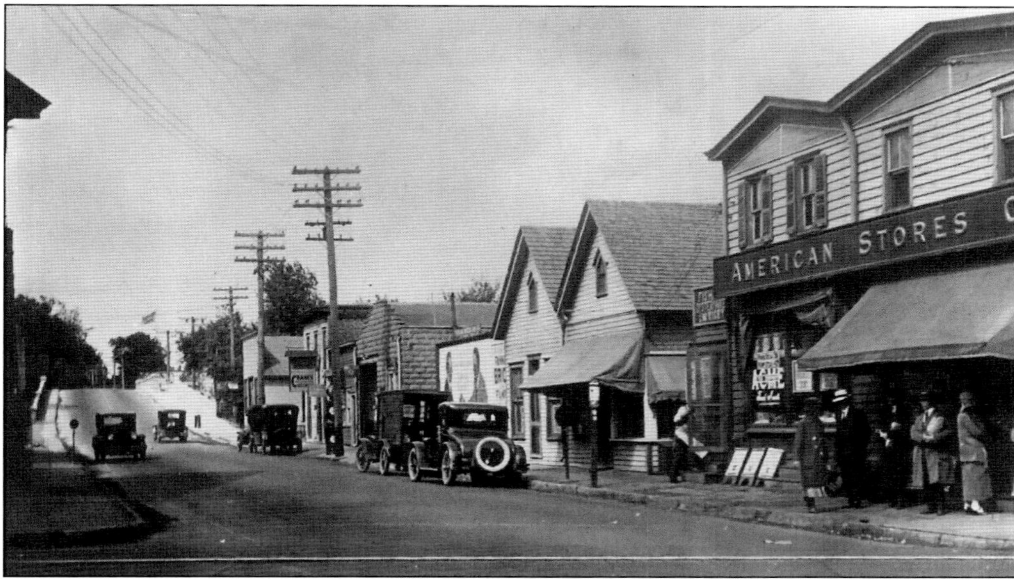

When American Stores took over the corner grocery at Bridge Street and Pennsylvania Avenue, it expanded to incorporate the building formerly occupied by James Cox. This picture shows the view farther out West Bridge Street, showing a "hump-backed" bridge over the canal, since leveled.

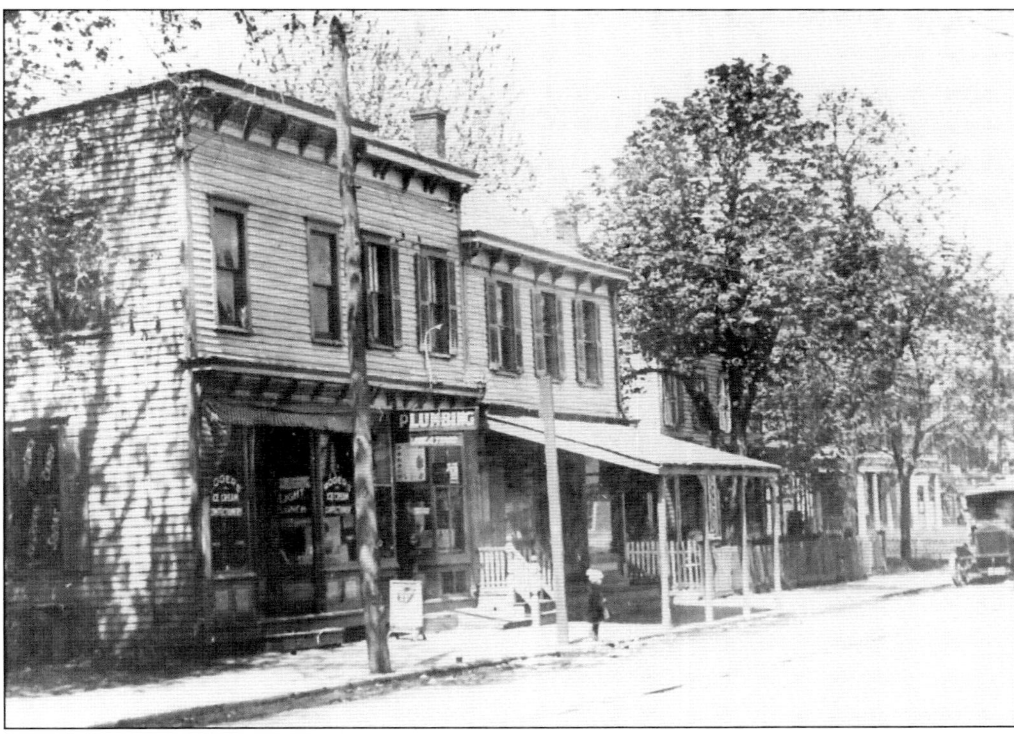

Along Bridge Street in what is still the downtown business district, Rogers' light lunch and ice cream store was flanked by a plumbing and heating supplies store at the turn of the century. The three stores pictured gave way to form a parking lot for the Morrisville (now CoreStates) Bank.

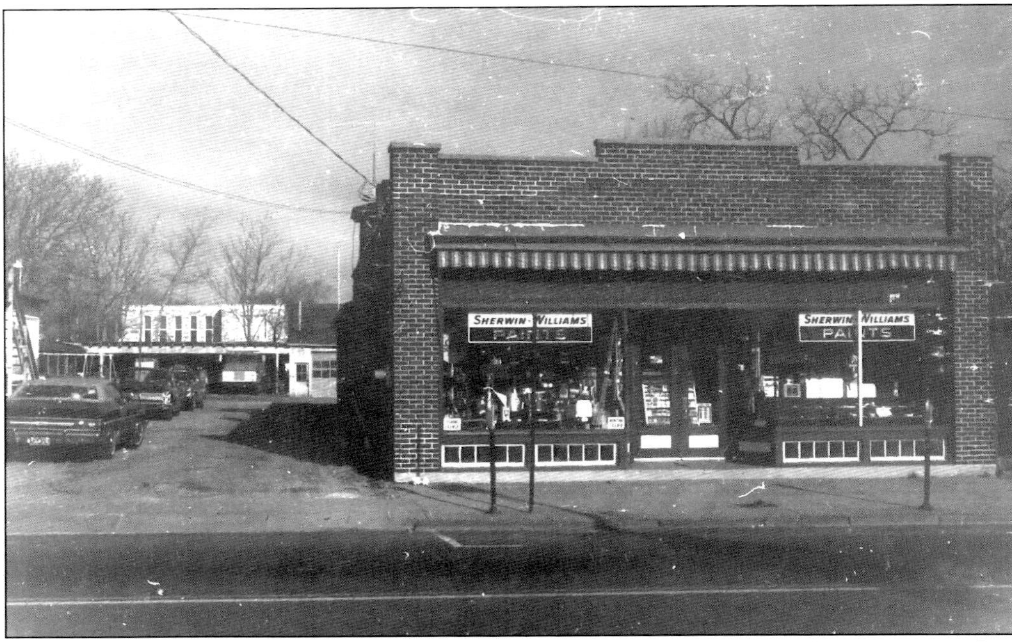

A business that survived on Bridge Street for half a century was Howell's hardware store, stocking a wide-ranging inventory of tools, nuts, bolts, nails, and screws, as well as paints, brushes, and fishing and hunting licenses to meet every non-ingestible need of borough residents.

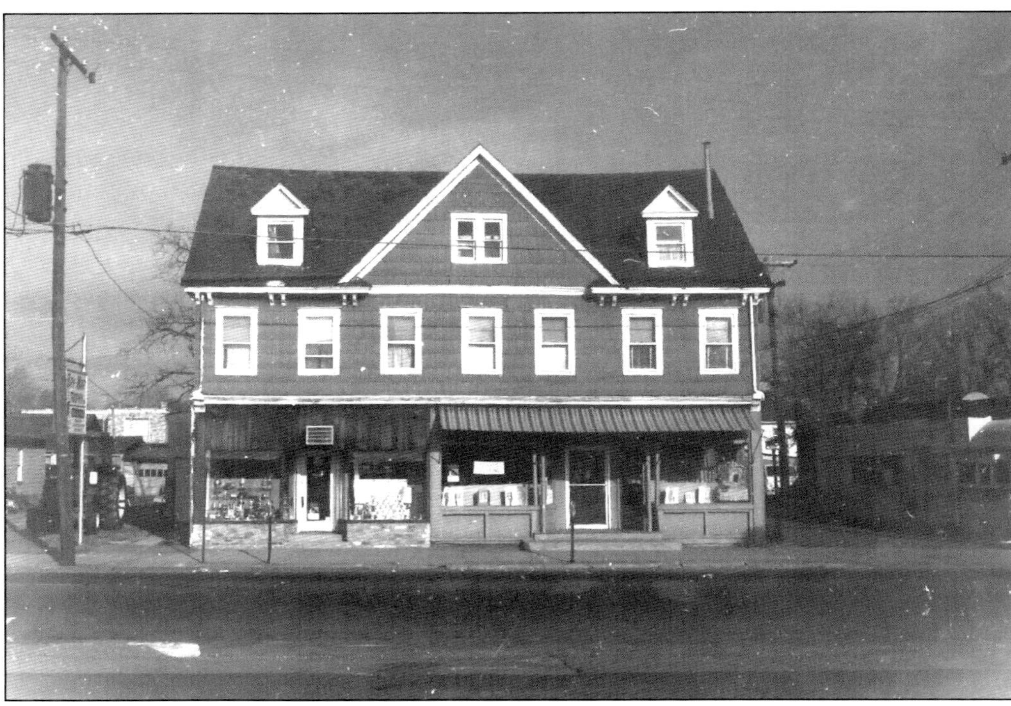

Among businesses along Bridge Street in the late 1940s and early '50s were a trophy shop and Tullio's Tailoring. There were apartments above the stores.

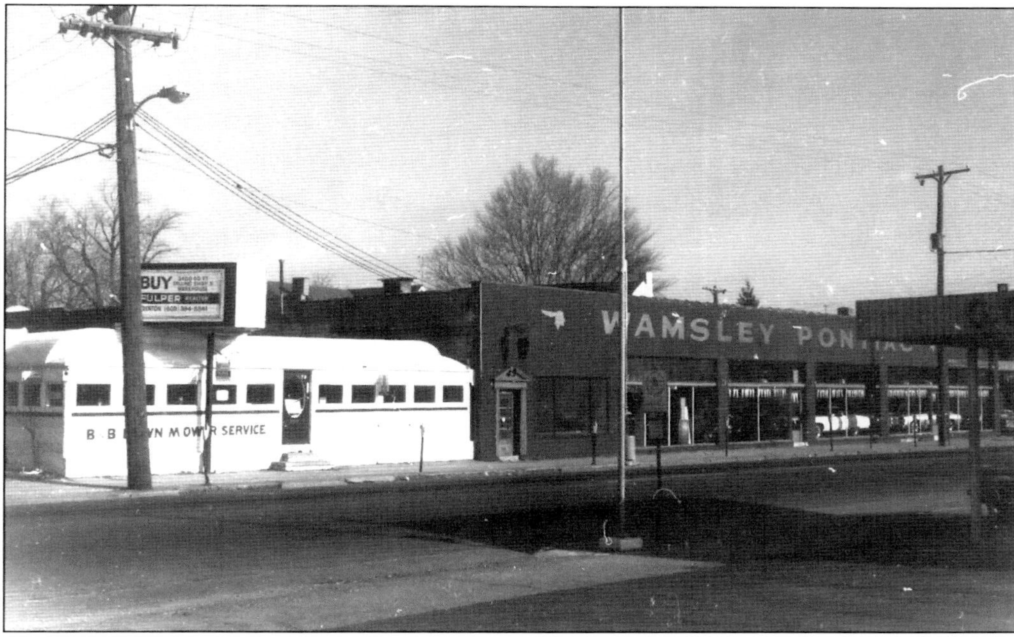

Continuing along Bridge Street toward the river, the B&B Lawn Mower Service (in the converted Morrisville Transit Diner) was next to the Wamsley Pontiac dealership.

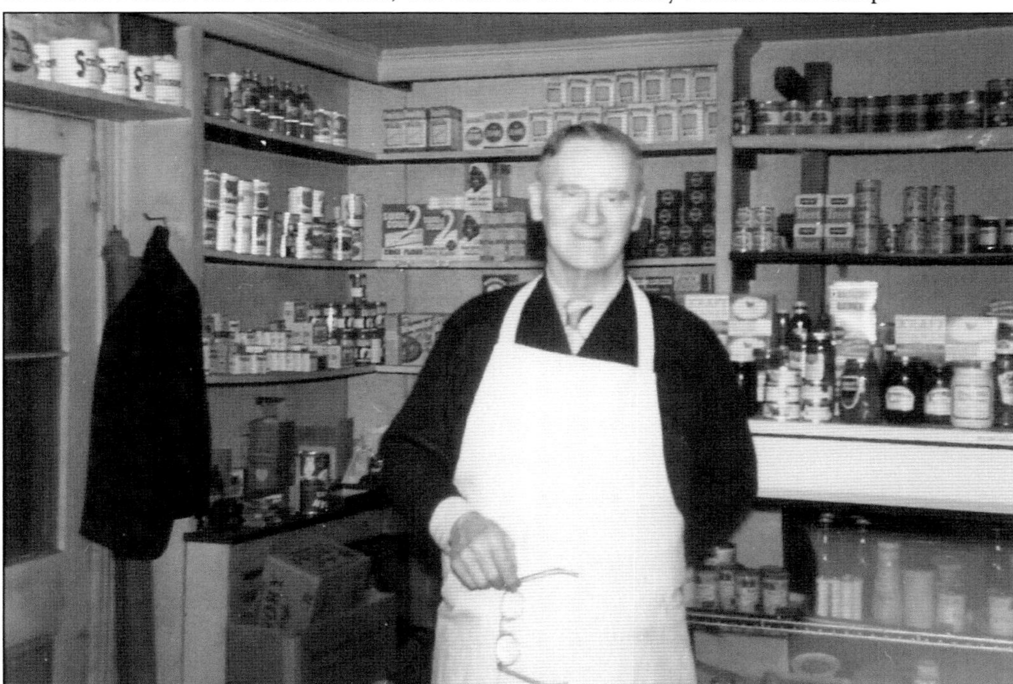

Not all businesses were in the business district. James Murray Sr. operated a neighborhood grocery store at the corner of Washington and Green Streets, across from the railroad, during the 1930s, '40s, and '50s. The wide variety of items stocked can be seen in the background, but there are not many of any one item since the business was small.

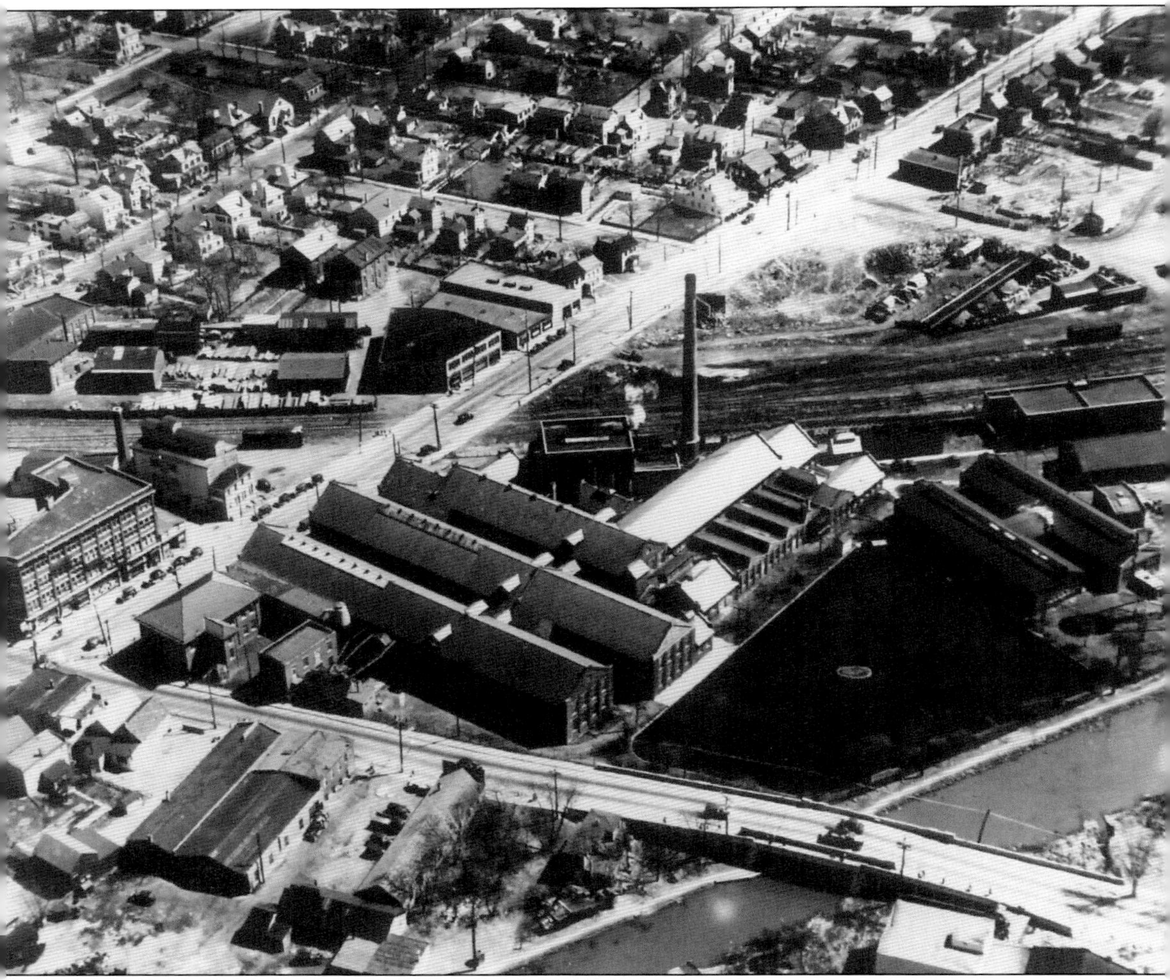

Rubber was first manufactured in Morrisville in 1873, when Dr. R.S. Dana and John W. Thompson operated a soft rubber factory in a large old brick building that had been the stables for a home built by Robert Morris and later owned by French General Jean Moreau. After being operated by a series of owners, the plant at the north end of Bank Street was sold for use as tenements and a new plant was constructed at Pennsylvania Avenue and Bridge Street in 1903. This aerial view shows the new plant with Bridge Street running left to right over the canal, which is next to the Vulcanized Rubber Company's large pond.

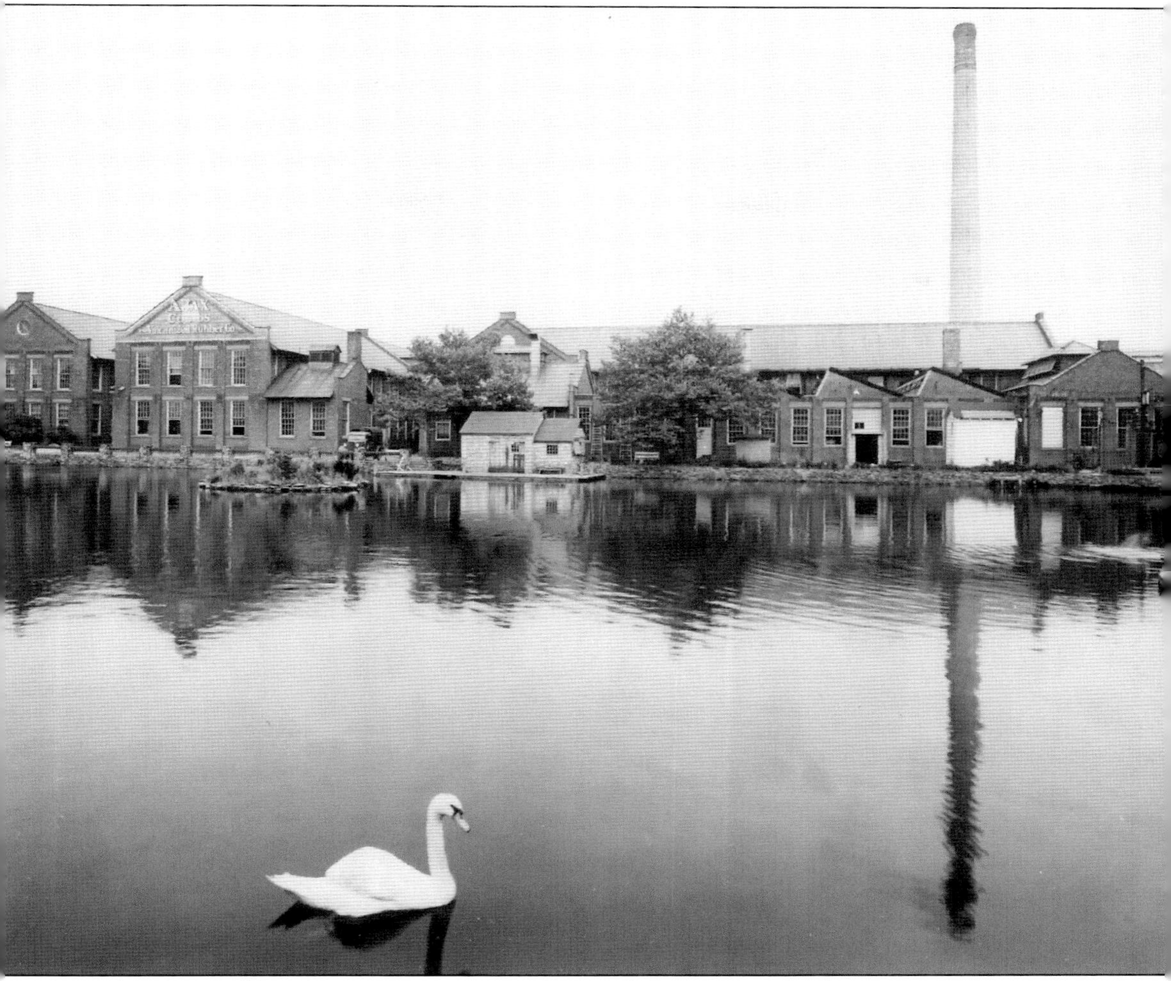

The Vulcanized Rubber Company's pond was clean and clear, attracting the swan swimming in the foreground. On any nice day during the early 1900s large fish could be seen swimming in its water, while Ajax combs and other rubber products were being manufactured in the buildings in the background.

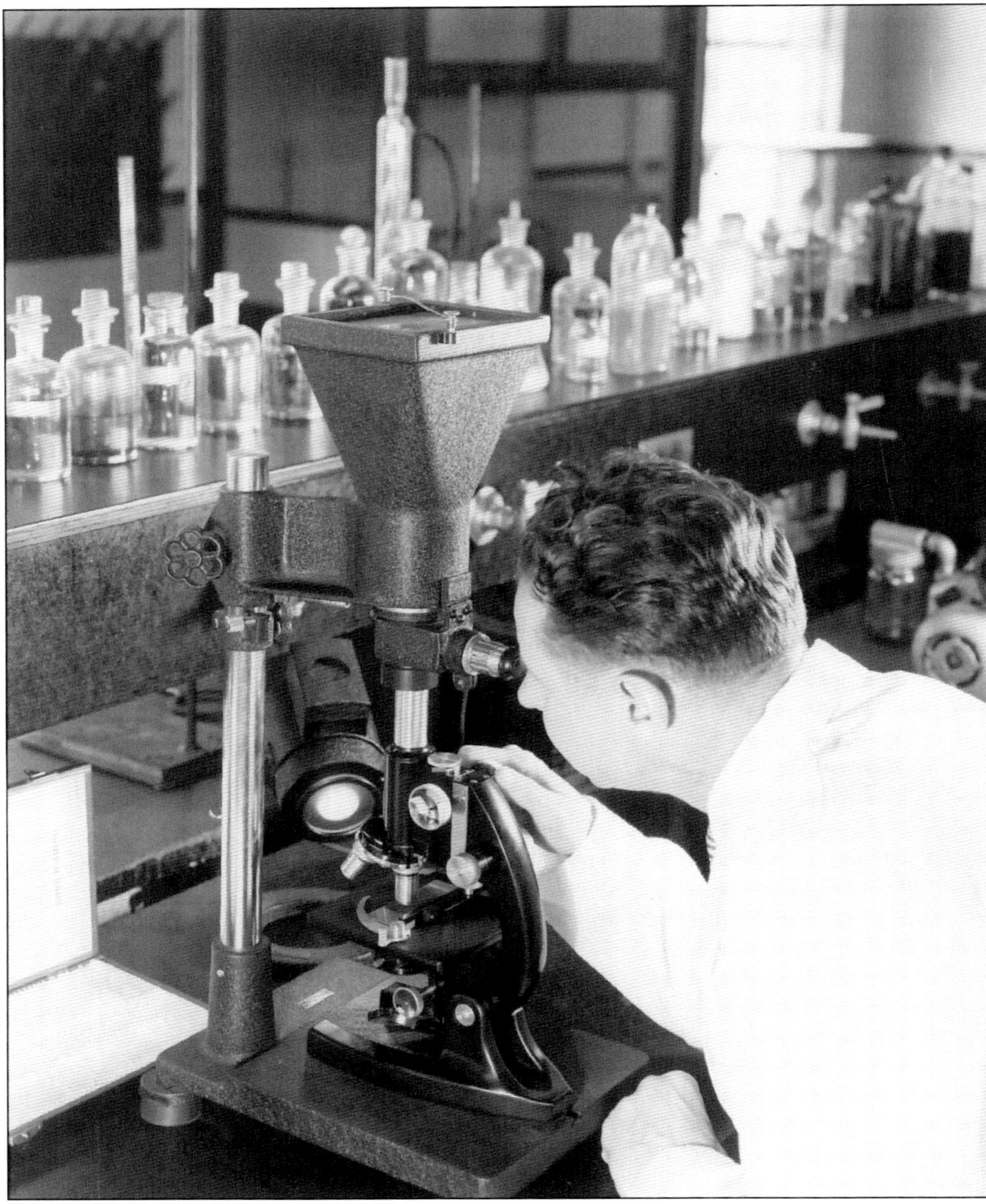

During World War I the Vulcanized Rubber Company produced large quantities of gas masks and other items used by the military. After World War I the company established a research laboratory and in 1940, after extensive experimentation, the injection molding of plastics was begun. In 1945 the firm's name was changed to the Vulcanized Rubber and Plastics Company. It was headed by Stanley H. Renton, president; John J. Noble, vice-president and sales manager; Prescott Beach, secretary and general manager; and Coleman P. Morgan, director of the development department, an expanded and very modern laboratory. Cole Morgan is shown examining experimental material through a microscope.

Another photograph taken in the Vulcanized Rubber and Plastics Company laboratory shows Ed Winarski fine-tuning what was then state-of-the-art equipment.

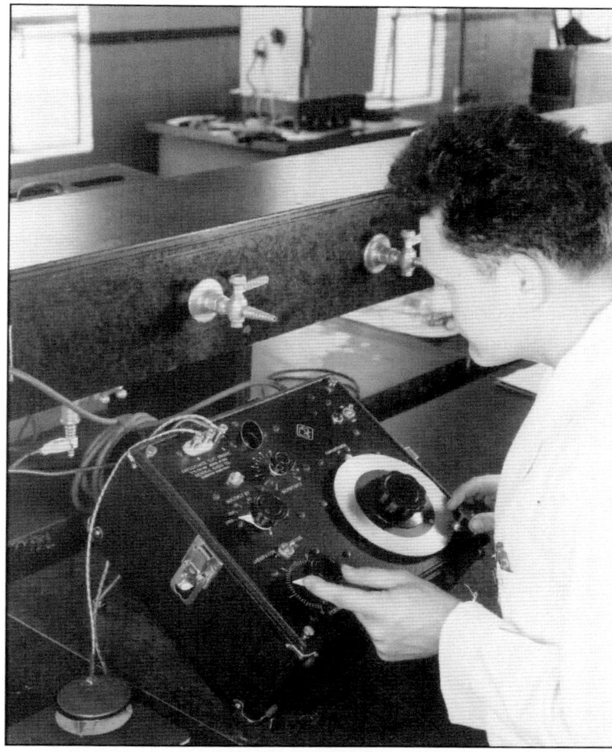

When Vulcanized Rubber and Plastics was turning out products made of both substances, the business boomed. In 1946 the company had seven hundred employees, but as the years passed business slowed and the work force was reduced to two hundred by the late 1970s.

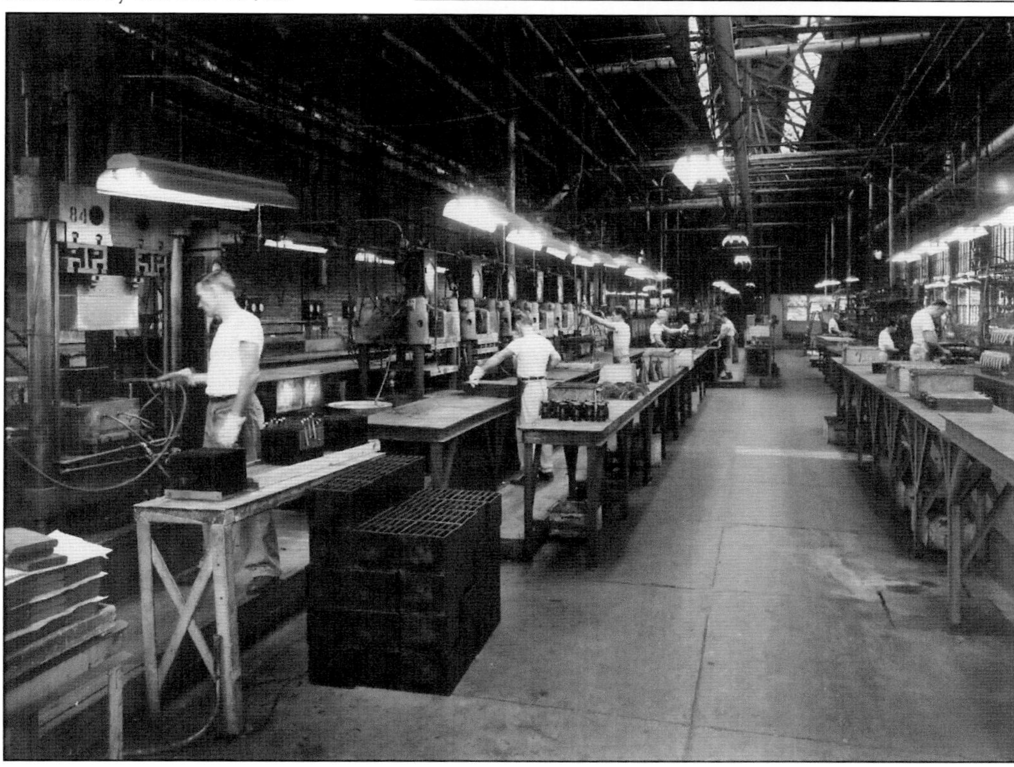

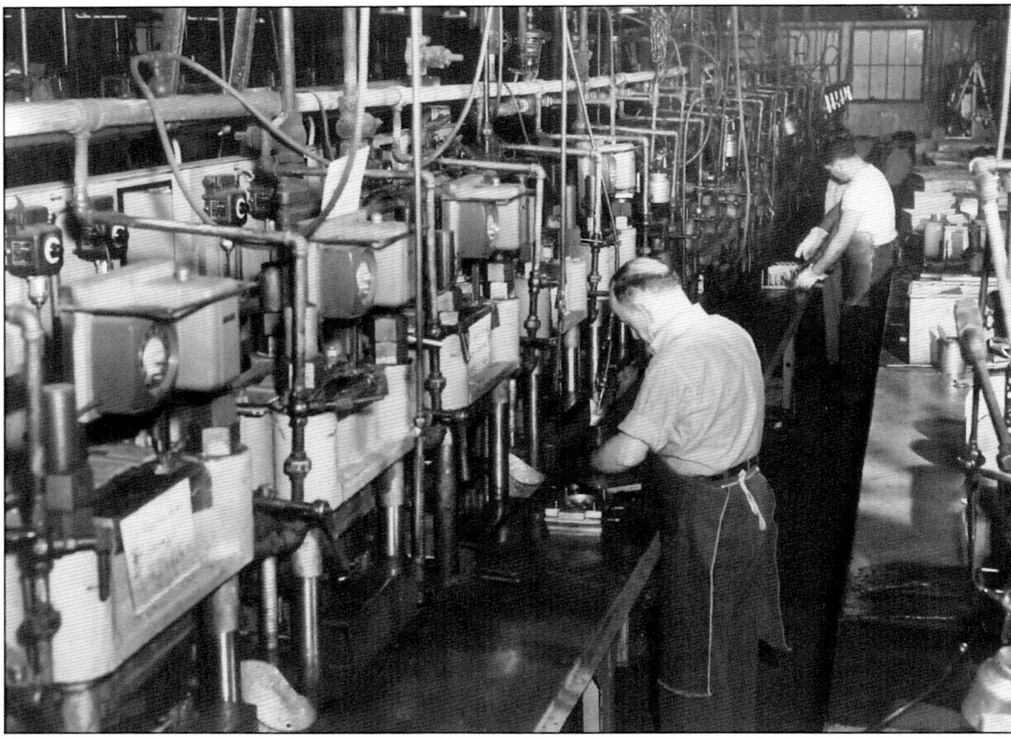

After a strike in 1978 and two costly fires, business continued to decline and the Vulcanized Rubber and Plastics Company finally closed its doors at midnight, May 20, 1980. This photograph shows activities in the plant when the rubber and plastics business was at its height, during the late 1940s.

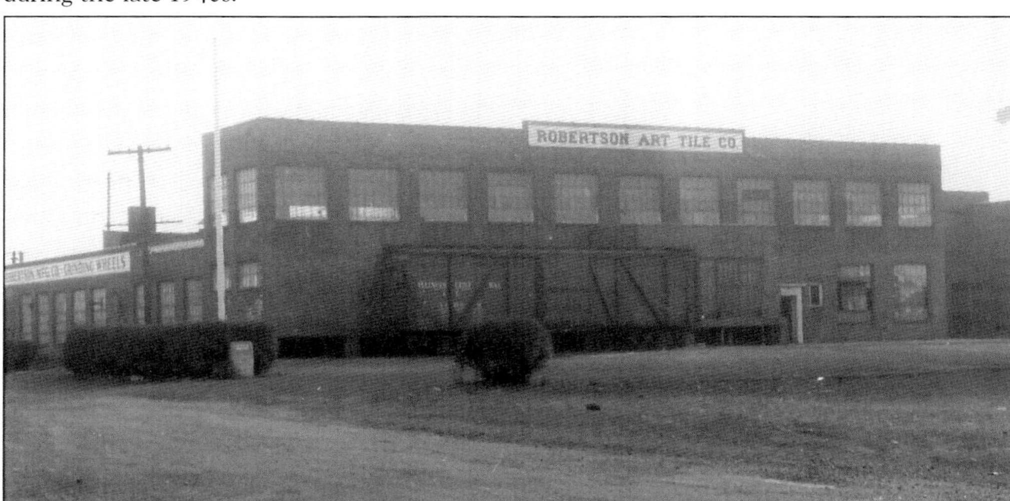

Seventeen years after rubber manufacturing was begun in Morrisville, a second major industry was founded by George W. Robertson, an English immigrant who was able to start a tile factory with financial assistance by Arthur D. Forst. Called the Robertson Art Tile Company until 1943, the "Tile Works" began in 1890 to produce white wall tile and a colored art tile used on fireplace mantels and facings, as well as for cornices and moldings.

A photograph taken in 1910 shows the Robertson Art Tile Company shipping office. The men pictured, from left to right, are Ed Watson, Pat Schisler, and Frank Smith.

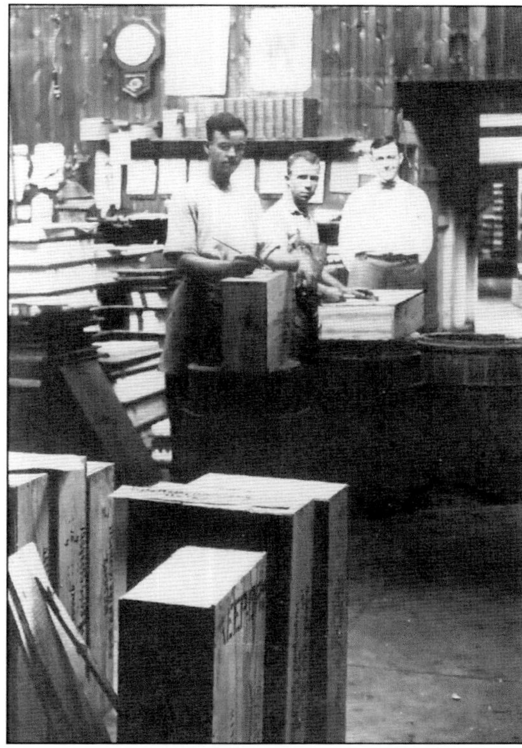

By 1959 the Robertson Manufacturing Company employed four hundred skilled workers, sixty in the Abrasives Division, and had a total annual payroll of some $2 million. The photograph shows Walt Miles and Lacy Austin at work in the plant *c.* 1965.

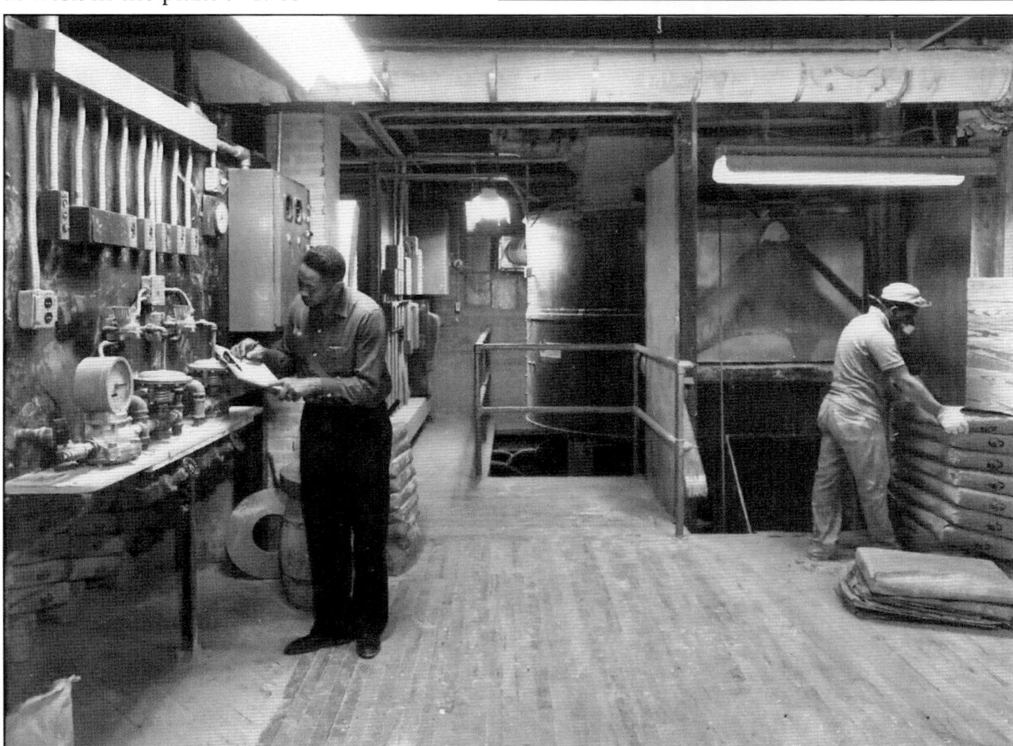

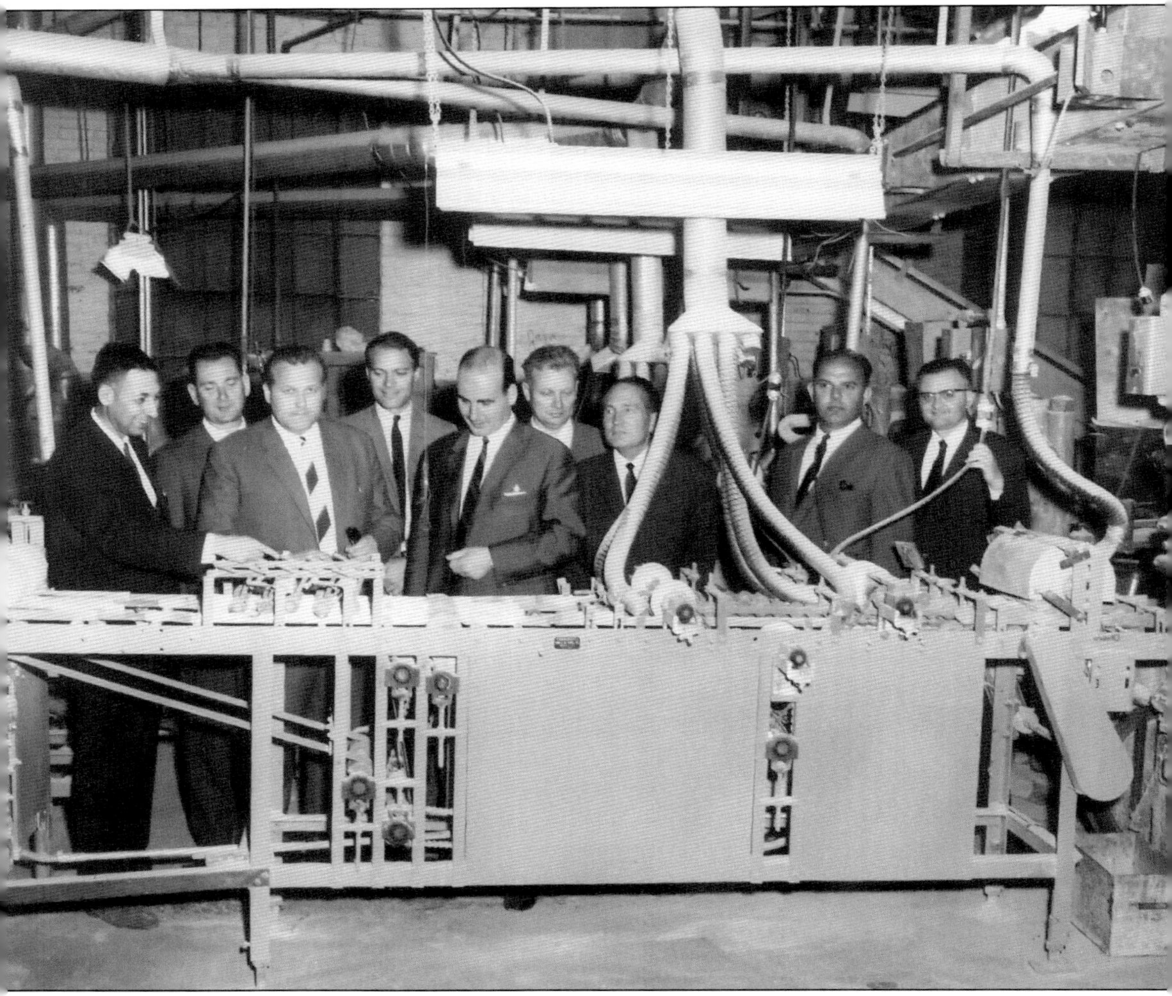

Robert E. Anderson Sr., who had joined the Robertson company in 1921 as a ceramics engineer, was president in 1960 and his son, Bob Anderson Jr., was vice-president. Raymond H. Rossell was also a vice-president as well as secretary and treasurer, and Horace T. Cook Jr. was vice-president in charge of sales. John C. Elder was plant manager with Donald C. Lansing as his assistant. Samuel Hershey was Abrasive Division sales manager with C. Richard (Dick) Anderson as his assistant. In the picture, Marty Parcel, vice-president of manufacturing in 1965, is showing some visitors from Germany how the tile production machinery functioned.

Three

Schools and Students

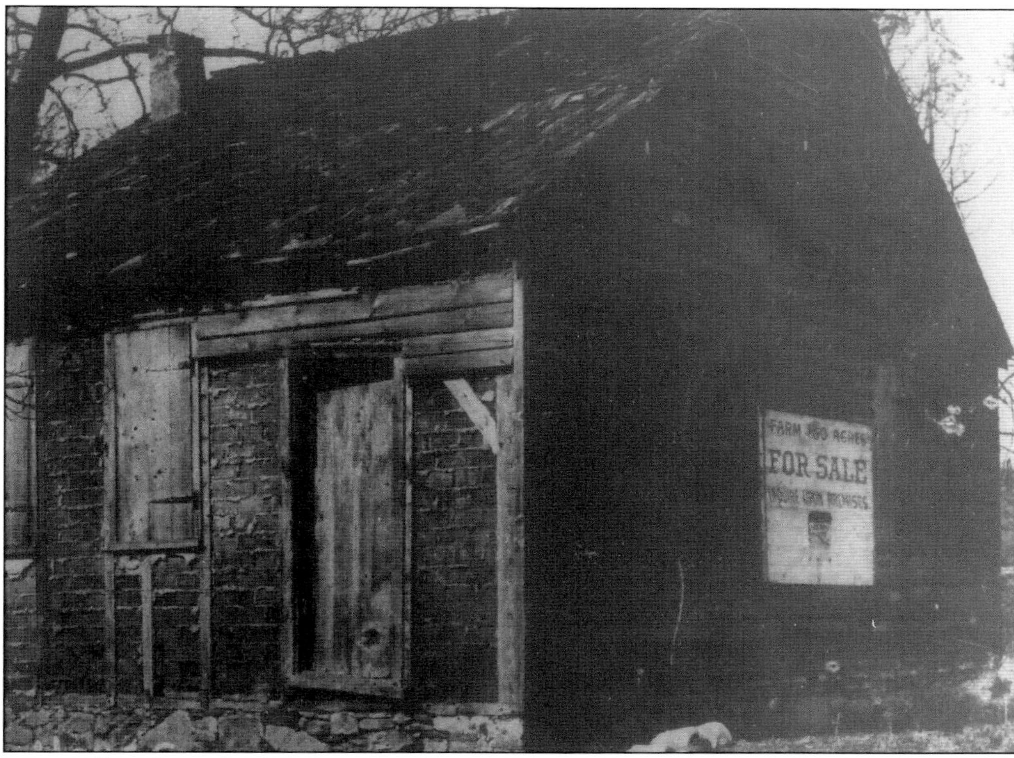

Morrisville's first school, one room where as many as fifty students could be crowded onto its rough wooden seats, was located at the western end of Union Street where it intersects Pennsylvania Avenue, on now land occupied by the Presbyterian Tower senior citizens' home. It was constructed on a half-acre of land set aside for a school by Josiah Wood in 1764, when he sold 70 acres to Adam Hoops. The school was used until 1857; it also served as a polling place and for meetings of borough council and other organizations.

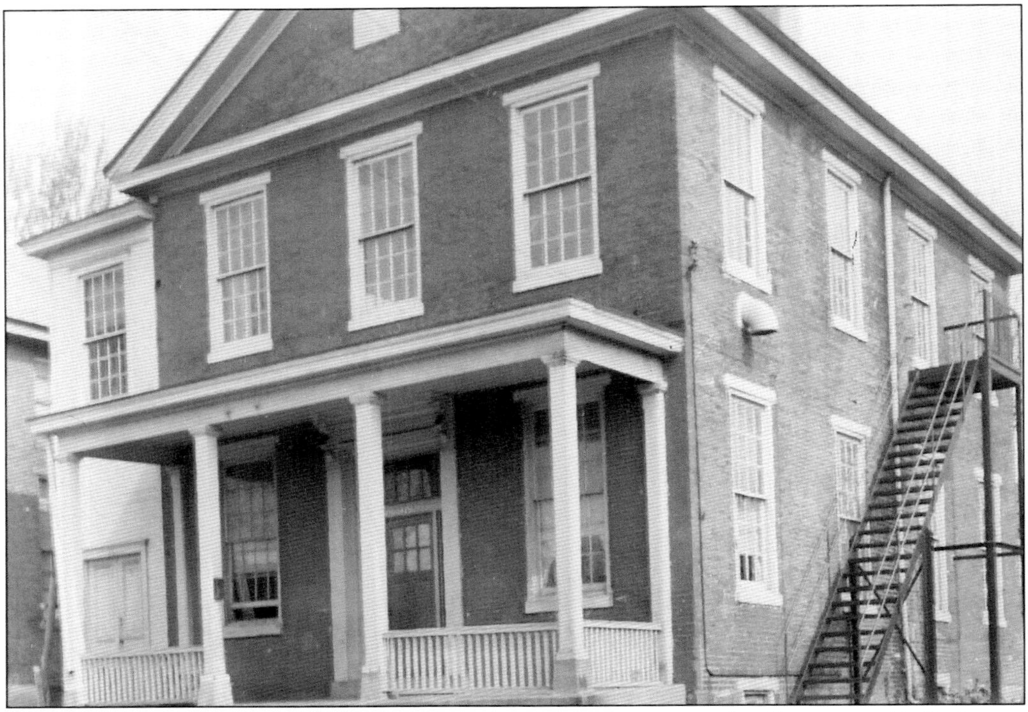

The Chambers Street School replaced the original one-room schoolhouse in 1857. It was expanded in 1876, and became a high school in 1892. Before 1892 Morrisville students who wanted to complete their education and obtain a high school diploma had to finish at Trenton High School across the river in New Jersey.

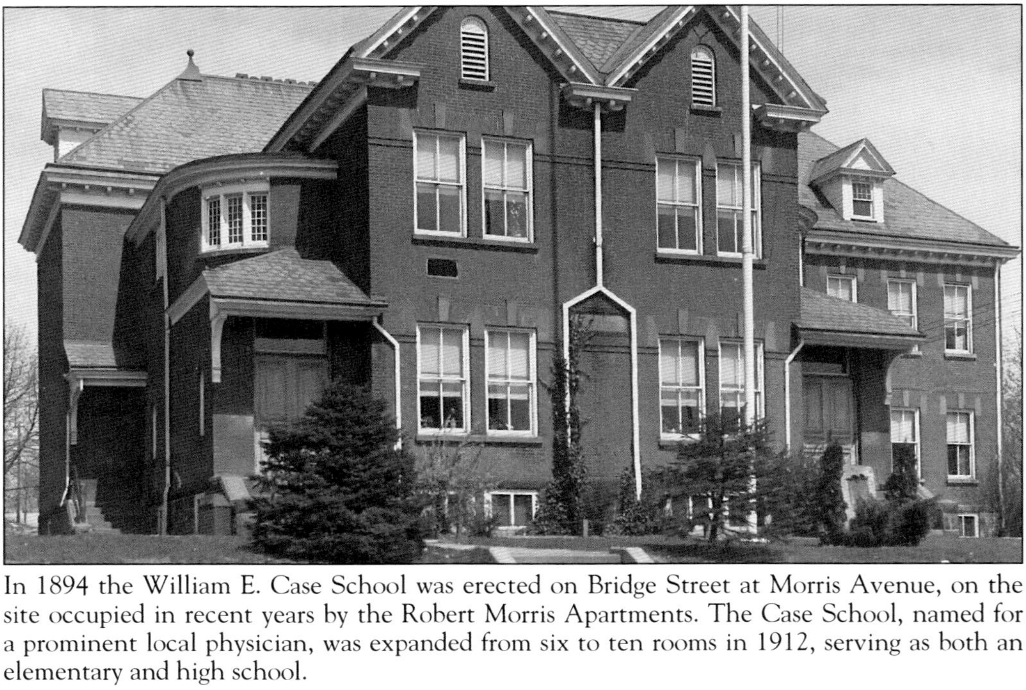

In 1894 the William E. Case School was erected on Bridge Street at Morris Avenue, on the site occupied in recent years by the Robert Morris Apartments. The Case School, named for a prominent local physician, was expanded from six to ten rooms in 1912, serving as both an elementary and high school.

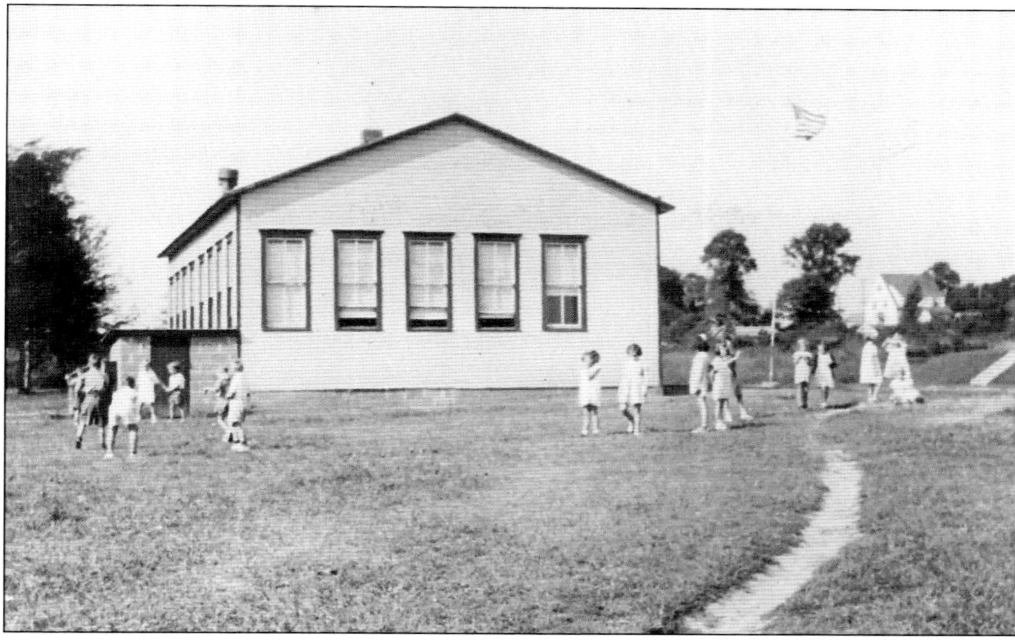

The first Capitol View Elementary School was erected during World War I, giving way to a more modern building in 1951. At present the school serves as a day care center.

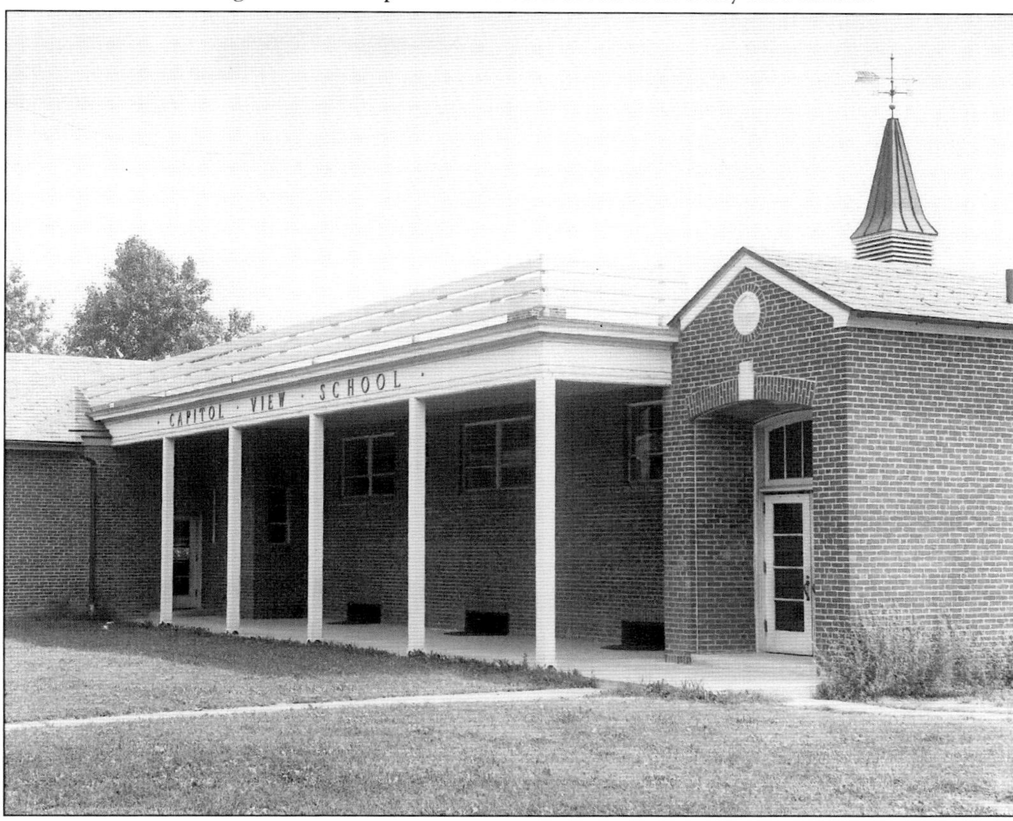

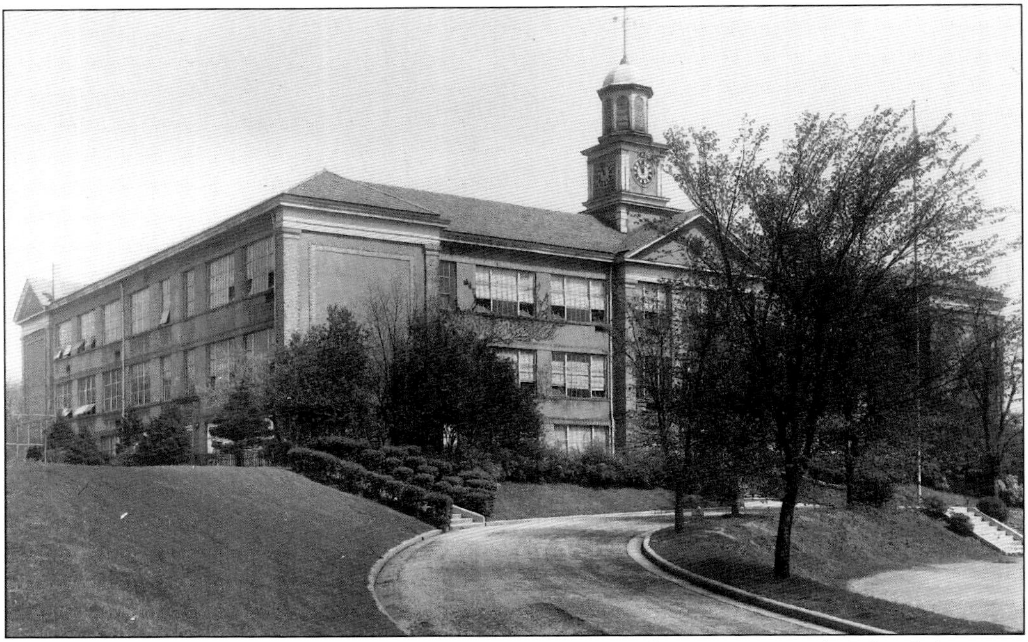

A four-room elementary school in Manor Park and the Robert Morris High School, between Hillcrest and Clymer Avenues, were both opened in 1924. The high school building was destroyed by fire in 1958 and the M.R. Reiter Elementary School was constructed on the site.

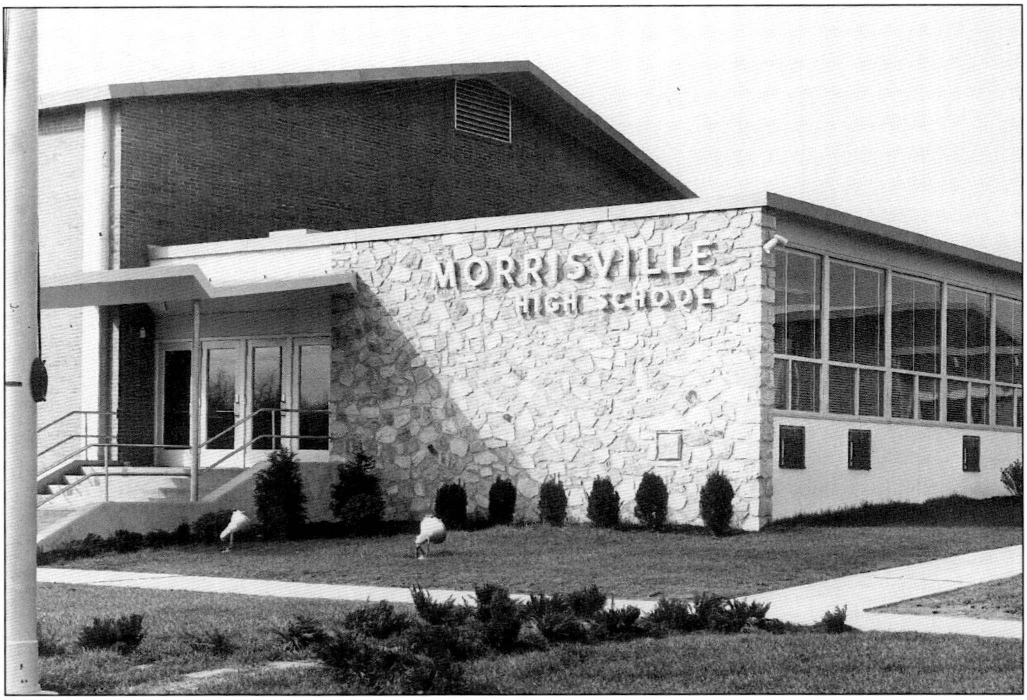

With increasing enrollment projected, a large middle-senior high school was opened on Palmer Avenue in 1958. As it turned out, enrollment did not increase appreciably and only about half of the space in the new school was needed.

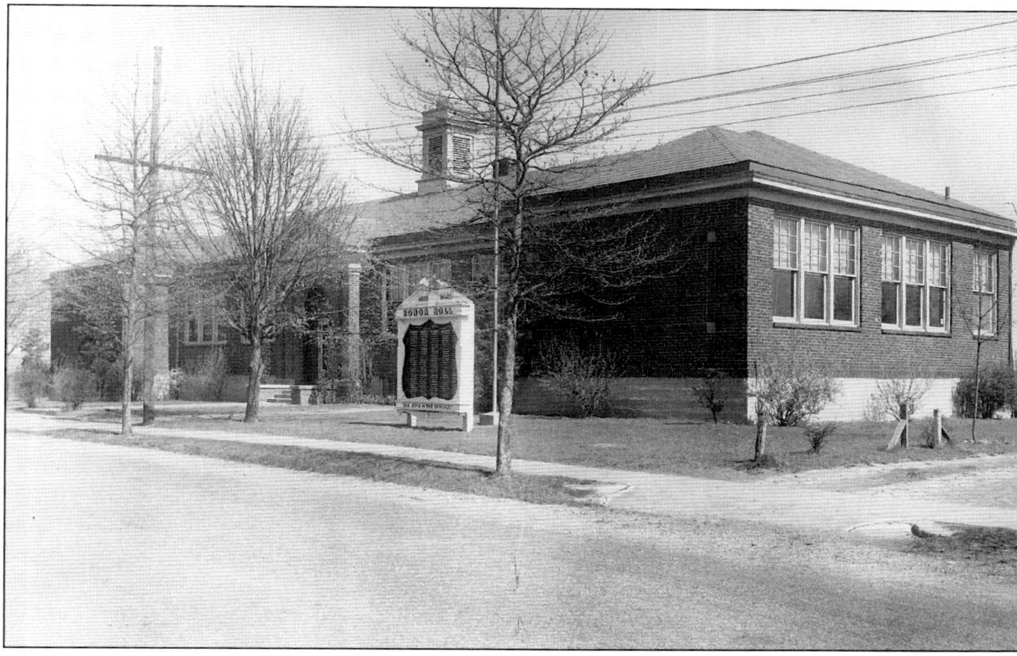

The Manor Park building, opened in 1924, was later converted to an office for the district justice and a senior citizens' center.

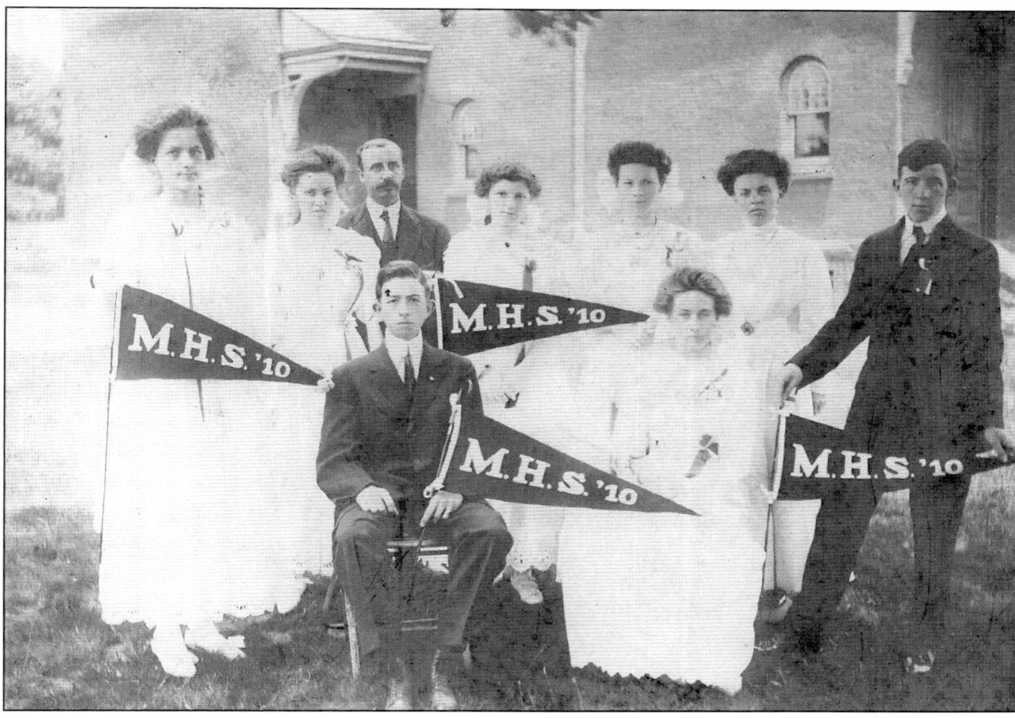

There were seven graduates in the Morrisville High School Class of 1910: Daisy Edney, Emma Elgerhauser, J. Headley Howell, Elmira Sine, Clarence Wharton, Stella Wharton, and Bessie Wildman.

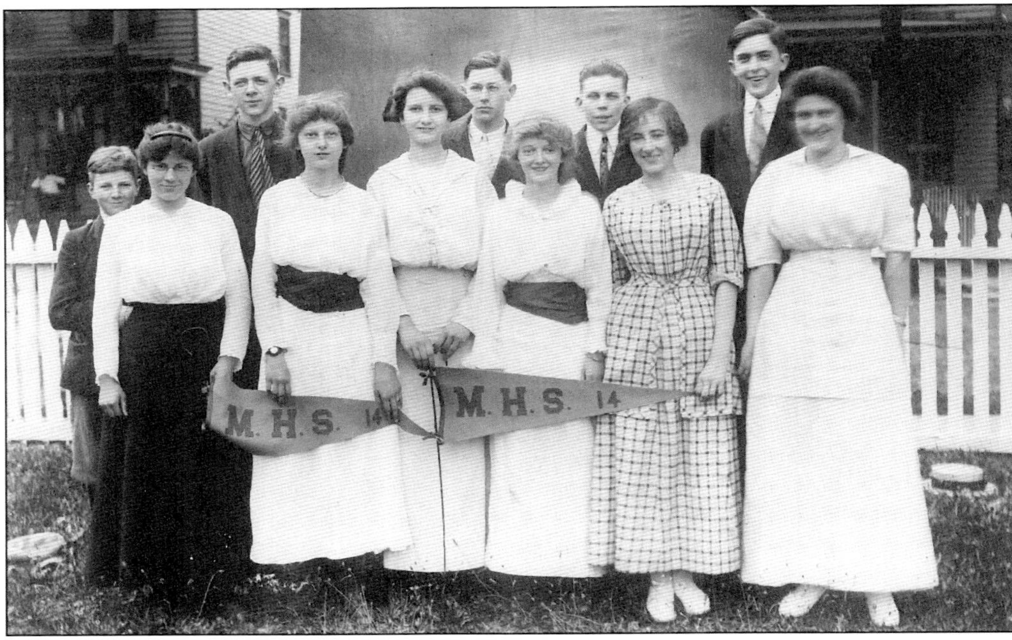

In 1914 Morrisville graduated six girls and five boys. The young ladies, from left, are Agnes Backes, Margaret Hunt, Blanche Taylor, Elsie Newman, Ruth McKenna, and Marian Muschert. The young men are John Backes, Cheston Hutchinson, J. Knowles Hogeland, Frank Gerbrick, and Harry Meredith.

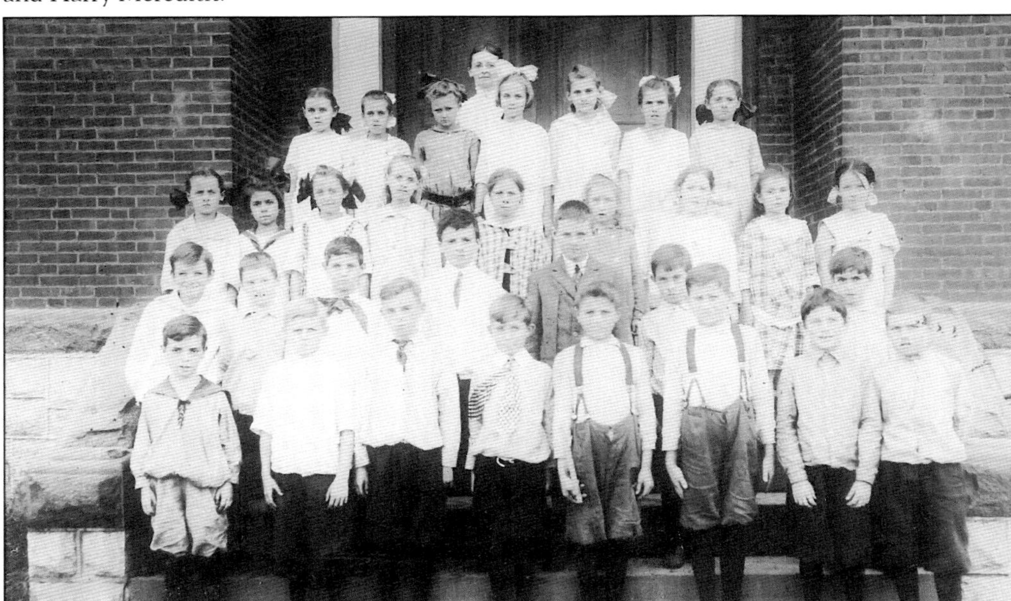

Not all of the students in Miss Kirkbride's fourth-grade class are identified on the back of the picture, but one who is easily recognizable is Willard Curtin, at left in the first row. He later was an attorney in Morrisville, a six-term congressman, and co-founder of the Curtin & Heefner law firm. Miss Kirkbride can be seen behind the large hair ribbon worn by the girl in the center of the top row. The picture was probably taken in 1916.

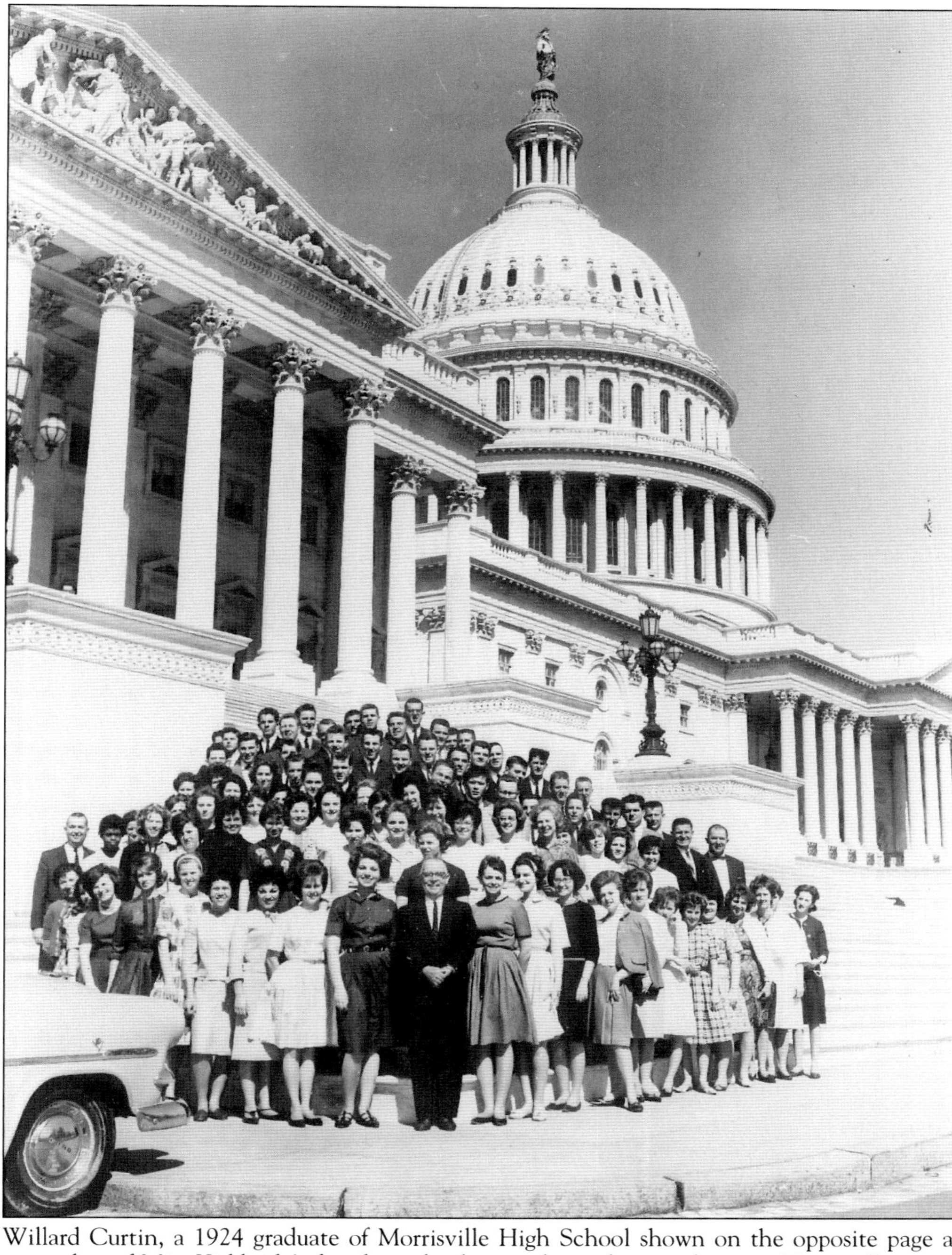

Willard Curtin, a 1924 graduate of Morrisville High School shown on the opposite page as a member of Miss Kirkbride's fourth-grade class, is shown here with many Morrisville senior classes on the steps of the Capitol in Washington, D.C., while he was serving in the U.S. House of Representatives. So popular was Curtin during his six-term congressional career that he was able to turn back a challenge by well-known author James Michener. Curtin appears here in the center of the front row of a class making the traditional senior trip to the nation's capital.

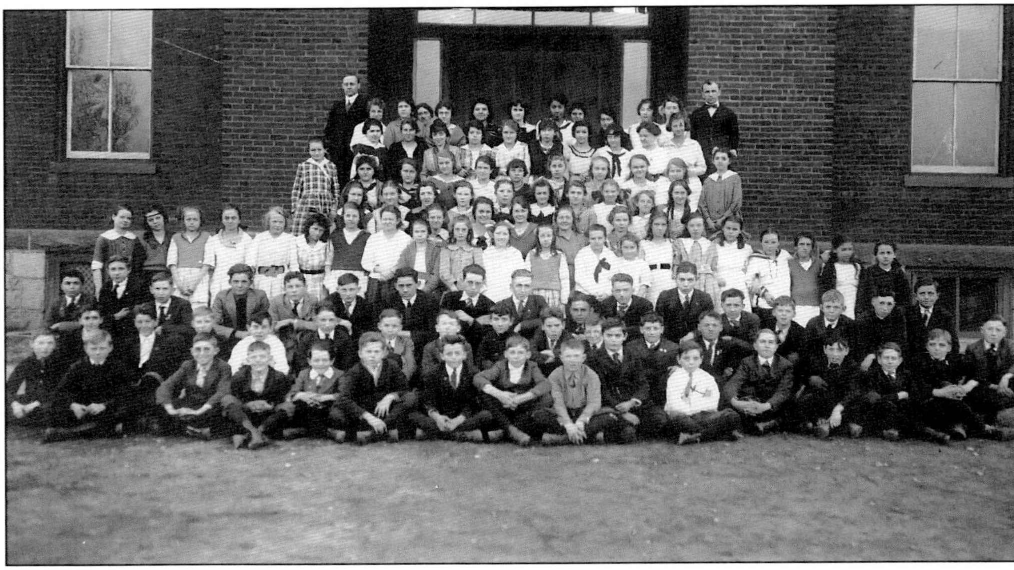

The town and its school population were both small enough in 1916 to show all the students, from all grades, in a single picture.

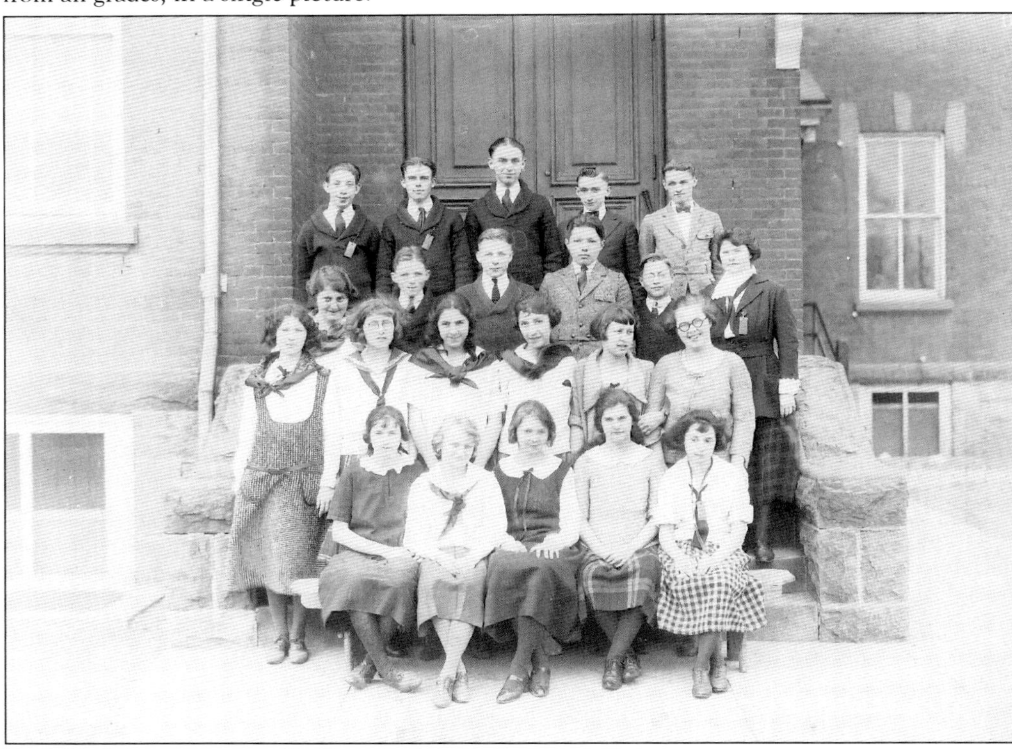

Space doesn't permit listing all members of the 1923 sophomore class, but third from the left in the third row, Victor Ellin, became a physician who practiced in Morrisville; fifth from the left, Harry Lee, later was Morrisville's borough engineer; the boy in the center, top row, Joseph Lebegern, became a Morrisville policeman; and the last boy on the right, top row, Isaac Scott, returned to be a member of the teaching and administrative staff.

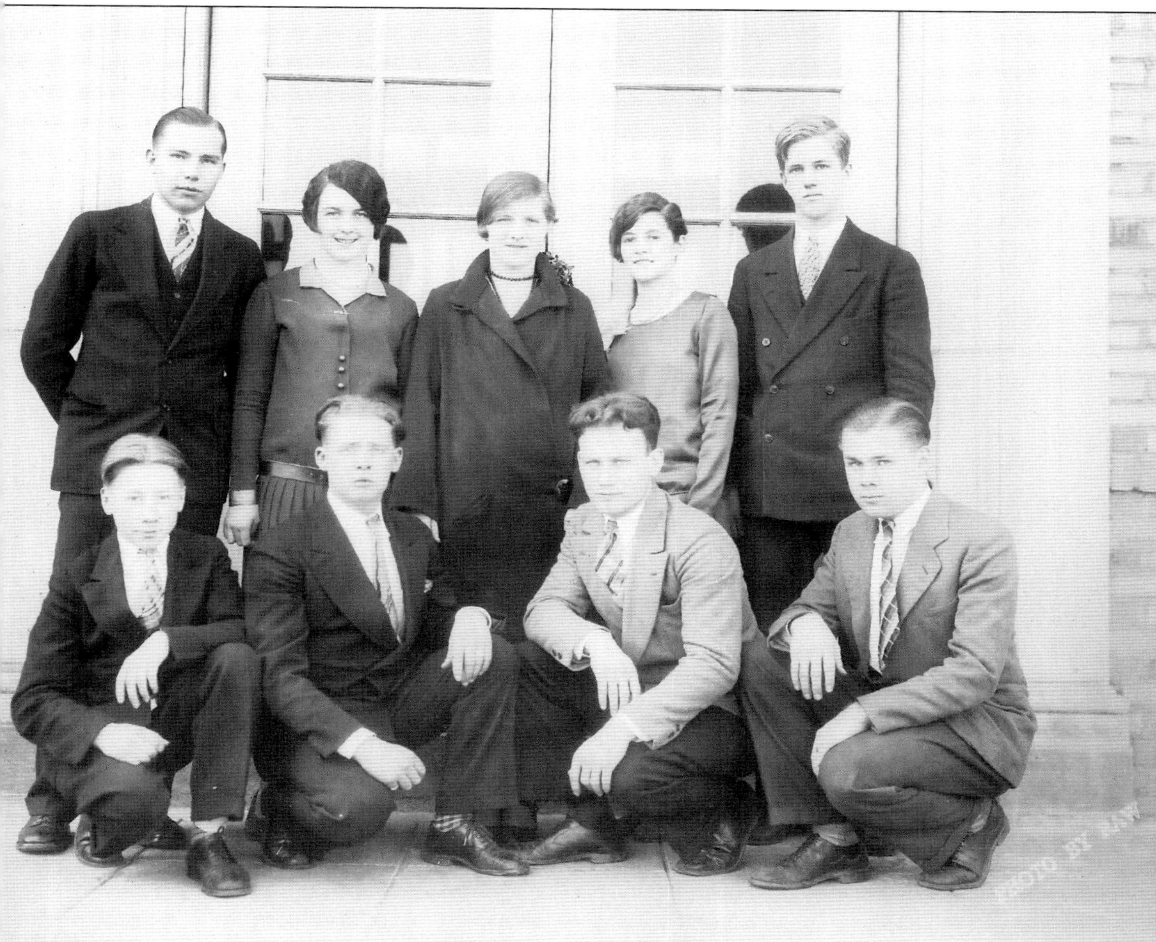

Dramatics always were popular at Morrisville High School. This is the cast of the operetta "Cherry Blossom," c. 1927. From left to right are as follows: (front row) Winifred Wright, Girton Greenlee, Richard Fox, and Harry Bunting; (back row) Ira Gunn, Edna Hale, Miss Florence Kunkel (teacher), Dot Melville, and Bob Stockham. About 40 years after this photograph was taken Harry Bunting became president of the Morrisville Bank.

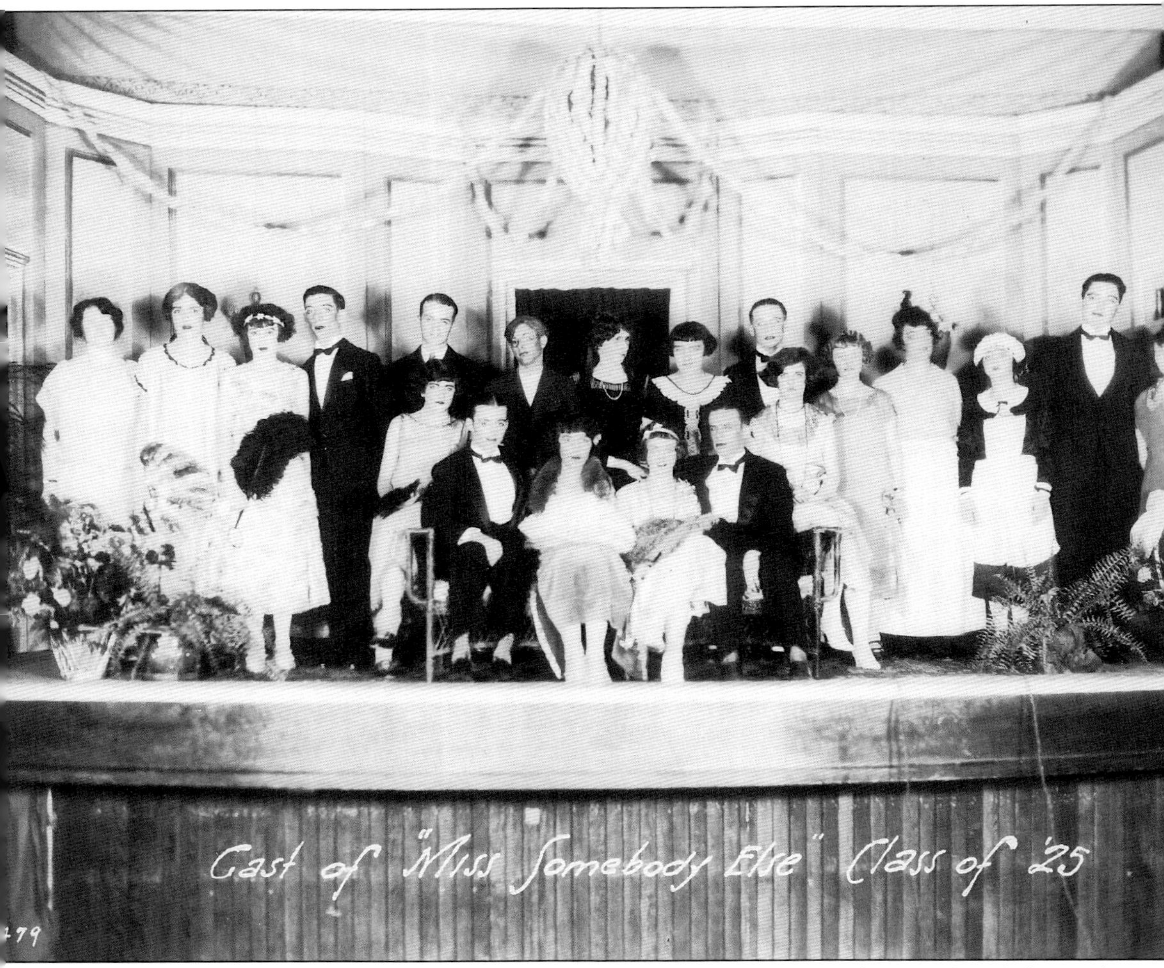

The traditional senior class play in 1925 was "Miss Somebody Else." The cast, from left to right, included: (front row) Anna Woodward, Ross Neagley, Grace Snook, Grace White, Herman Johnson, and Mary Wurst; (back row) Miss Helen Taylor (teacher), Sylvia Naylor, Jessie Margerum, Charles Delaney, Isaac Scott, Harry Lee, Jean Custer, Mildred Dietrick, Victor Ellen, Annie Phillips, Suzanne Bellardo, Bessie Katz, William Schofield, and Miss Christine Clymer (teacher).

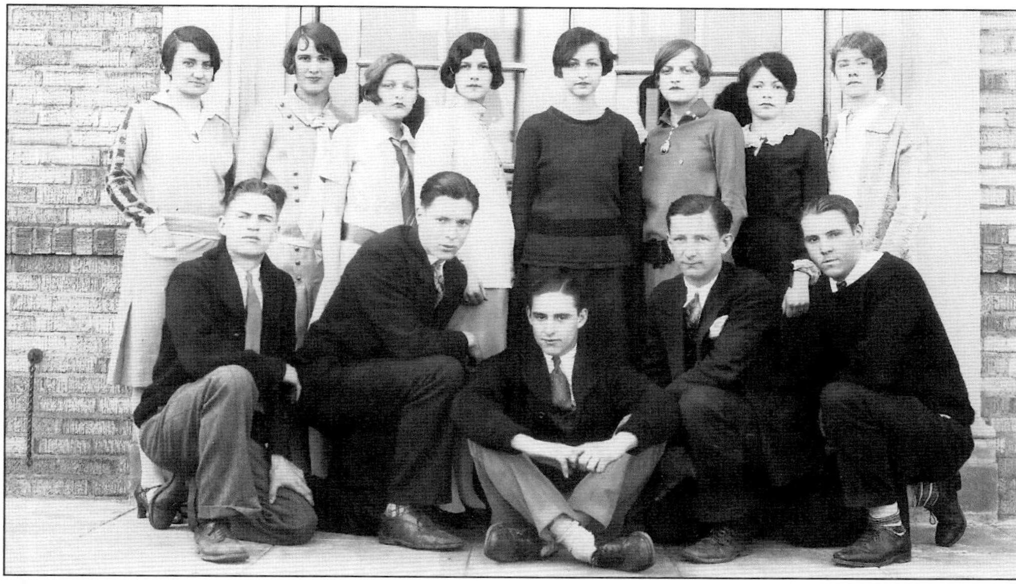

The occasion for this group photograph taken in 1927 or '28 was not noted, but the people are all identified. From left to right are as follows: (front row) Barton Ames, Tom Stockham III, Jack Donaldson, Adam Kupiec, and Floyd Kerr; (back row) teacher Helen Bucher, Violetta Greenlee, Dorothy Ruetter, Grace Hendrickson, Marie Sanford, Virgelia Davis, Miriam Gerber, and Maud Temple. Floyd Kerr returned to Morrisville High School as a popular teacher and coach.

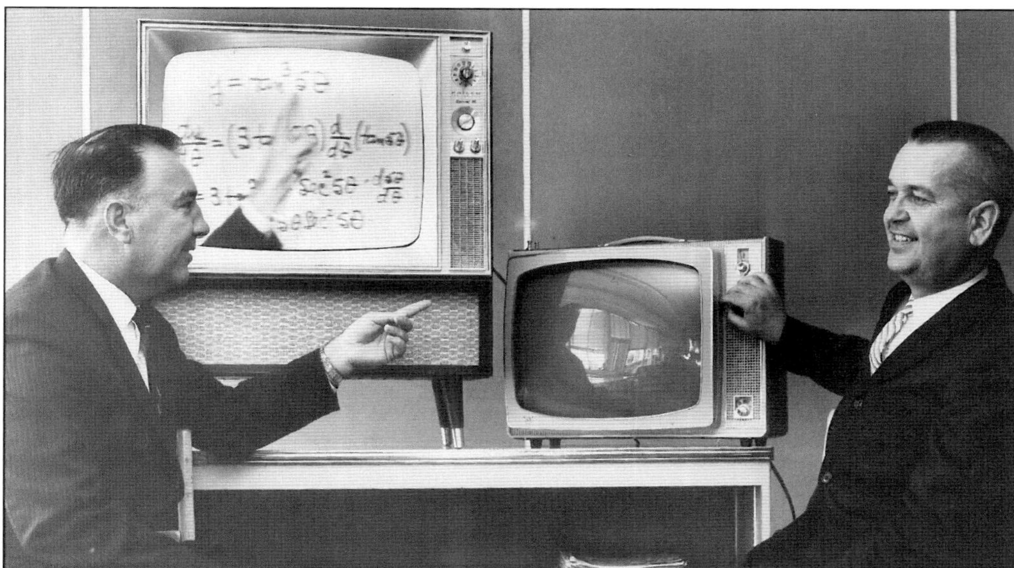

Under the leadership of Superintendent Paul Phillips (left) and Principal James Wood, Morrisville schools began using television for instructional purposes during the 1960s and '70s. A quarter century later one of their protégés, Superintendent Elizabeth Fineburg, and Technology Coordinator Earl Davis pioneered in computer applications, creating a borough-wide intranet among the public schools, parochial school, public library, historic society, borough hall, and senior residence—all connected to the Internet.

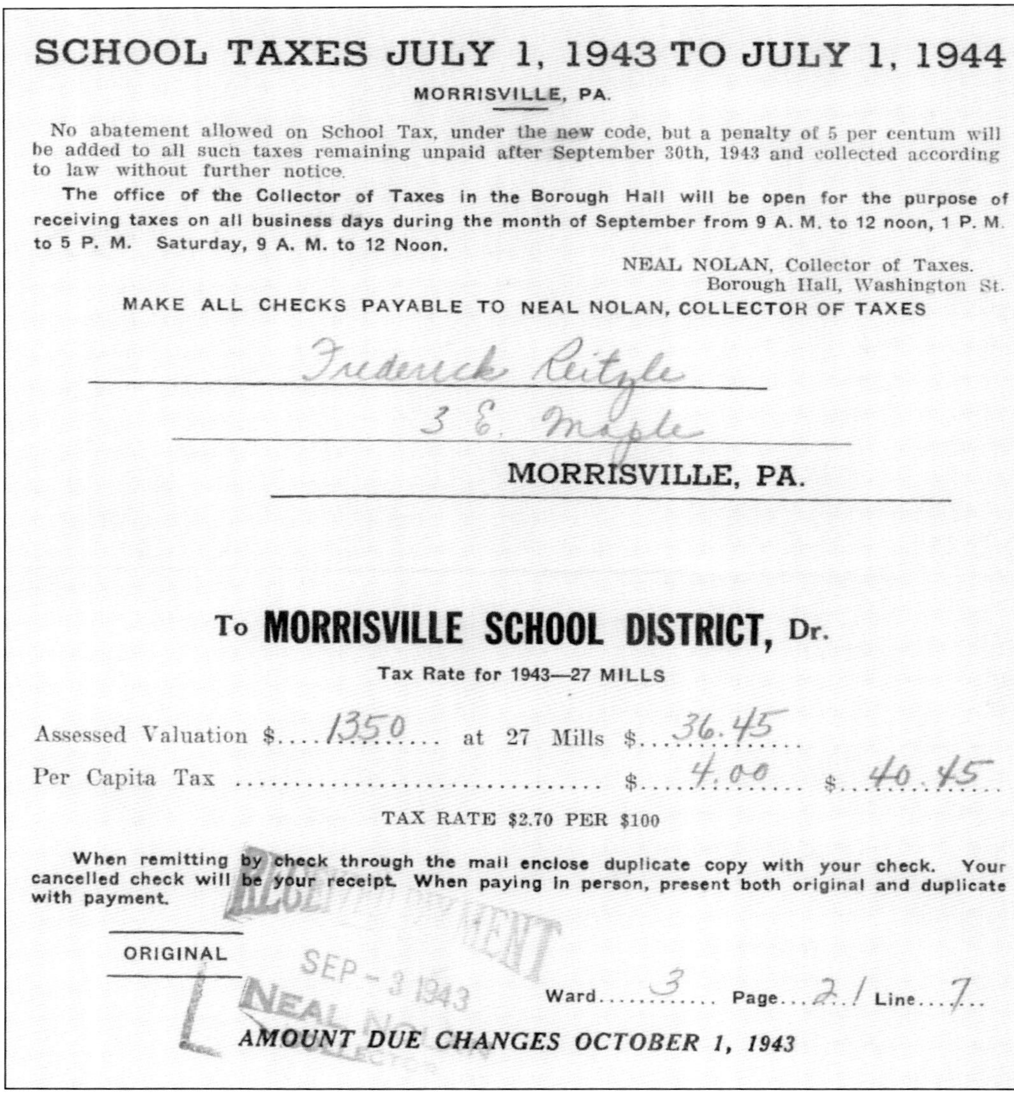

SCHOOL TAXES JULY 1, 1943 TO JULY 1, 1944

MORRISVILLE, PA.

No abatement allowed on School Tax, under the new code, but a penalty of 5 per centum will be added to all such taxes remaining unpaid after September 30th, 1943 and collected according to law without further notice.

The office of the Collector of Taxes in the Borough Hall will be open for the purpose of receiving taxes on all business days during the month of September from 9 A. M. to 12 noon, 1 P. M. to 5 P. M. Saturday, 9 A. M. to 12 Noon.

NEAL NOLAN, Collector of Taxes.
Borough Hall, Washington St.

MAKE ALL CHECKS PAYABLE TO NEAL NOLAN, COLLECTOR OF TAXES

Frederick Reitzle
3 E. Maple
MORRISVILLE, PA.

To **MORRISVILLE SCHOOL DISTRICT,** Dr.

Tax Rate for 1943—27 MILLS

Assessed Valuation $....1350.... at 27 Mills $....36.45....

Per Capita Tax .... $....4.00.... $....40.45....

TAX RATE $2.70 PER $100

When remitting by check through the mail enclose duplicate copy with your check. Your cancelled check will be your receipt. When paying in person, present both original and duplicate with payment.

ORIGINAL

SEP - 3 1943 NEAL NOLAN

Ward....3.... Page....21.... Line....7....

AMOUNT DUE CHANGES OCTOBER 1, 1943

School taxes for 1943–44 on a typical Morrisville home on Maple Avenue, plus a per capita tax, totaled only $40.45!

Four

Some Notable Residents

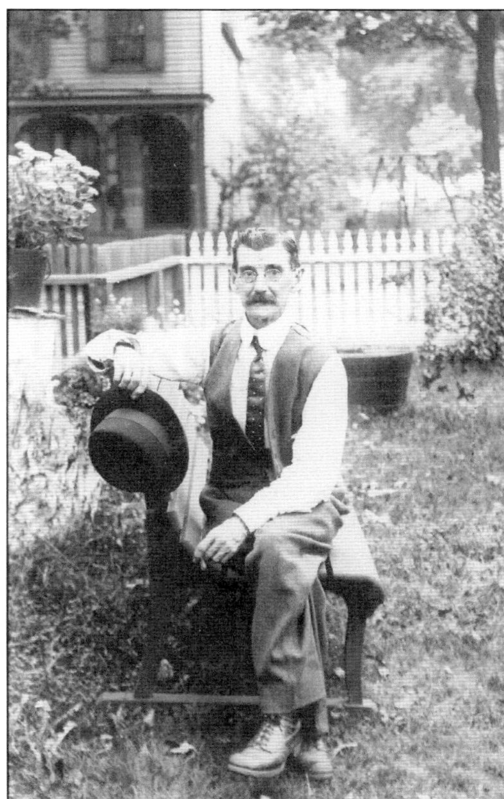

William Jackson (Billy) Pope, Morrisville's only photographer for years, took many of the pictures in this book. He photographed school classes, weddings, and scenes throughout the town. A collection of his photographs was donated to Historic Morrisville Society by his granddaughter, Mabel Whittaker.

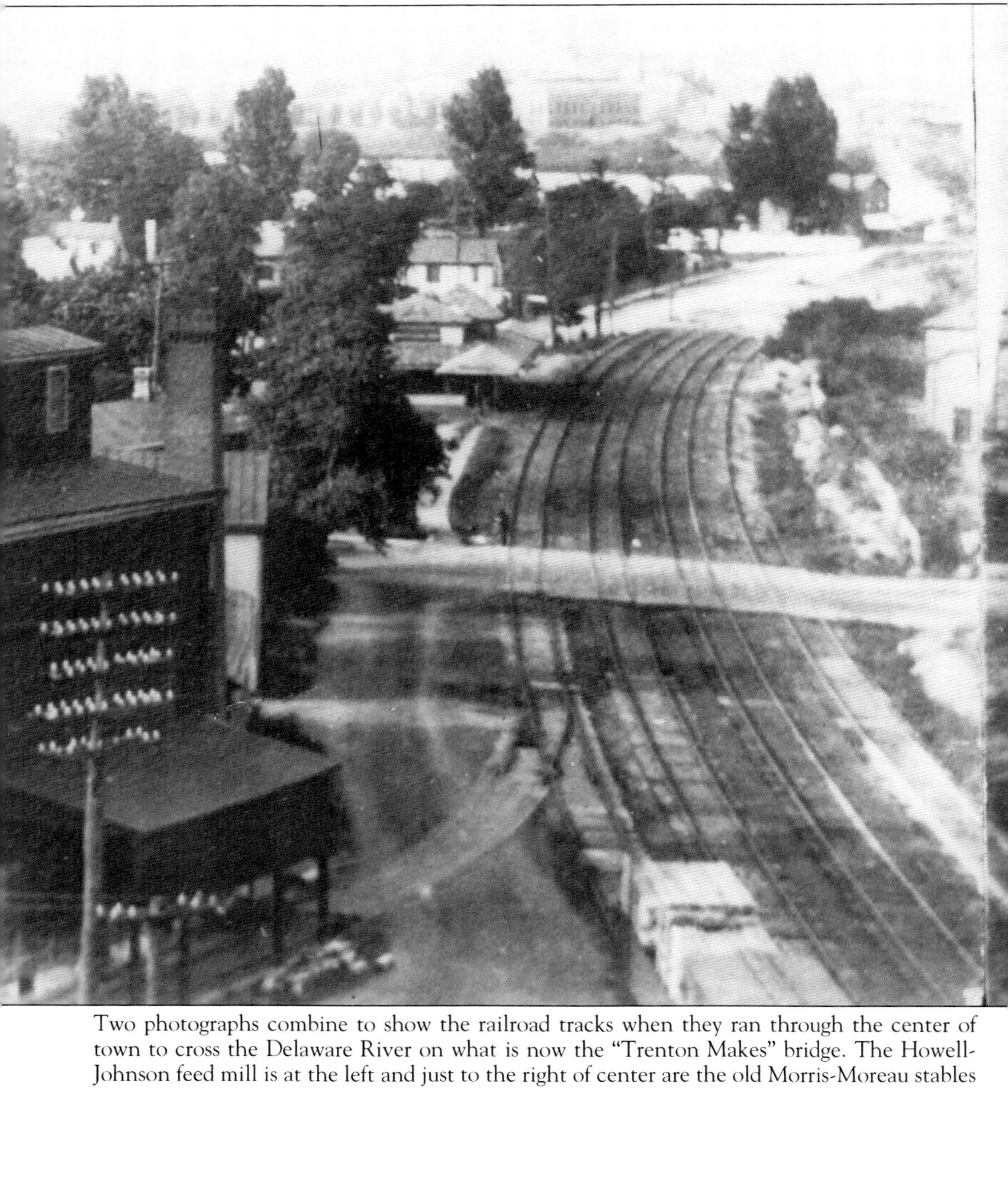

Two photographs combine to show the railroad tracks when they ran through the center of town to cross the Delaware River on what is now the "Trenton Makes" bridge. The Howell-Johnson feed mill is at the left and just to the right of center are the old Morris-Moreau stables

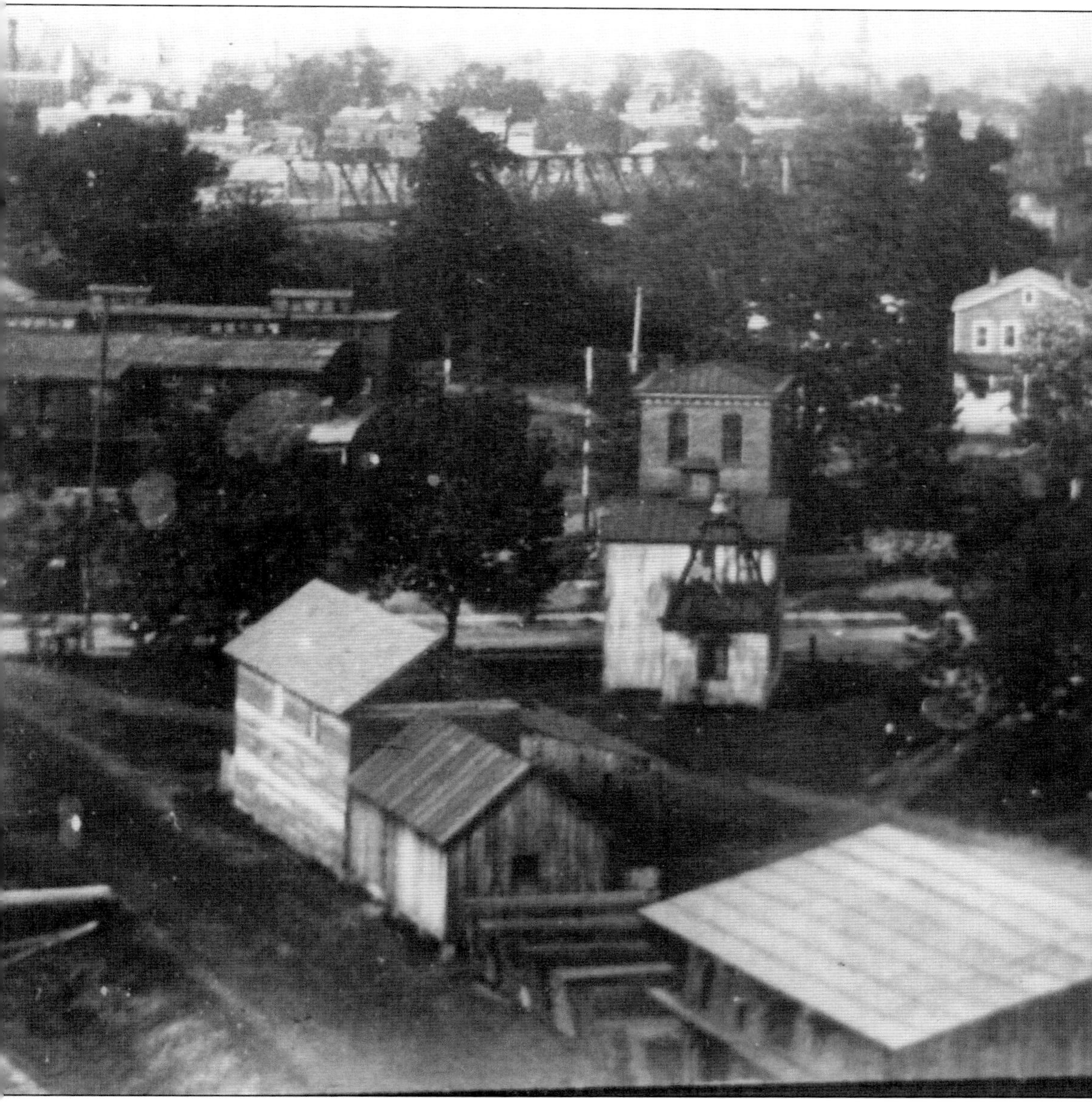

that became the town's first rubber mill. The thoroughfare crossing the tracks is Washington Street. Pennsylvania Avenue is just out of the picture, at the bottom.

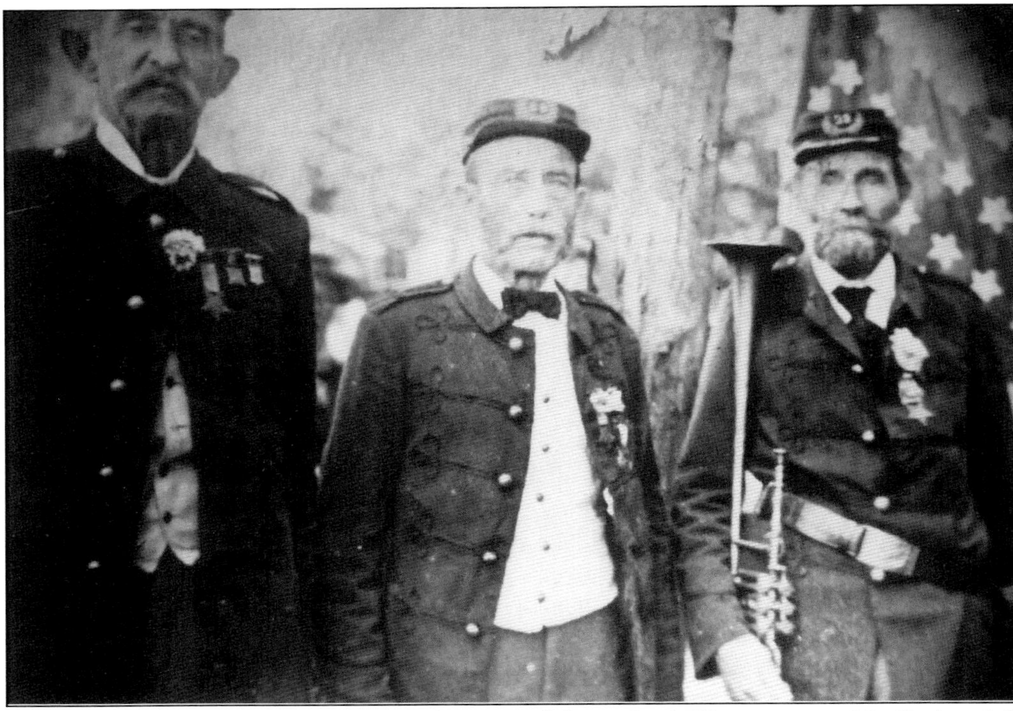

Among Billy Pope's photographs was this one of three Civil War veterans: Mr. Barber, Mr. Burns, and Mr. Dana.

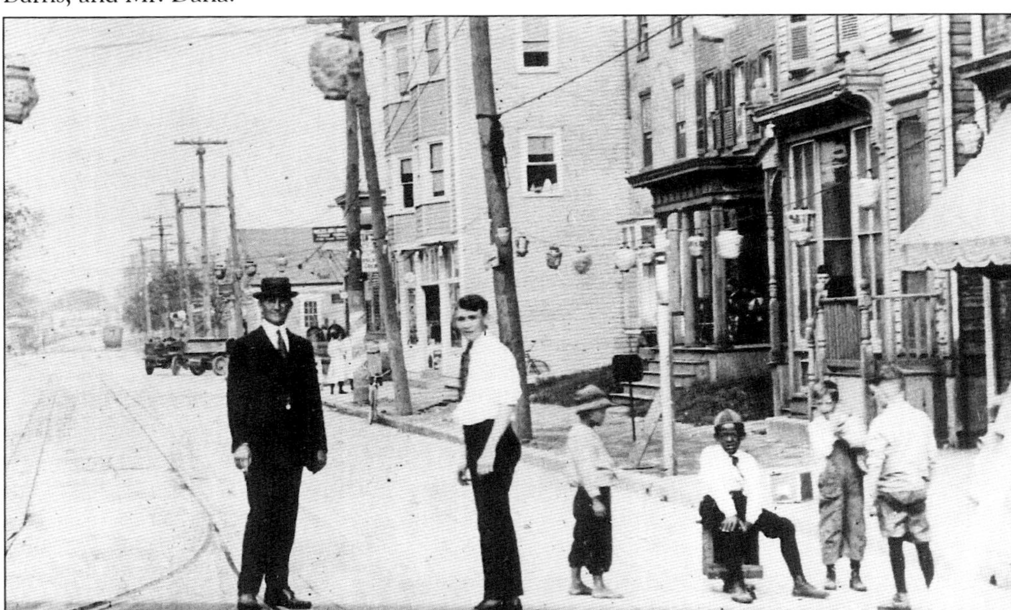

This group is shown on Bridge Street in the heart of Morrisville's downtown business district, not far past the intersection with Pennsylvania Avenue. The trolley tracks can be seen curving from the left. The reason for the decorative lanterns strung across the street and in front of the buildings is not known, but it appears that a celebration of some kind was under way.

Weddings in old time Morrisville prompted a lot of horseplay by friends of the groom—with the fun mostly at the groom's expense. This downtown business is festooned with tin cans, old shoes, and signs—lots of signs. One reads, "I love the cows and chickens, but this is the life." Another offers the usual blessing, "May all your troubles be little ones," and another offers a pointer: "When you feel down at the mouth, think of Jonah. He came out all right."

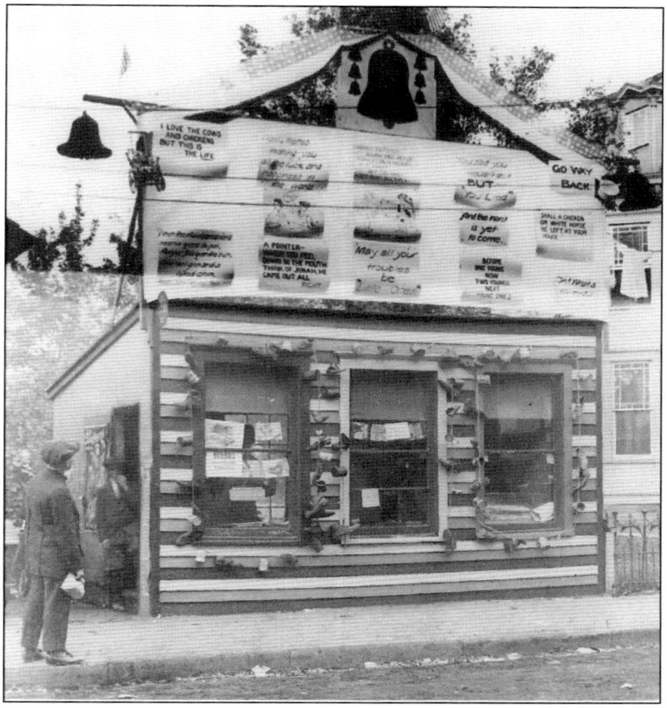

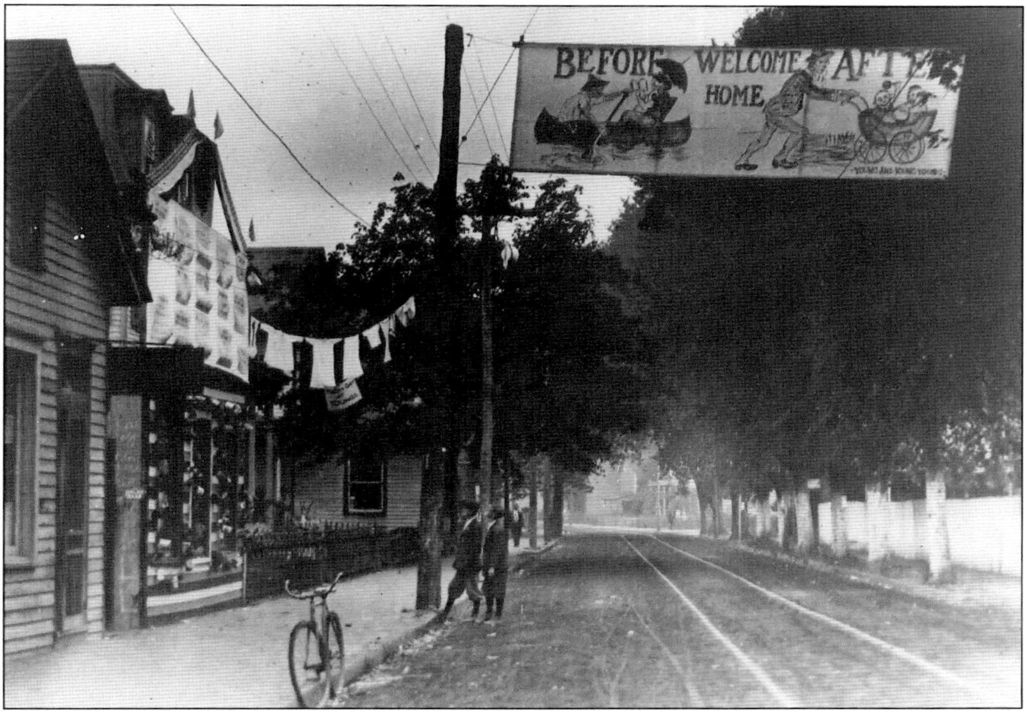

Another view of the post-wedding decorations shows a wash line rigged from the store to the nearest telephone pole and a banner across the street showing the groom before and after, "before" happily paddling along with his bride-to-be and "after" pushing a baby carriage.

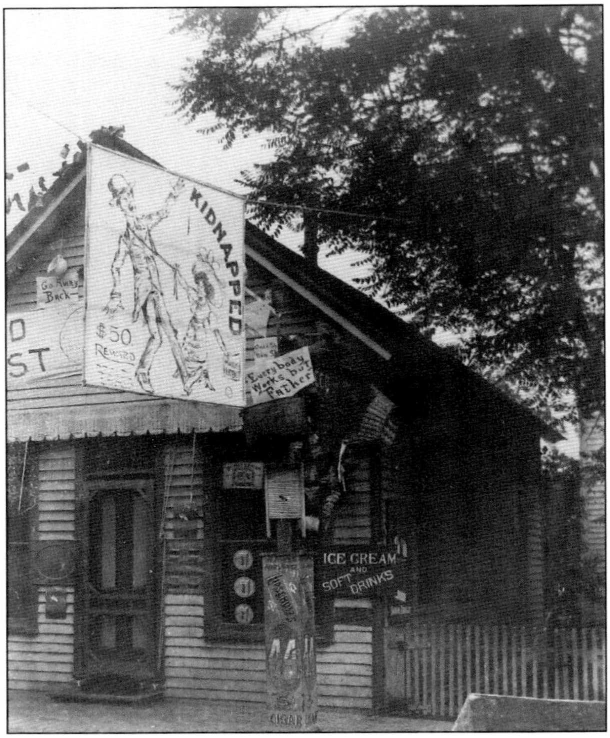

Wedding high jinks included "art," as the sign suspended in front of this ice cream store shows. The groom is again the victim, "kidnapped," with a "$50 reward," and a sign proclaiming that "Everybody works but father."

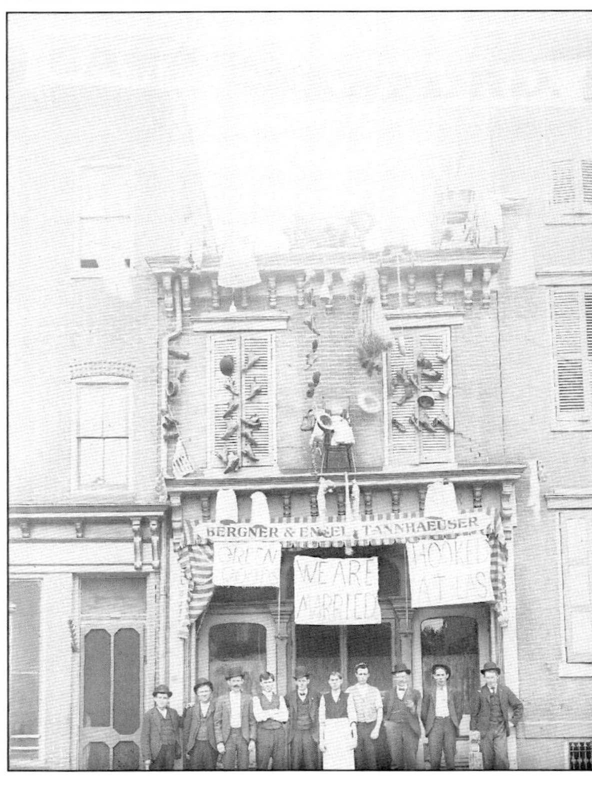

Among elaborate tributes to married life was this one at a business on Bridge Street showing old shoes, clothing, and signs: "We are married," "Green goods," and "Hooked at last." Despite the humor, men in front of the store show nothing but grim expressions.

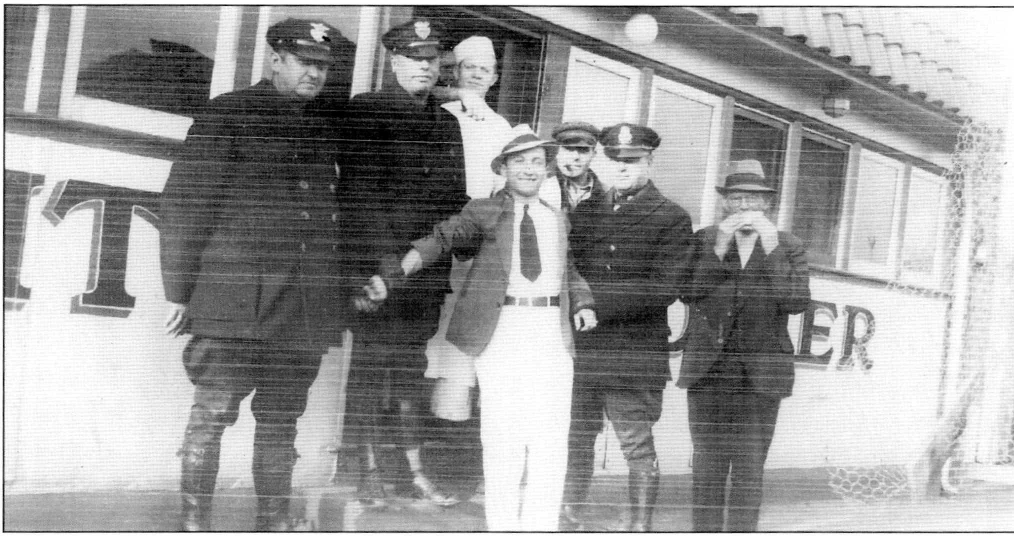

Not only were grooms made fun of with signs and banners, but they also were "arrested." This picture shows three arresting officers; from left to right (in front of the Transit Diner on Bridge Street) are George Rose, Al Cooper, and Andy Thompson. The diner's proprietor (white shirt and cap, in the doorway) was John Bekia. The "victim" and the other two men are not identified.

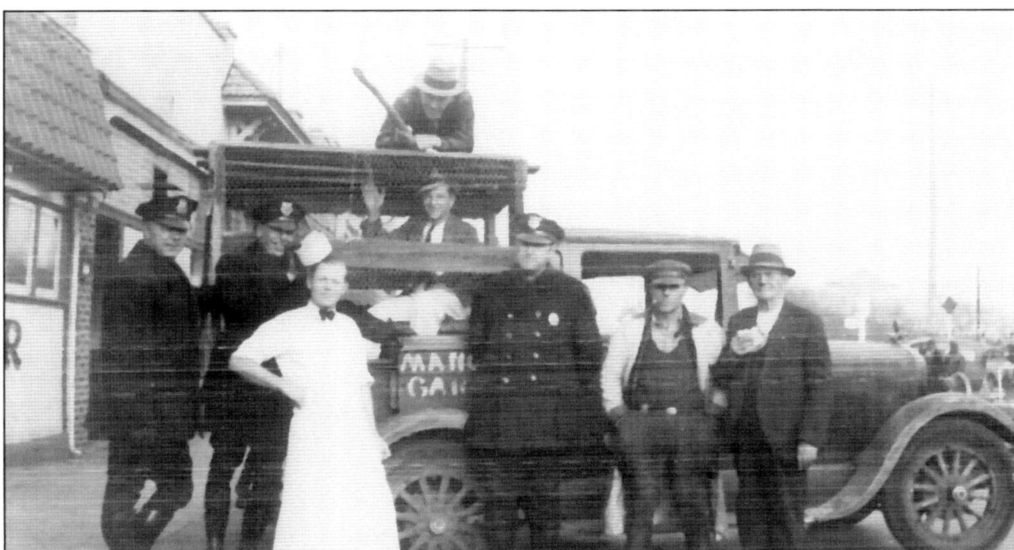

After his arrest, the newlywed groom was placed in a cage on the back of a truck and driven around town so everyone could see that he was no longer a free man. The groom, undismayed, can be seen waving from his mobile prison.

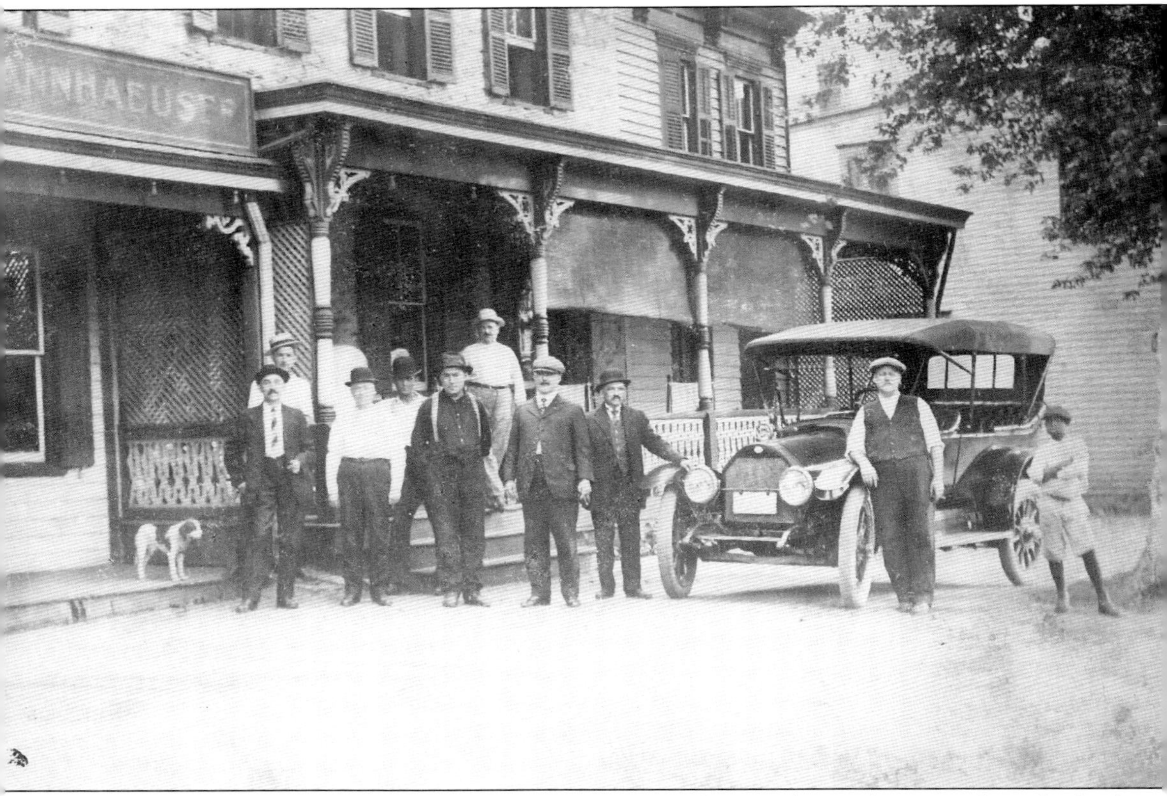

The Hogeland House, at the corner of Bridge Street and Pennsylvania Avenue, where the bank now stands, was a favorite gathering spot for Morrisville's men and, on the day the picture was taken, for two children and a dog.

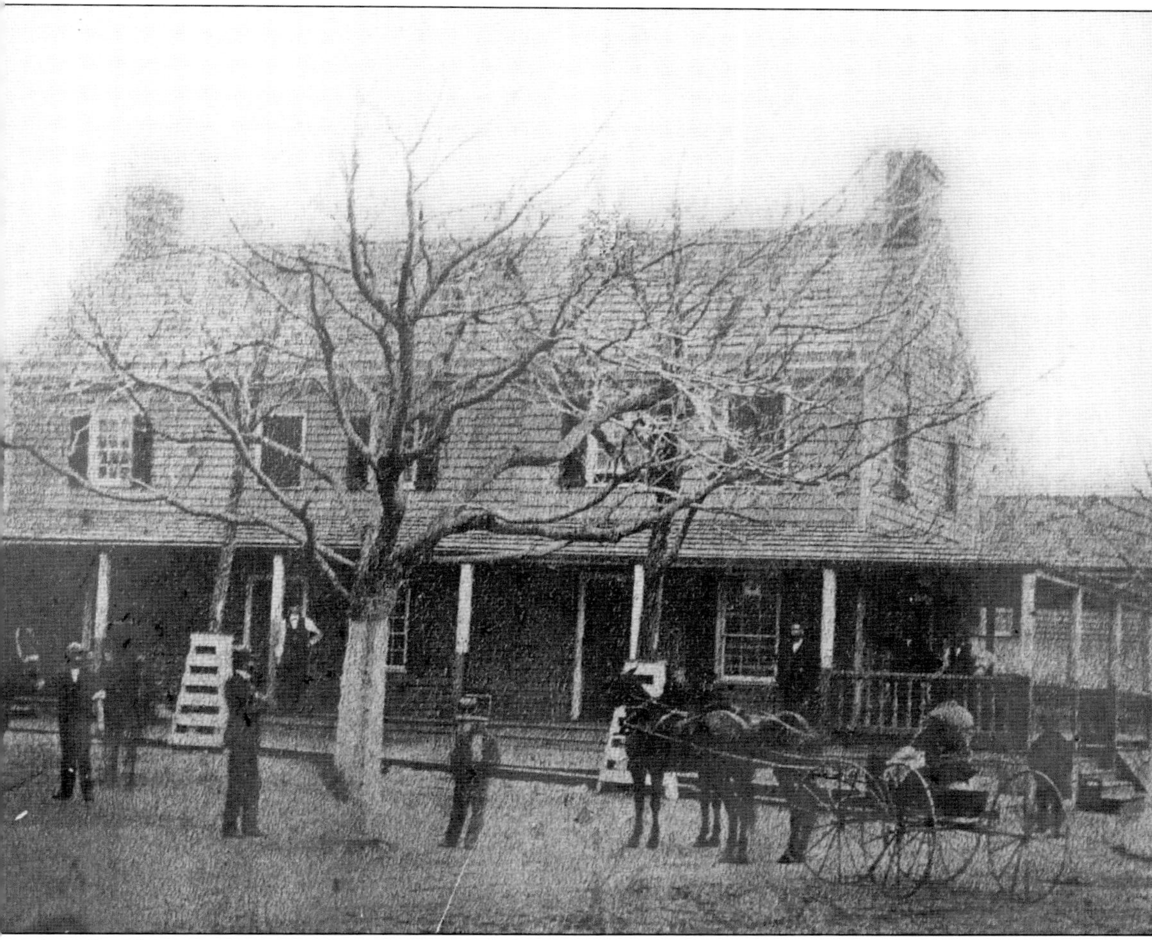

Another favorite meeting place in nineteenth-century Morrisville was the Robert Morris Hotel at Bridge and Mill Streets (Mill is now Delmorr Avenue). This photograph, taken before 1890, shows immigrant Frederic Reitzle holding a horse at left and a buggy with two horses at right.

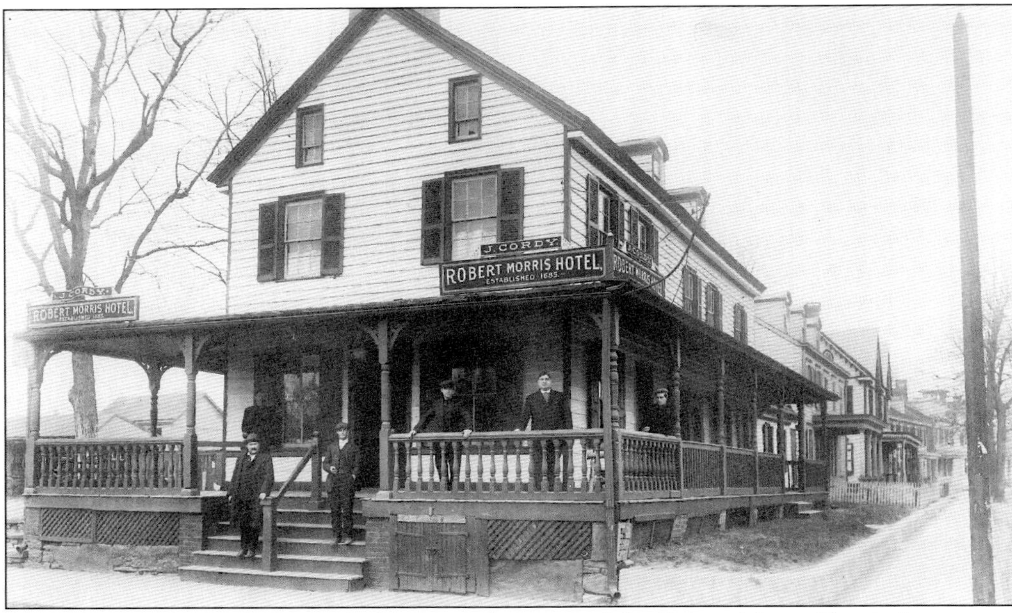

This picture, taken around 1914, shows another view of the Robert Morris Hotel. A successor, also named the Robert Morris, is located on Bridge Street about halfway between Pennsylvania and Delmorr Avenues.

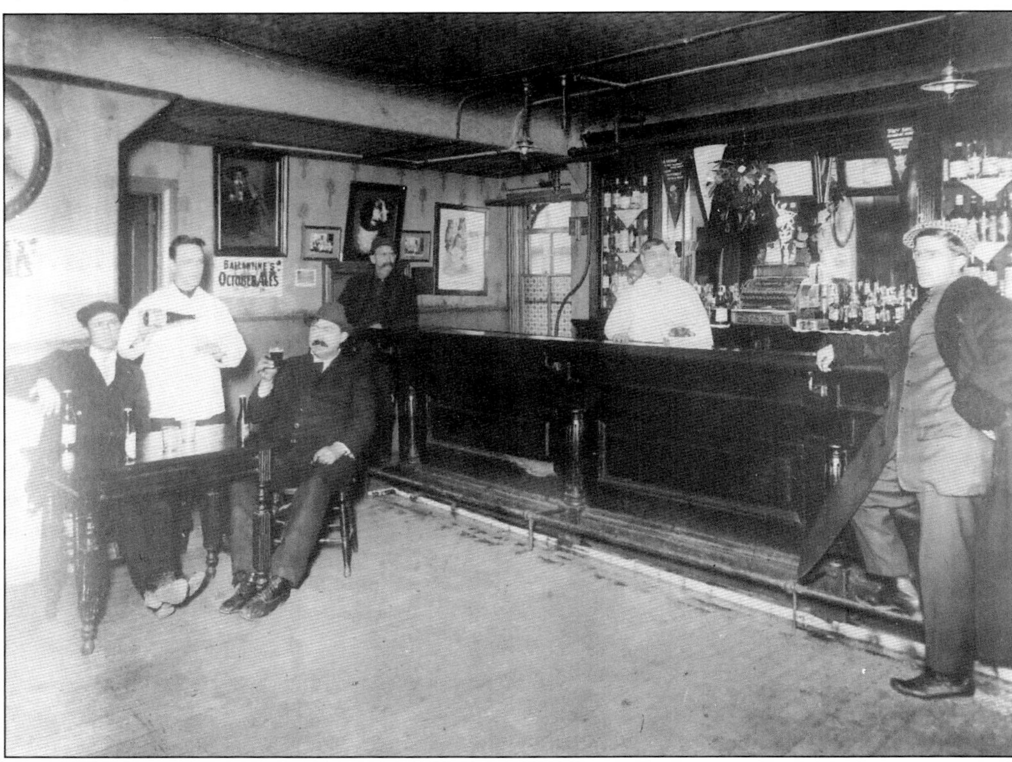

Inside the Robert Morris Hotel, citizens gathered for convivial refreshment and conversation. The seated man raising his glass is Frederic Reitzle.

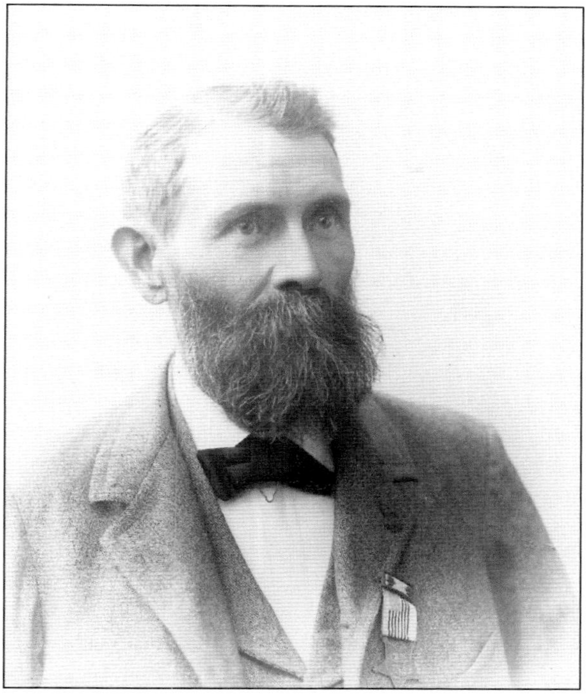

Dr. R.S. Dana, with John W. Thompson, established Morrisville's first rubber manufacturing plant in the old Morris-Moreau stables building at the north end of Bank Street.

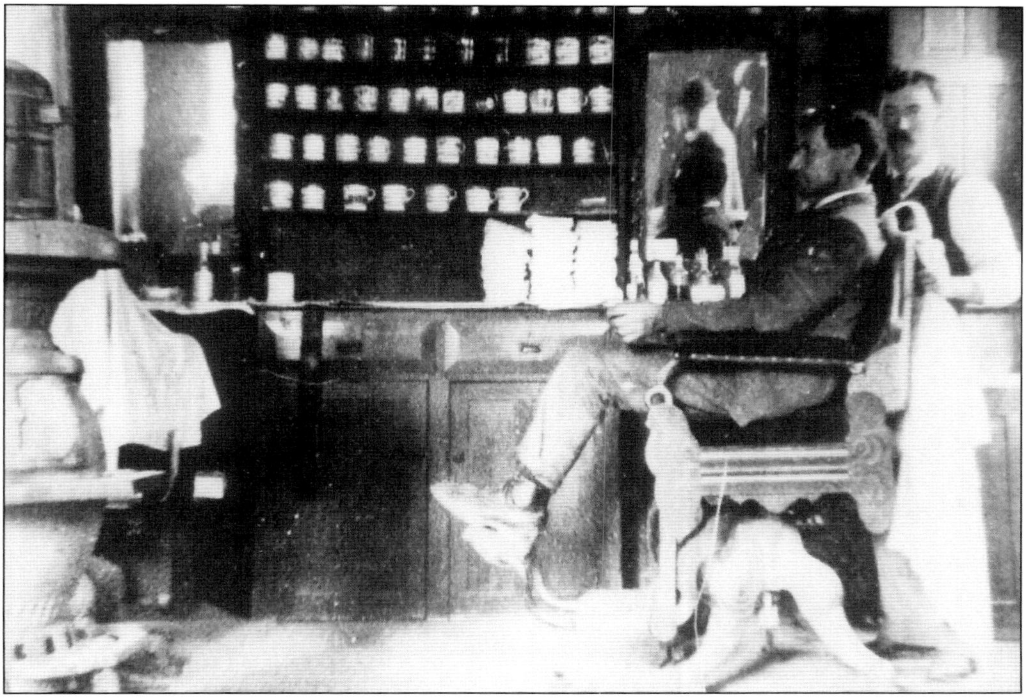

Emory Cox's barber shop was located near the intersection of Pennsylvania Avenue and Bridge Street. This photograph, by Billy Pope, shows Abram Service of Fallsington admiring his shave and haircut. Regular patrons had their own shaving mugs, on the wall, and there was a pot-bellied stove for heat in the winter.

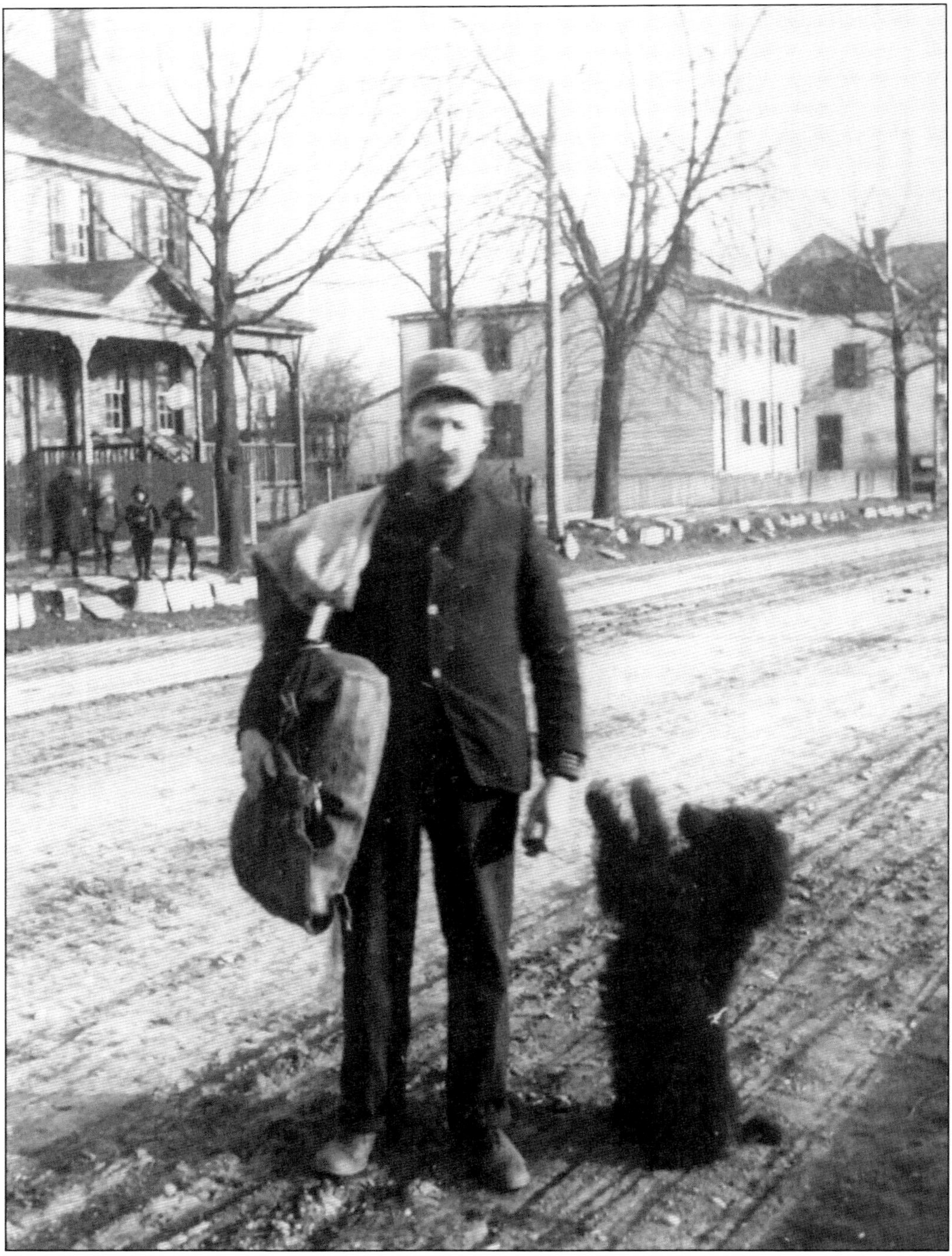

Postman Ely Lefferts was on his way up Pennsylvania Avenue when he paused to greet a friendly dog and have his picture taken. The photograph was taken around the turn of the century.

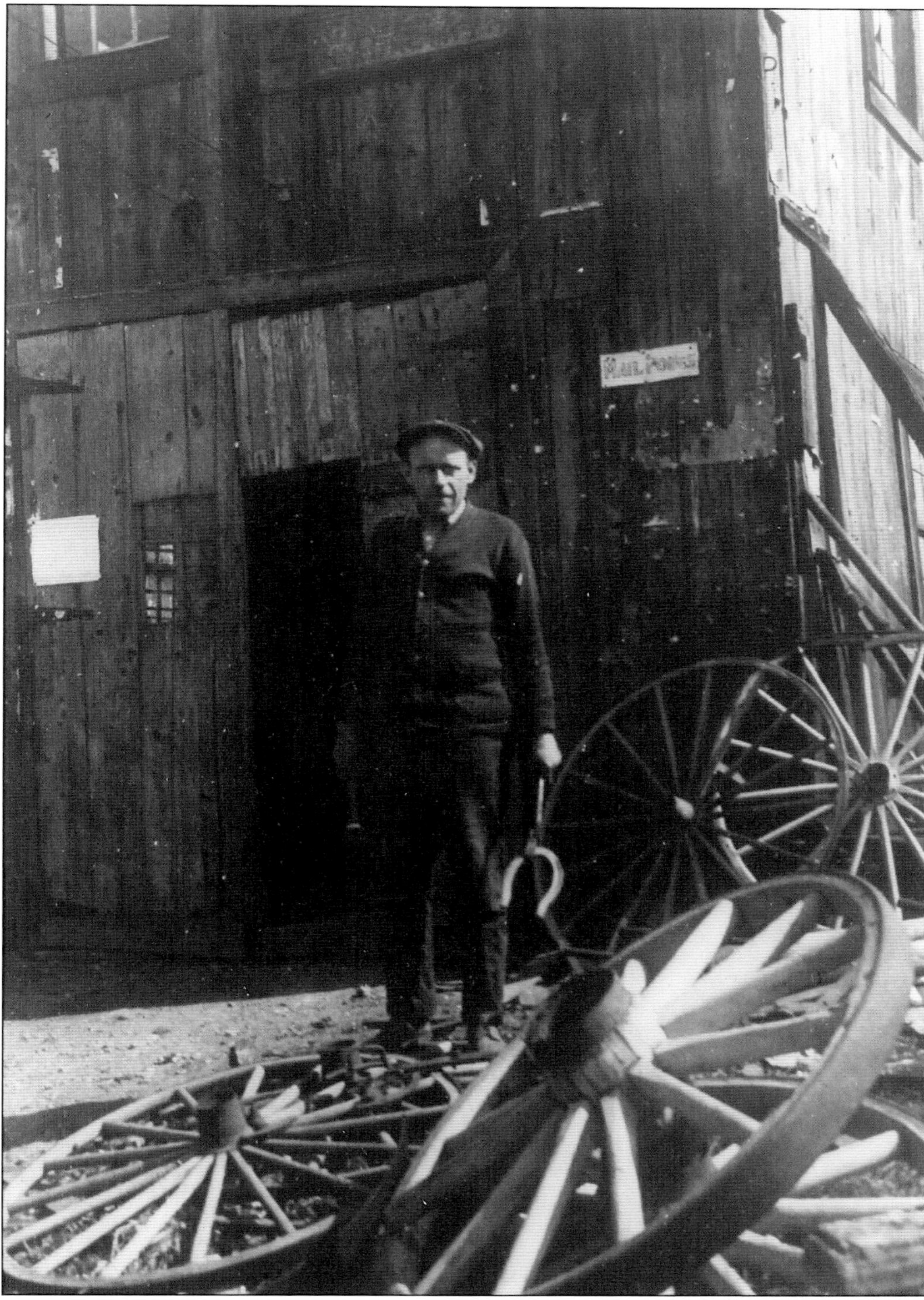

One of Morrisville's early blacksmiths, Fred Harm, is pictured outside his shop, located at the corner of South Pennsylvania and Delaware Avenues. The sign at the right of the door reads "Mail Ponies."

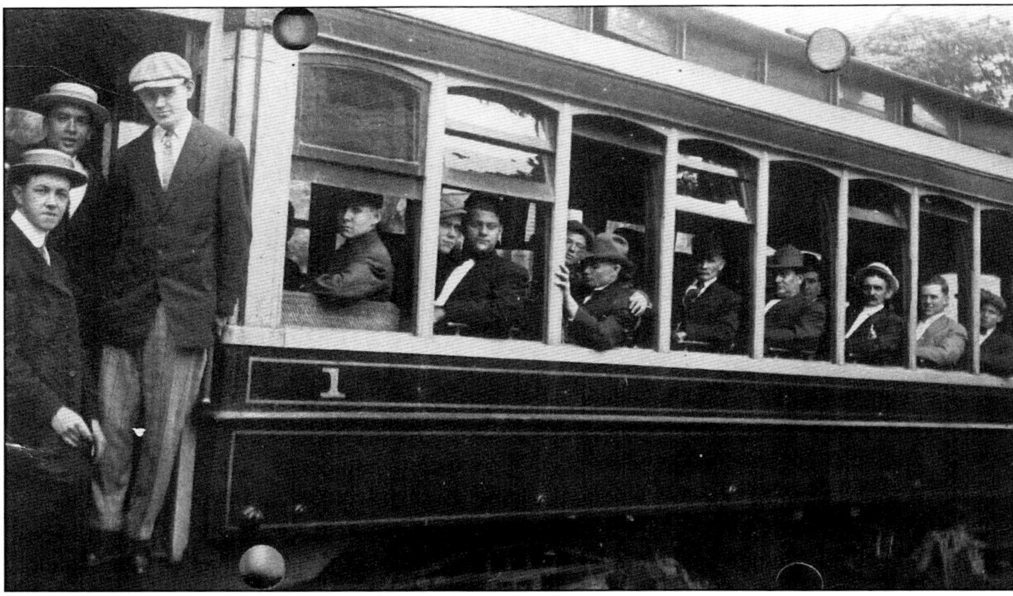

A 1911 photograph shows Morrisville's baseball team about to depart by trolley for a game at Newtown. From left to right are Frank Smith, Martin Wright, William Howell, Bill Hohweiler, Joe Dice, Fred Nolan, unidentified, Henry Roth, Bob Biedleman, Willard McCummings, and Mahlon Hendrickson.

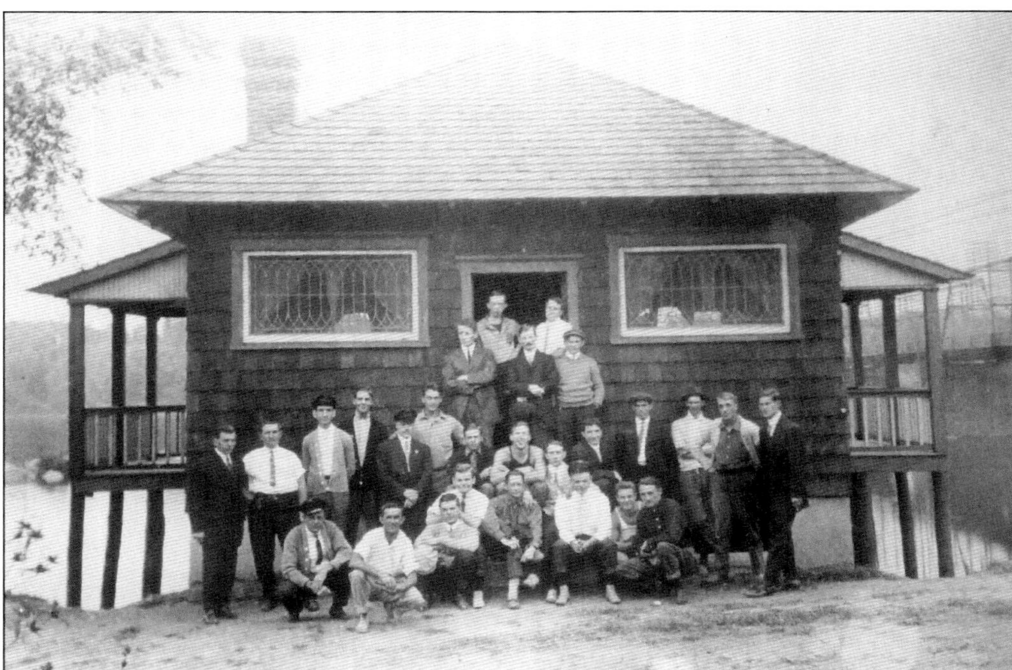

The Chippewa Canoe Club was a busy athletic and social organization. The club building was located just north of the Calhoun Street bridge. Members canoed for exercise, recreation, and as a competitive sport.

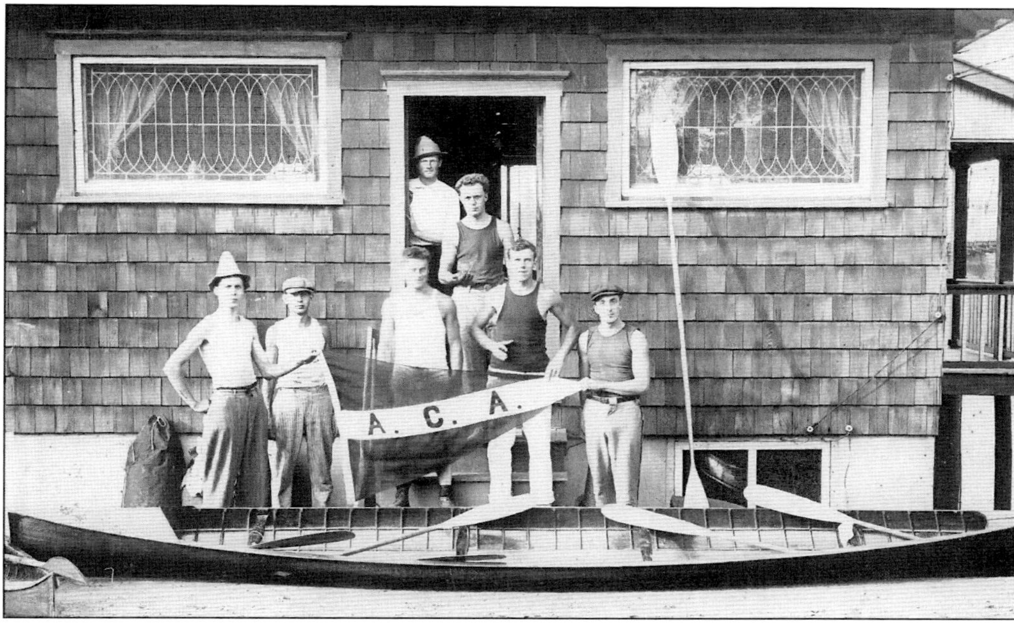

Members of the Chippewa Canoe Club pose with a banner and (small) trophy won at a canoeing competition held at Bordentown, New Jersey, in American Canoe Association races. The man in the doorway wearing a hat is probably Les White. The man in front of him is holding the trophy in his right hand. Bill Johnson is holding the A.C.A. banner at the right.

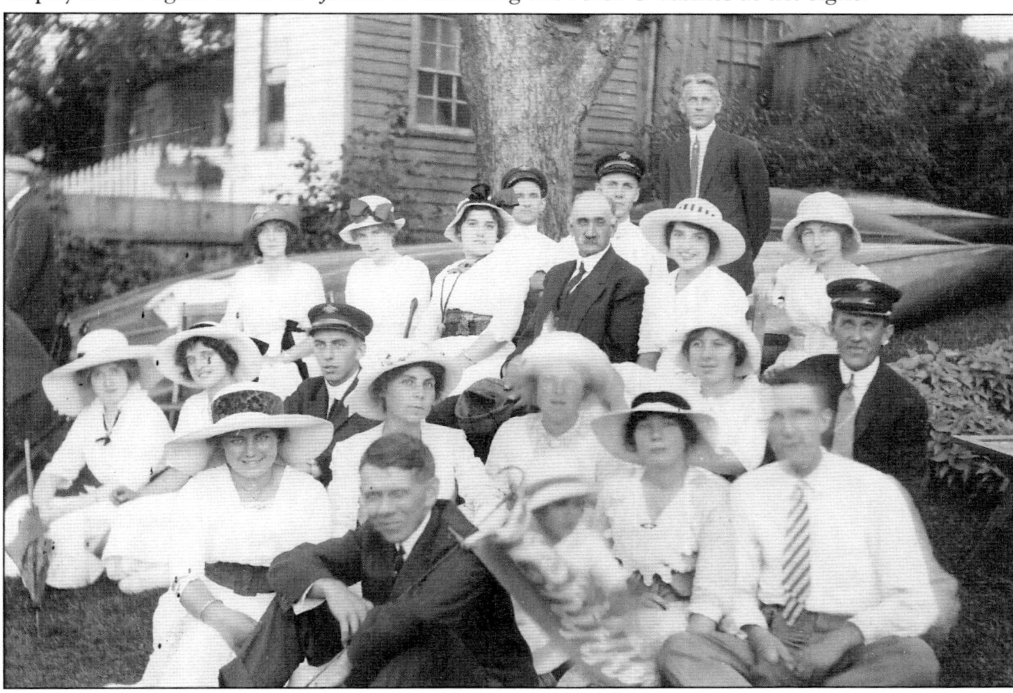

Another gathering of Chippewa Canoe Club members and guests was at a regatta held at Burlington, New Jersey. Gertrude Gentry is seated next to Harry Burns (wearing cap), at right in the second row.

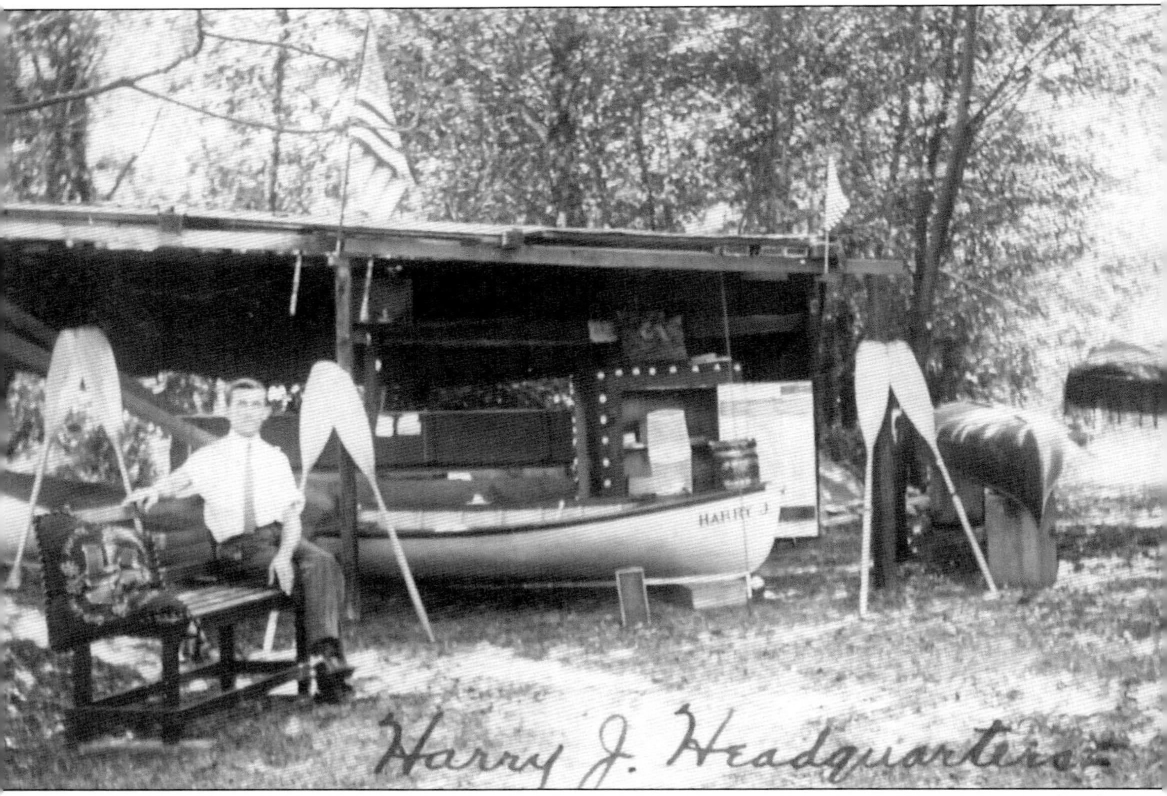

Not all Chippewa members kept their canoes at the clubhouse. Harry Burns is pictured at his personal canoe shelter located near Union Street alongside the canal. The shelter appears to have all the comforts of home.

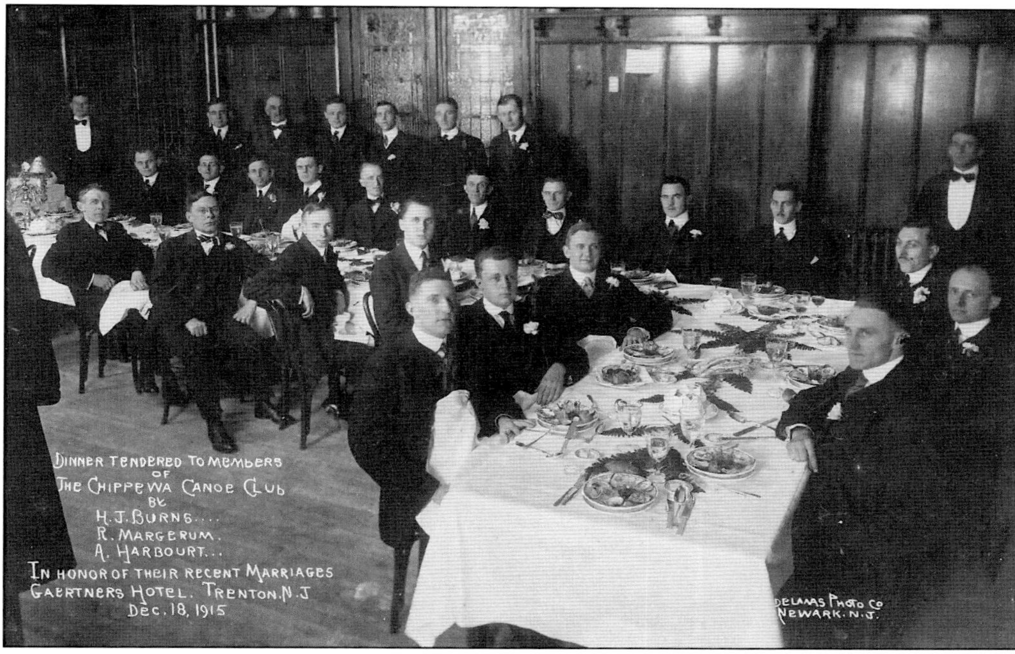

When the Chippewa Canoe Club members had a dinner, they did it in style. The event pictured was a dinner tendered to members of the club by H.J. Burns, R. Margerum, and A. Harbourt in honor of their recent marriages. The place was Gaertner's Hotel in Trenton, New Jersey, and the date was December 18, 1915.

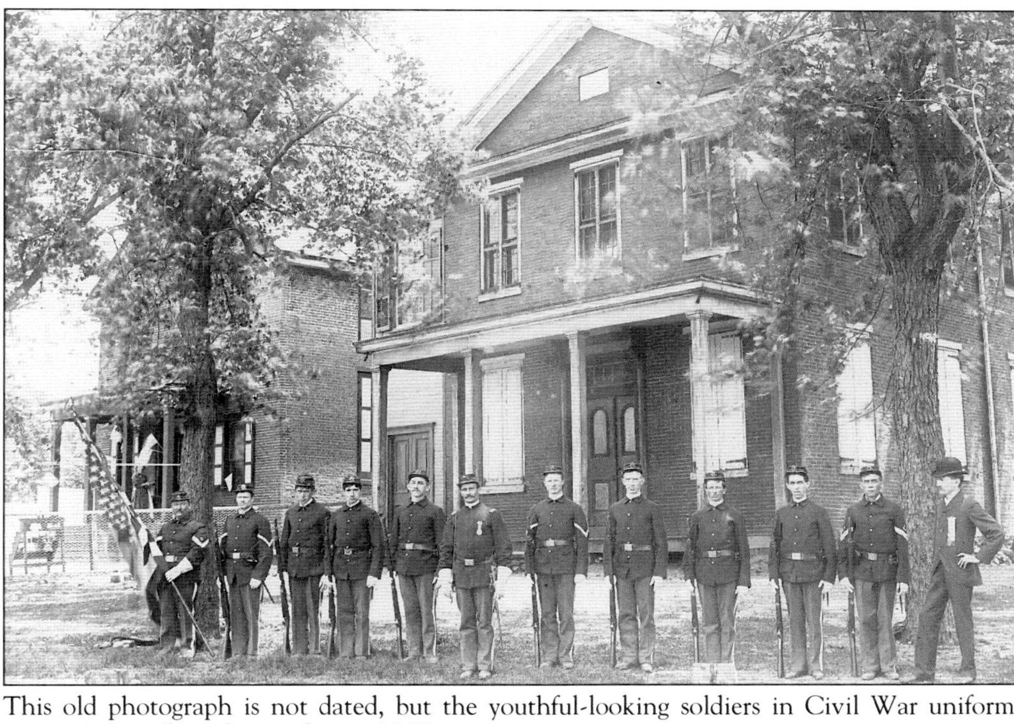

This old photograph is not dated, but the youthful-looking soldiers in Civil War uniforms suggest it must have been taken *c.* 1860.

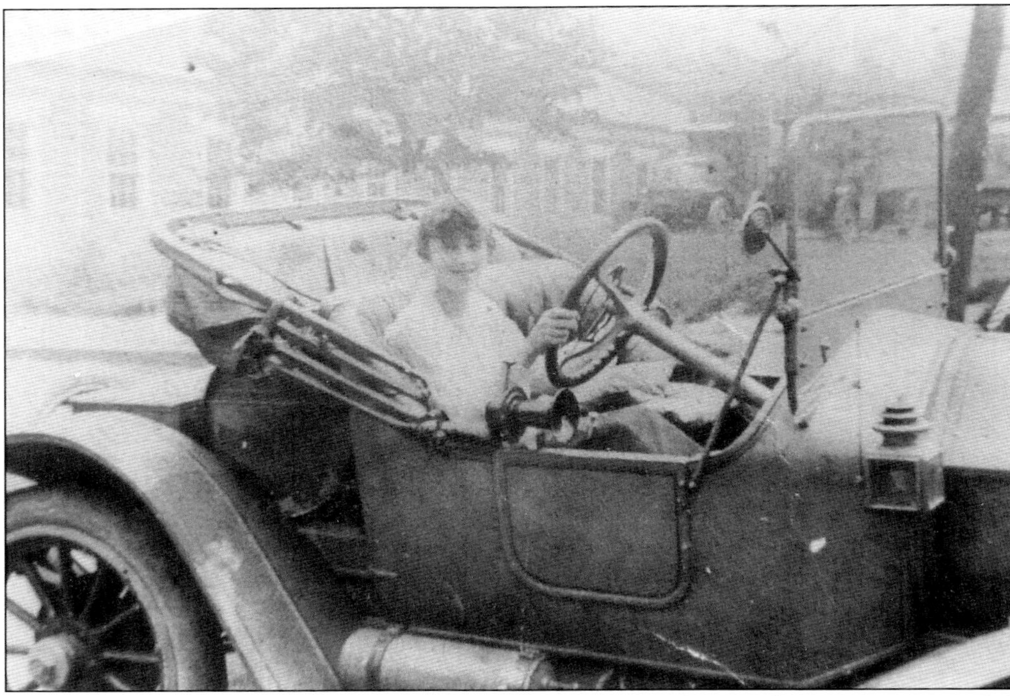

In 1917 Margaret Cooper, then seventeen, had her picture taken in this vintage automobile in front of number 40 East Bridge Street, near Washington Street. Note the steering wheel on the right.

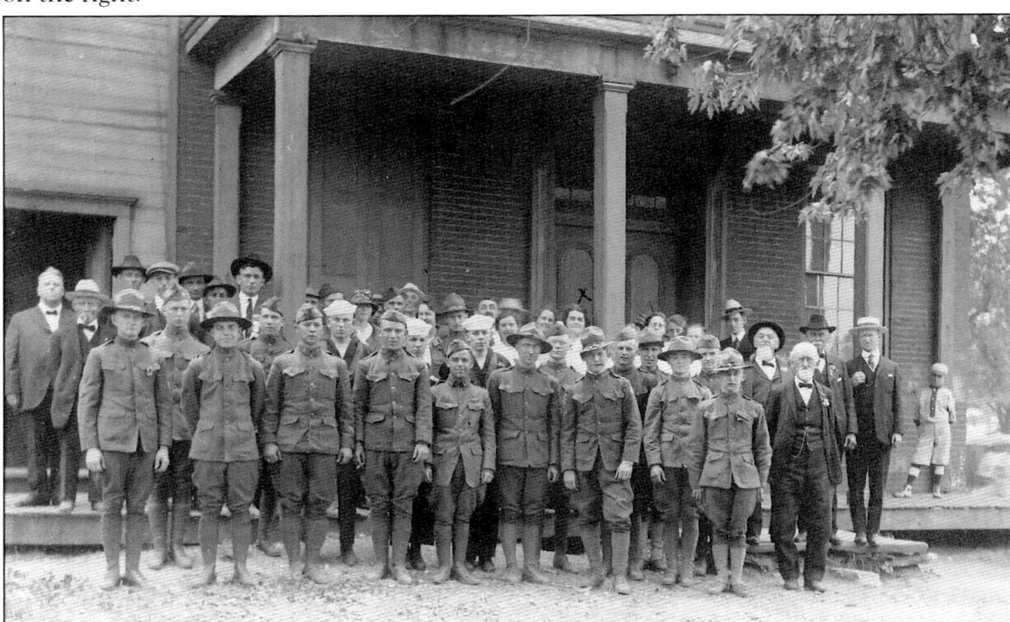

A picture taken in 1918 or '19 shows a group of World War I soldiers attending a "Welcome Home" party held by the local Red Cross. Mrs. Byron W. Meredith, Red Cross president, is the lady to the left of the center column, at the back.

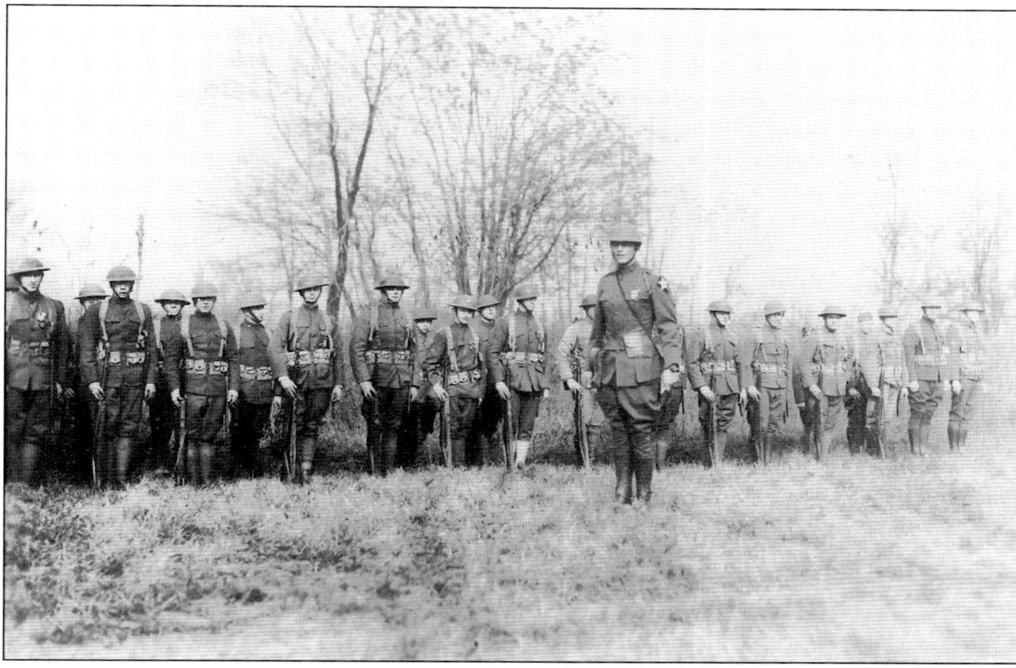

A mock battle was staged by American Legion Post 433 in 1920, in a field near Summerseat. As the photograph shows, the area was completely undeveloped at the time.

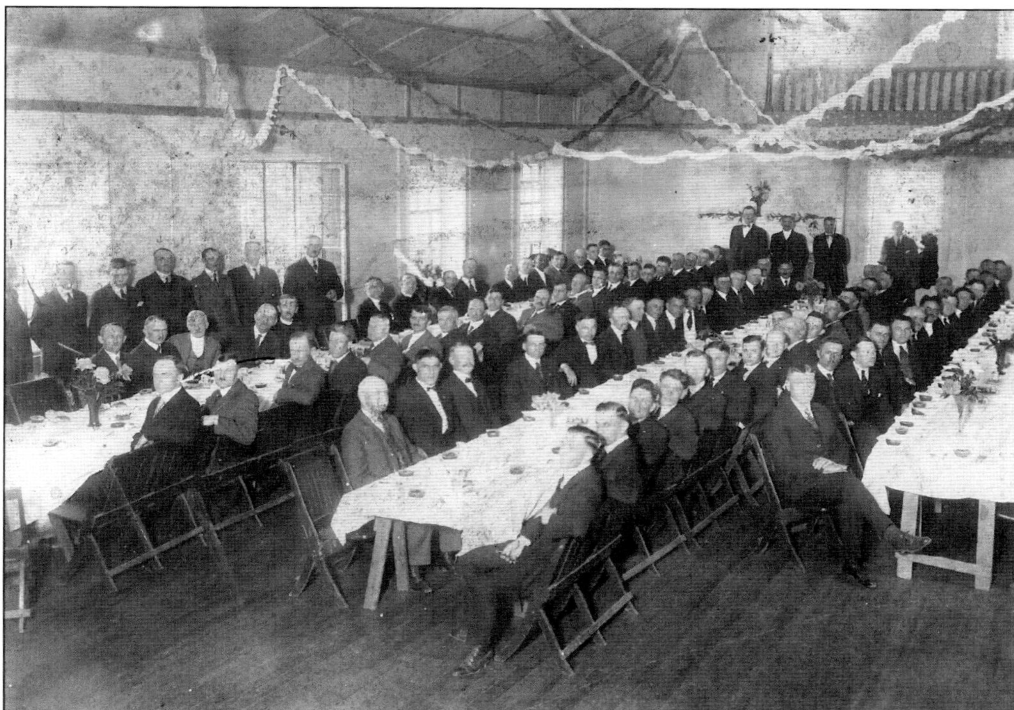

Morrisville's Chamber of Commerce had an impressive membership of approximately one hundred when this picture was taken at a dinner meeting.

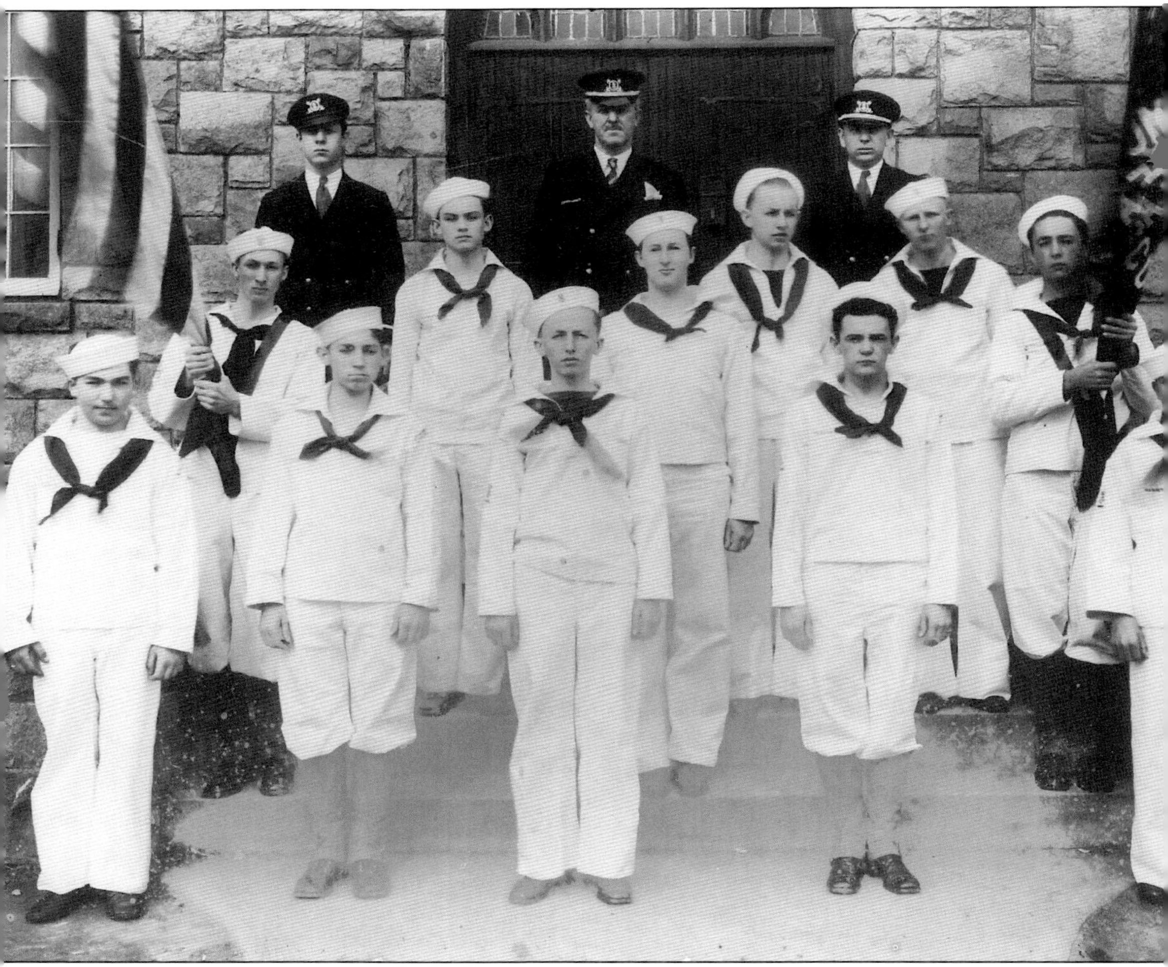

For years Morrisville had a Sea Scouts troop that took to the Delaware River in a 26-foot power launch donated by the U.S. Navy. Not all in the picture are identified, but the officers are, from left to right, Harper Stockham, Commodore Thomas Stockham, and Cliff Nelson. Bill Anderson is between the two Stockhams and to his left, one step down, is Bob White. Clarence "Huck" Landis is next to the young man holding the flag at right, and Bud Whalen is at the right in the front row. The troop continued to be active into the 1950s under the leadership of Harper Stockham, Charles Burgess, and Richard Landis. This picture was taken on the steps of Morrisville's Community House.

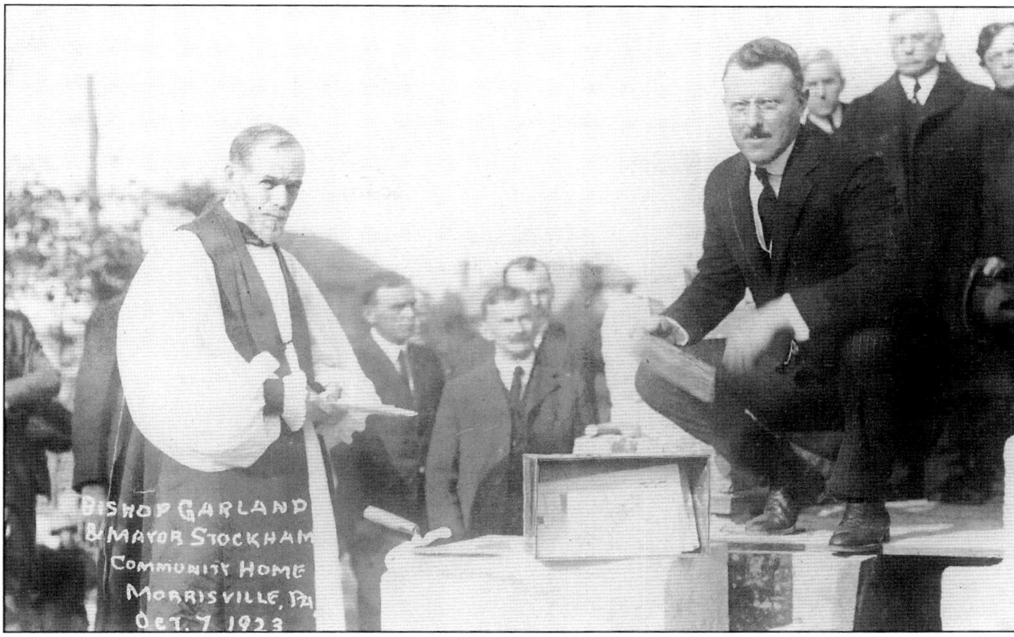

The Community House on North Pennsylvania Avenue, a building now occupied by the Curtin & Heefner law firm, was dedicated on October 7, 1923. The clergyman is Bishop Garland and the man kneeling is Mayor Thomas Stockham.

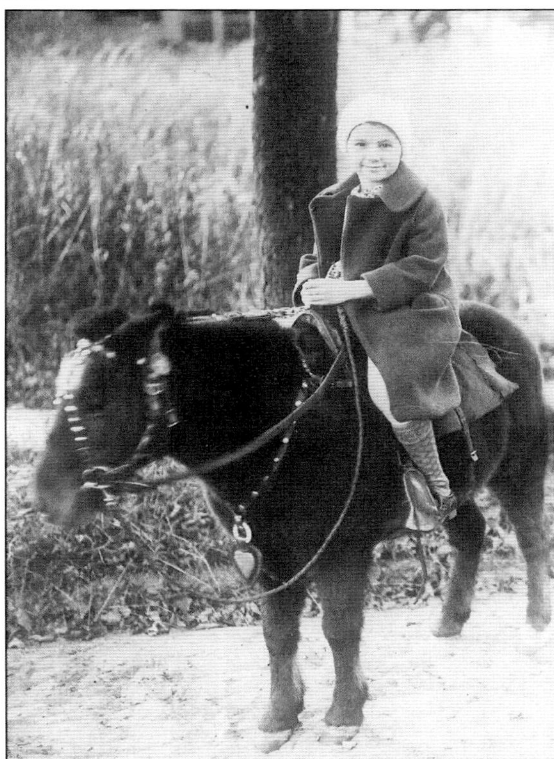

Once upon a time entrepreneurs with ponies would travel about and charge a small fee to take a youngster's picture sitting on a pony. Jean Reitzle smiles happily for the camera on one such traveling pony for this 1930s-era photograph.

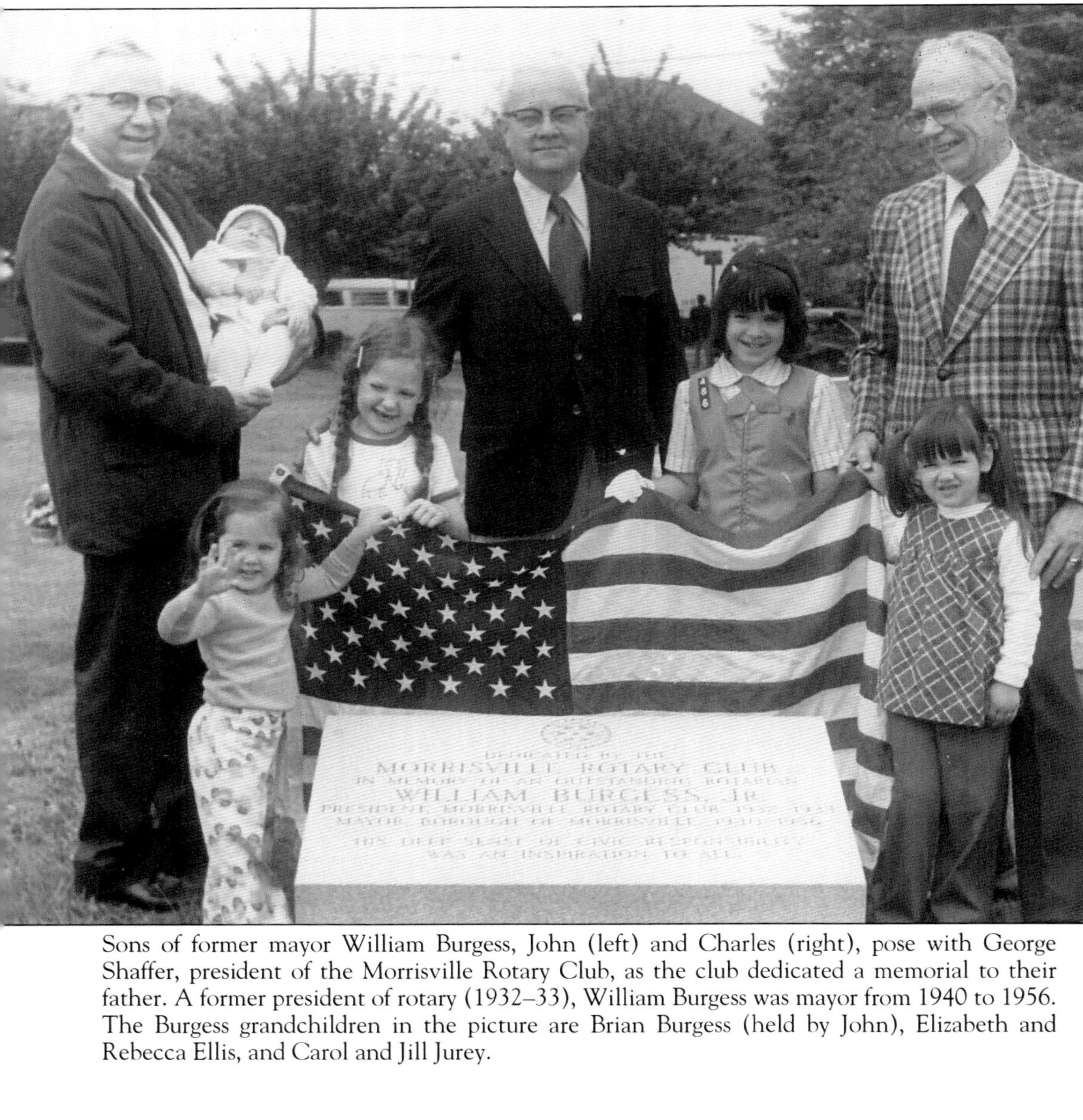

Sons of former mayor William Burgess, John (left) and Charles (right), pose with George Shaffer, president of the Morrisville Rotary Club, as the club dedicated a memorial to their father. A former president of rotary (1932–33), William Burgess was mayor from 1940 to 1956. The Burgess grandchildren in the picture are Brian Burgess (held by John), Elizabeth and Rebecca Ellis, and Carol and Jill Jurey.

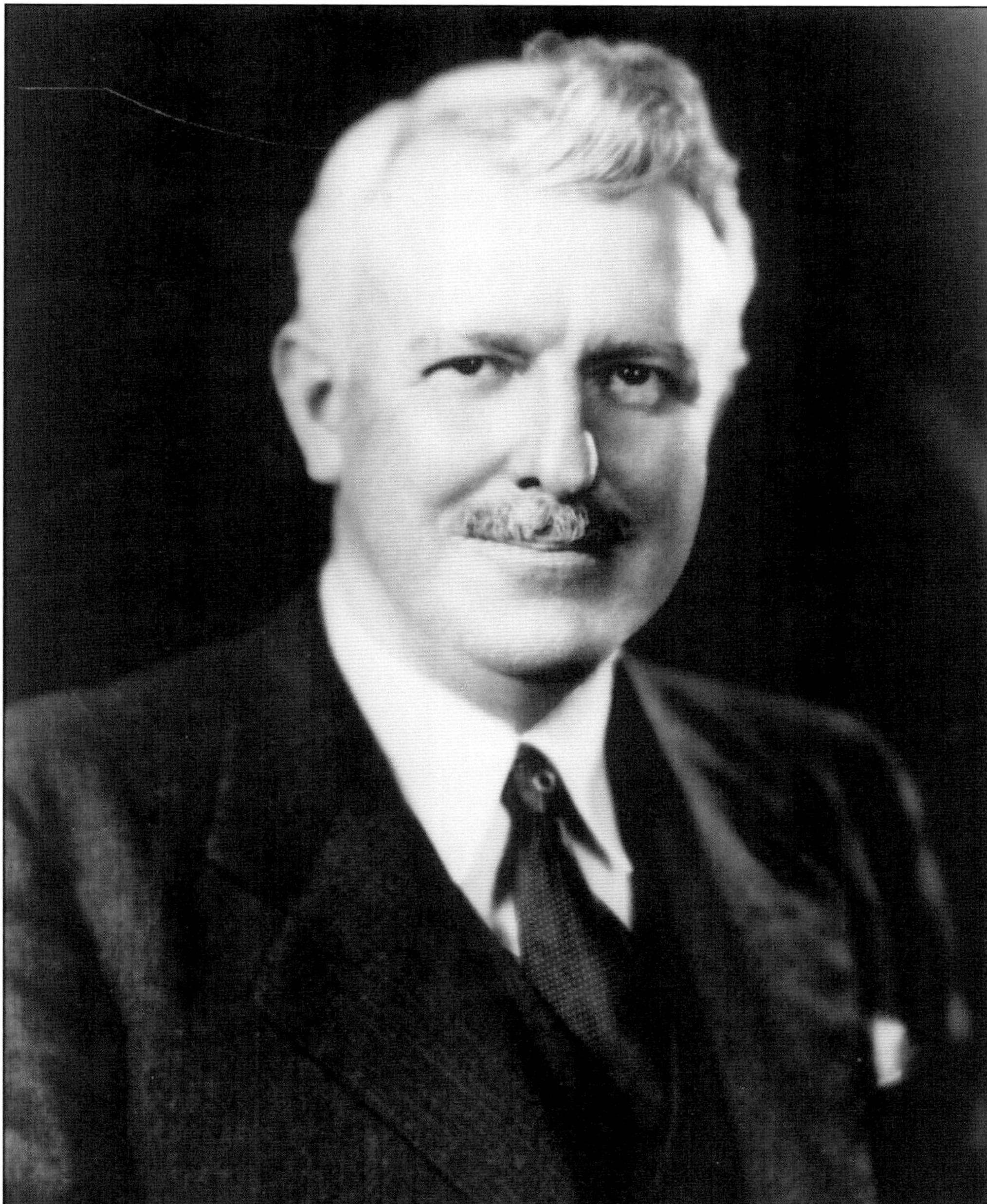

This portrait photograph of Thomas B. Stockham was taken in 1940. He was a civil engineer and architect, and his business activities included real estate and insurance. A lifetime resident of Morrisville, he was active in a multitude of civic affairs—most impressively serving as mayor for sixteen years and for six terms as Bucks County's member of the Pennsylvania House of Representatives. His skills as an engineer and architect, coupled with his interest in the history of the borough, were especially valuable when he devoted himself to the restoration of Summerseat, one of the nation's most significant landmarks.

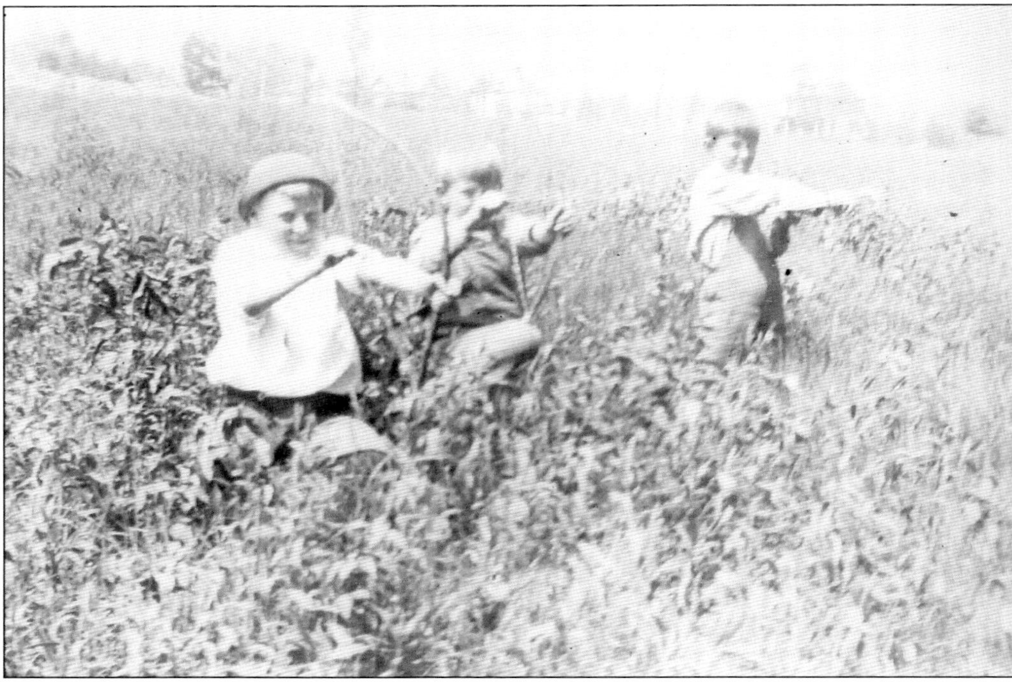

These young archers, playing Robin Hood or pretending to be Indians *c.* 1915, were photographed in a field that is now covered by the Morrisville Shopping Center's blacktopped parking lot. From left to right are Richard Landis, and Frank and Louis Reitzle.

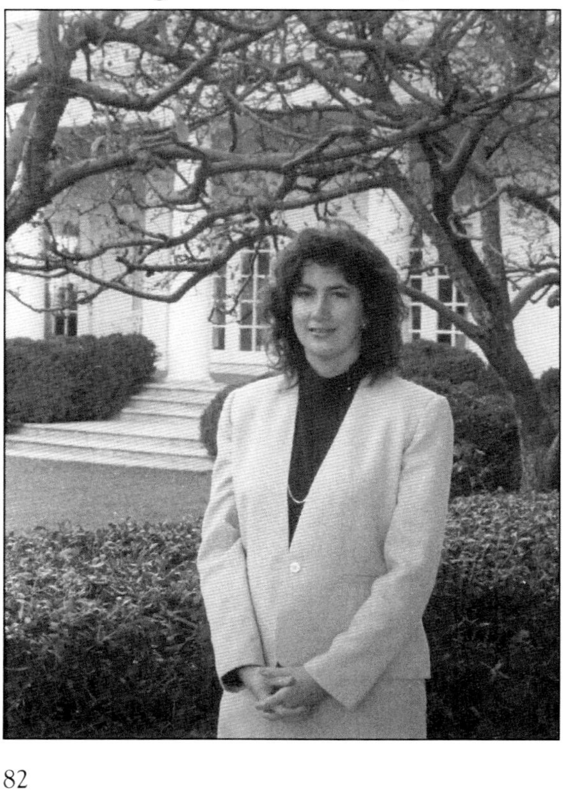

One Morrisvillean made it to the White House. Pictured standing in the Rose Garden outside the West Wing of the Presidential mansion, Barbara Borden Wood was a member of the staff of Max Friedersdorf, President Ronald Reagan's first Assistant for Legislative Affairs, and later served in the same capacity with his successor, M.B. Oglesby. Their office was located one floor above the Oval Office and she was often greeted by a cheery "Good morning, Barbara" as the President passed on his way to or from work. Barbara graduated from Morrisville High School in 1967 and earned an associate's degree from Rider University in 1969.

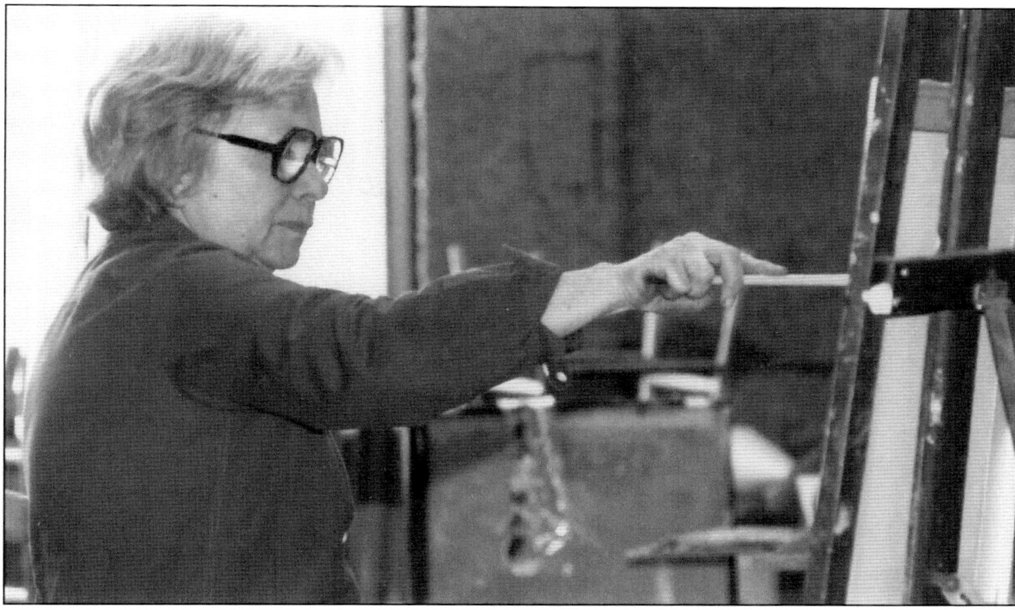

At one time Morrisville seemed to be somewhat of an artists' colony, with J. Gordon White and Daniel Garber, among others, living in the town. One who is still active is Elizabeth Ruggles, shown at work in her studio on Osborne Avenue. For years she was the only Bucks County woman to earn a full-time living as an artist, working as a commercial artist for the New Jersey State Health Department for thirty years, selling her paintings at galleries in Pennsylvania and New Jersey, and teaching art classes at the School of Industrial Arts in Trenton, the Yardley Art Center in Pennsylvania, the Pennington Art Center in New Jersey, and the Princeton Art Association. Born in Sunbury, Pennsylvania, she was educated at Colorado University, the National Academy of Design in New York, and the Pennsylvania Academy in Philadelphia.

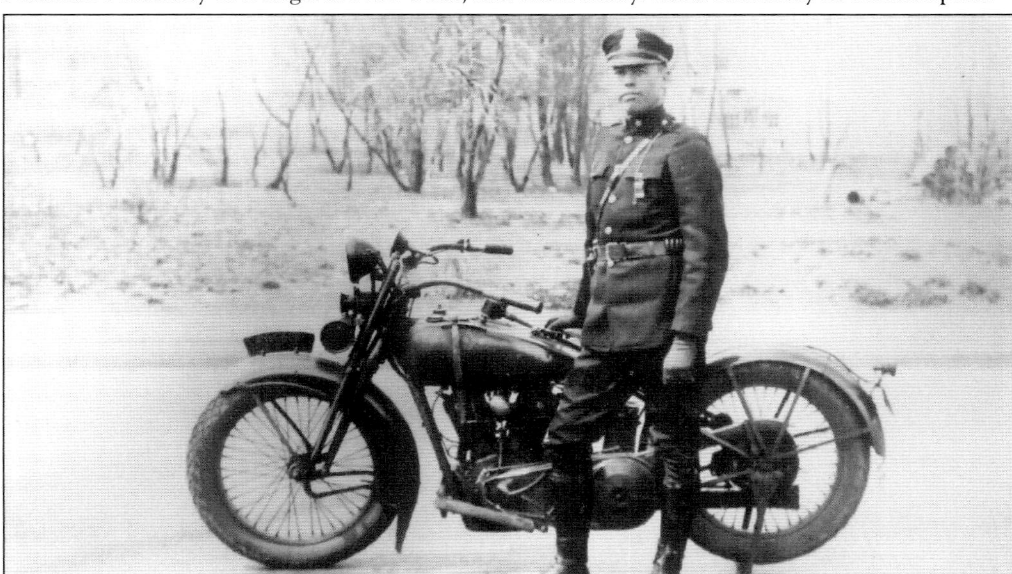

In 1925 Al Cooper was chief of police. In fact, he was Morrisville's police force. This photograph shows him with the motorcycle he rode while patrolling the town.

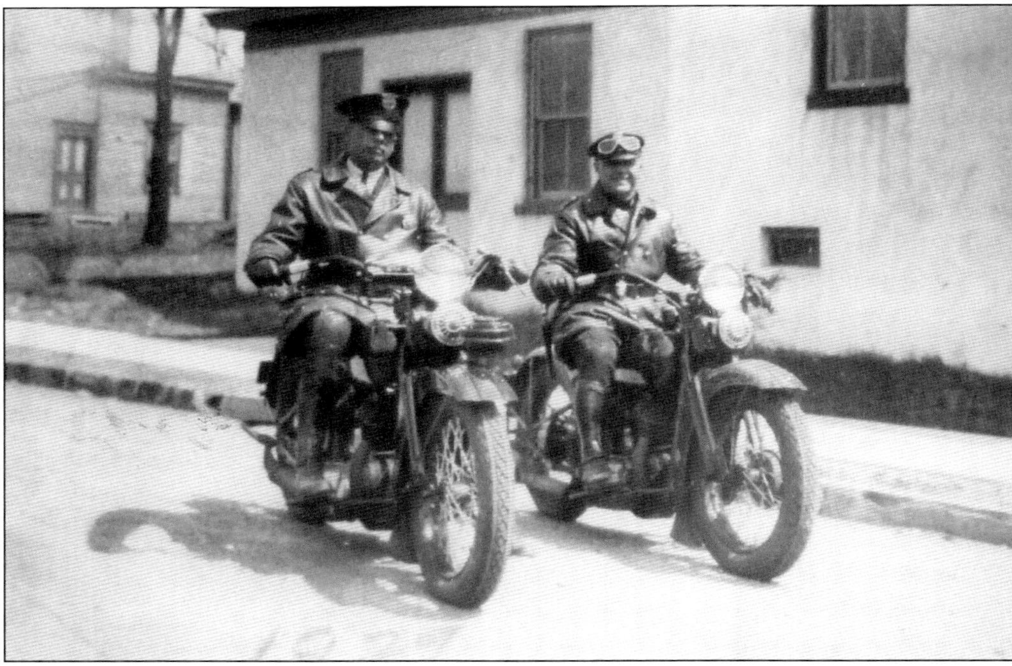

Morrisville's police force doubled when Constable Andy Thompson (right) joined Chief Al Cooper in responding to calls for assistance or to investigate an accident. This picture was taken in 1929 next to the entrance to the jail at the rear of borough hall on Washington Street.

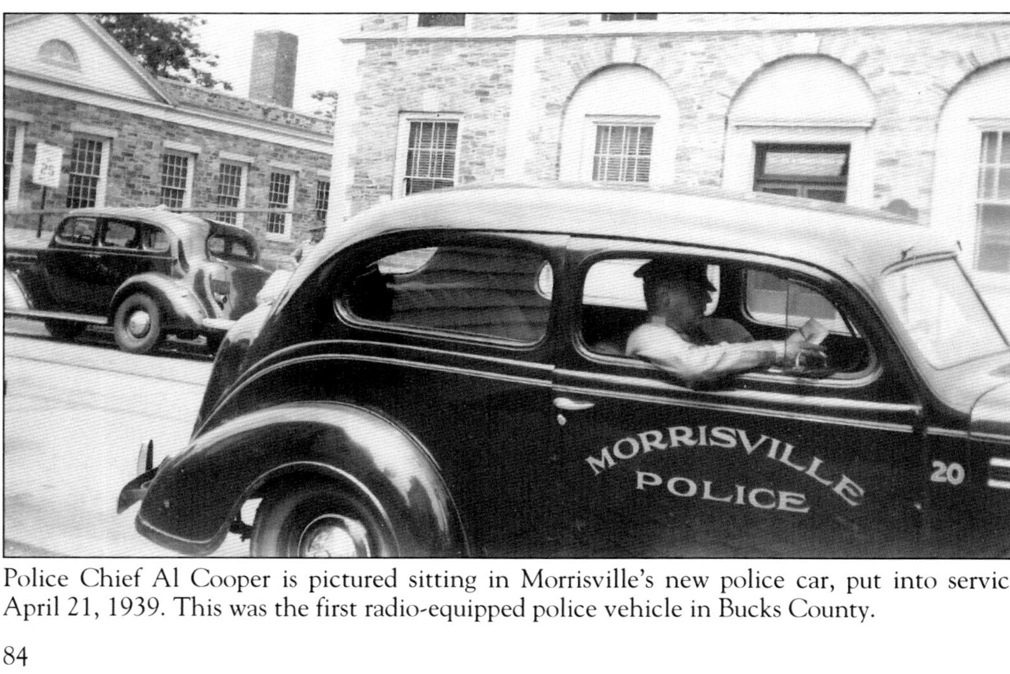

Police Chief Al Cooper is pictured sitting in Morrisville's new police car, put into service April 21, 1939. This was the first radio-equipped police vehicle in Bucks County.

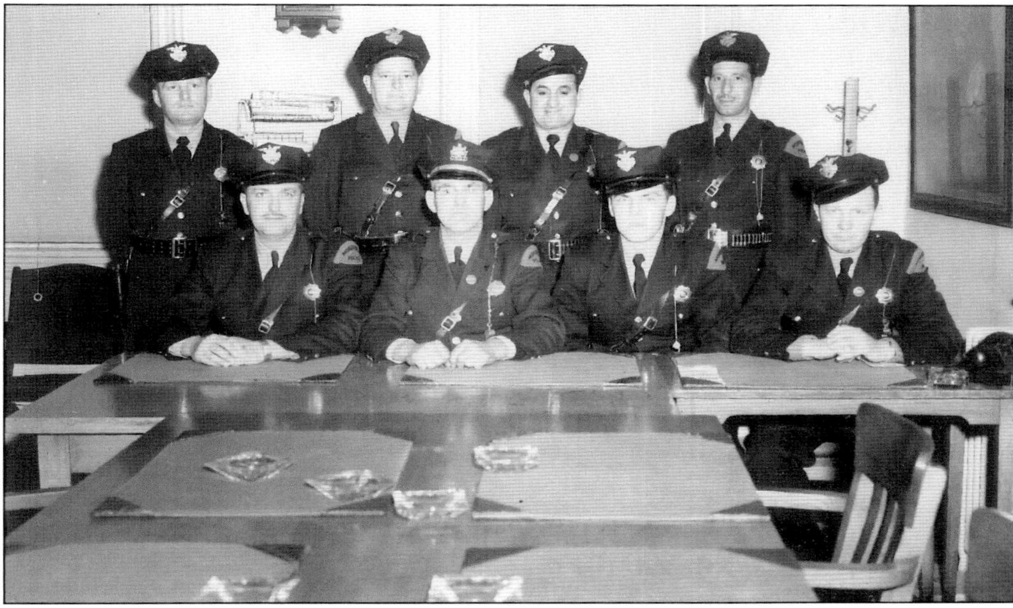

A few years later, in 1954, Morrisville's police force had expanded to eight officers. From left to right are as follows: (front row) Harry Tomlinson, Chief John Davis, Joe Cavanaugh, and Stan Naprawa; (back row) Mahlon Cummings, Clifton Morris, Frank Picciotti, and Joe DiGiorgio.

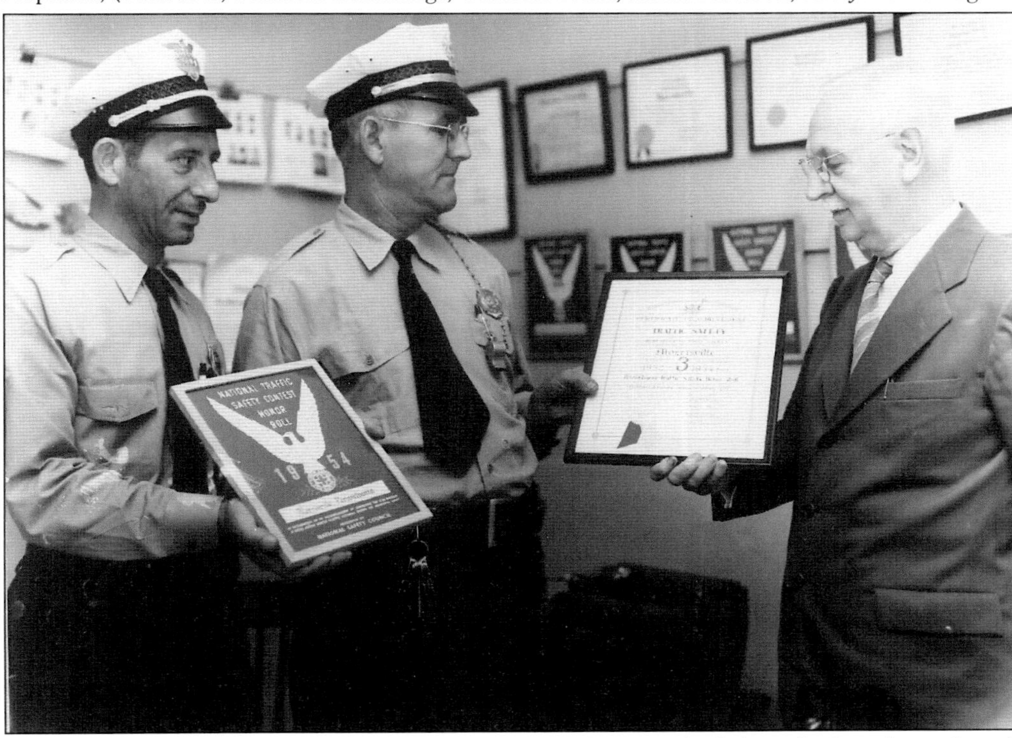

Another photograph taken in 1954 shows Mayor Burgess (right) with Patrolman Joseph DiGiorgio (left) and Police Chief John Davis as they examine national traffic safety awards won by the borough.

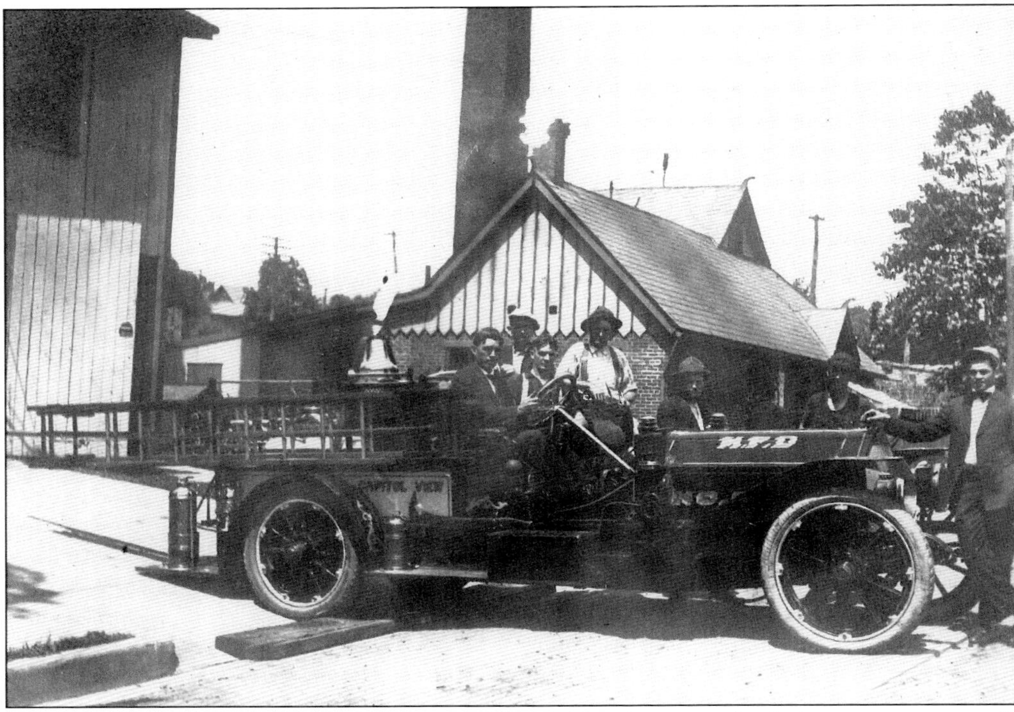

In 1919 volunteer firemen from the Capitol View Fire Company built their own engine, by converting a Palmer Singer automobile, a vehicle that had been a pleasure car.

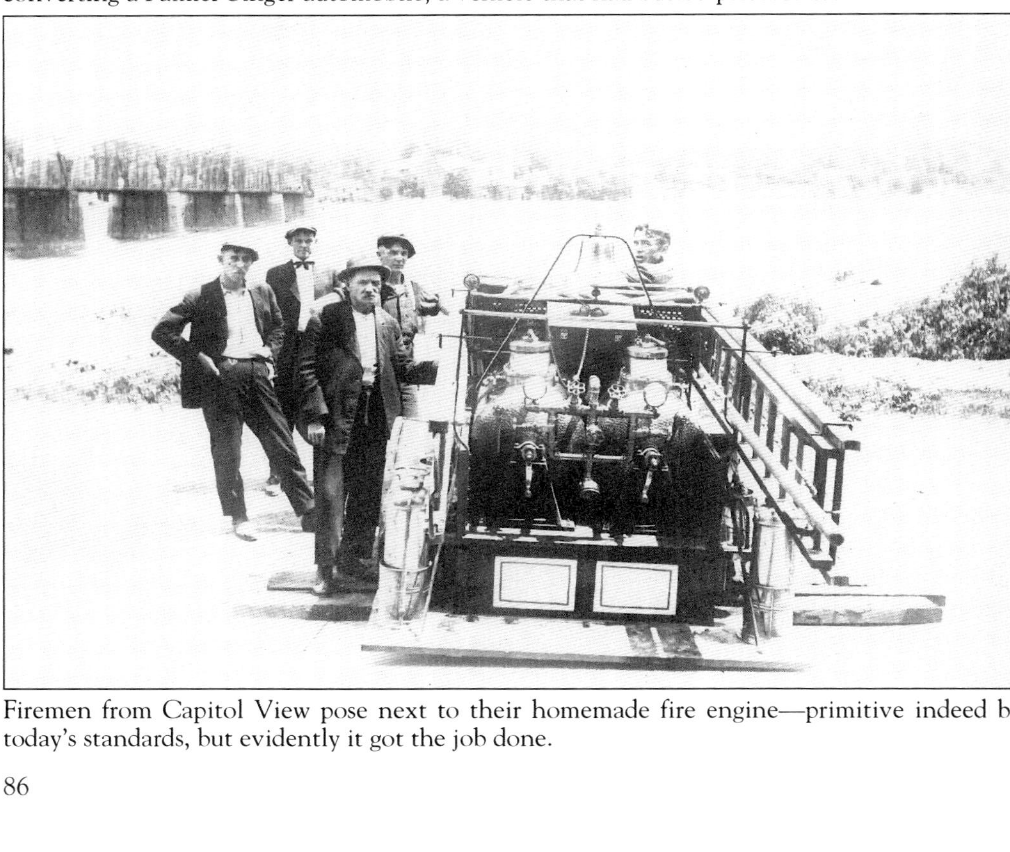

Firemen from Capitol View pose next to their homemade fire engine—primitive indeed by today's standards, but evidently it got the job done.

Five

Good Sports in Morrisville

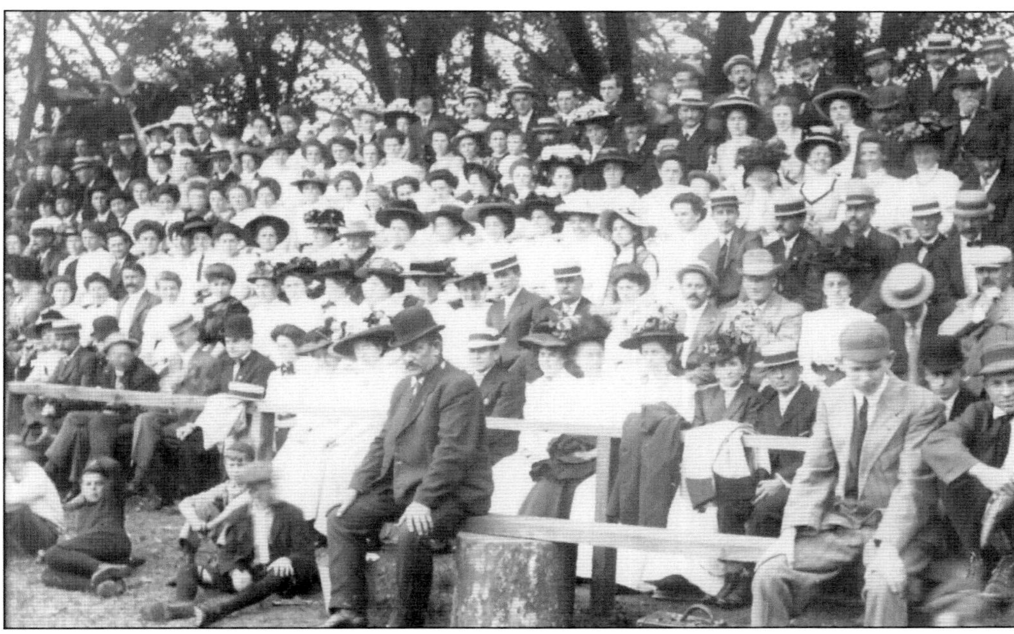

With no television to distract them in 1909 the fans turned out in large numbers to watch local sports teams in action. During the summertime the Morrisville Reds baseball team was a crowd pleaser, especially since it won most of its games.

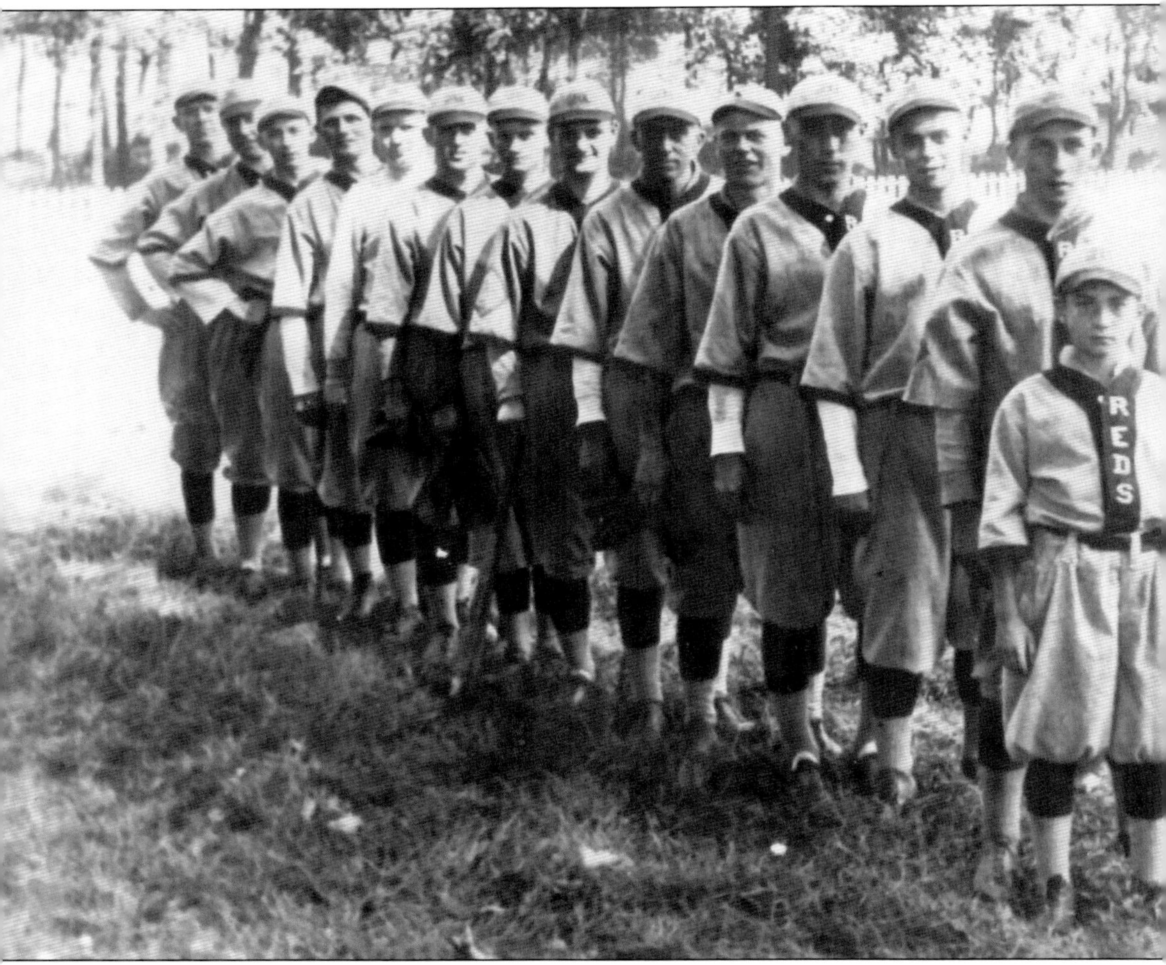

During the early 1900s the Morrisville Reds were a semi-pro baseball team that dominated the Delaware River League. Identifiable, from left, are W.O. "Ortie" Justice (first), Dave "Pug" Lukens (sixth), Neal Nolan, and Lew Wright (ninth). This picture was taken on "The Island" (now Williamson Park) in 1919. In 1927 Lukens played third base on an all-star team in Trenton that included barnstorming Babe Ruth in right field and Lou Gehrig at first base. The all-star team beat the Brooklyn Giants 9–4 with Ruth hitting three home runs. Gehrig had two hits, one a double, and Lukens hit for a single.

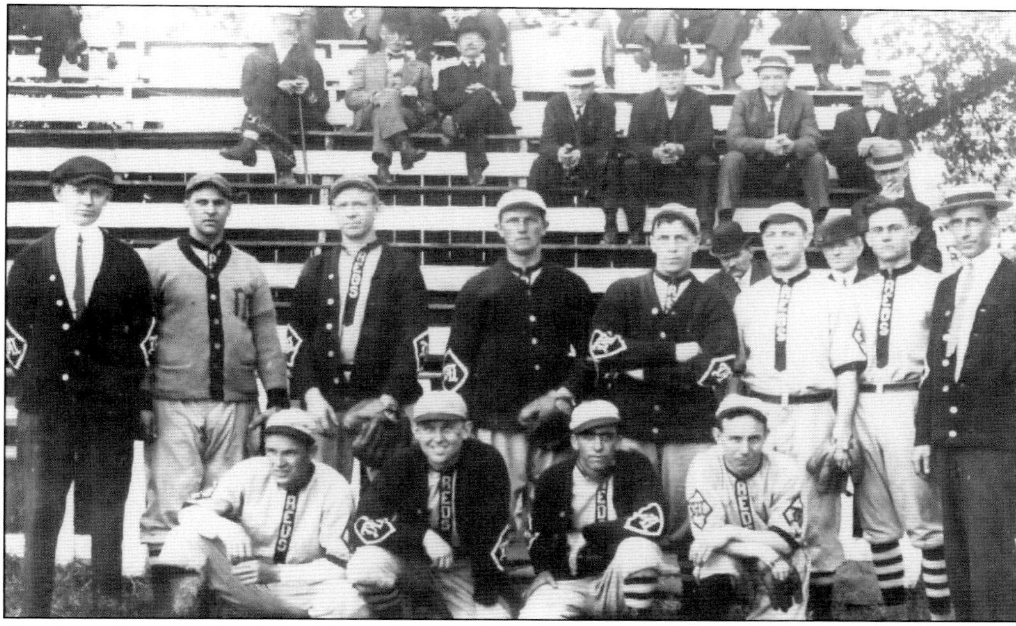

Another photograph of the Morrisville Reds has manager Bill Howell at left, standing, with Ortie Justice third from left, Bill Mason, and Bob Chapman. Kneeling at right are Neal Nolan and Lew Wright. Bill Howell, a World War I veteran, was commander of the American Legion post in 1923 and 1943, and served as Morrisville's borough secretary for a quarter century.

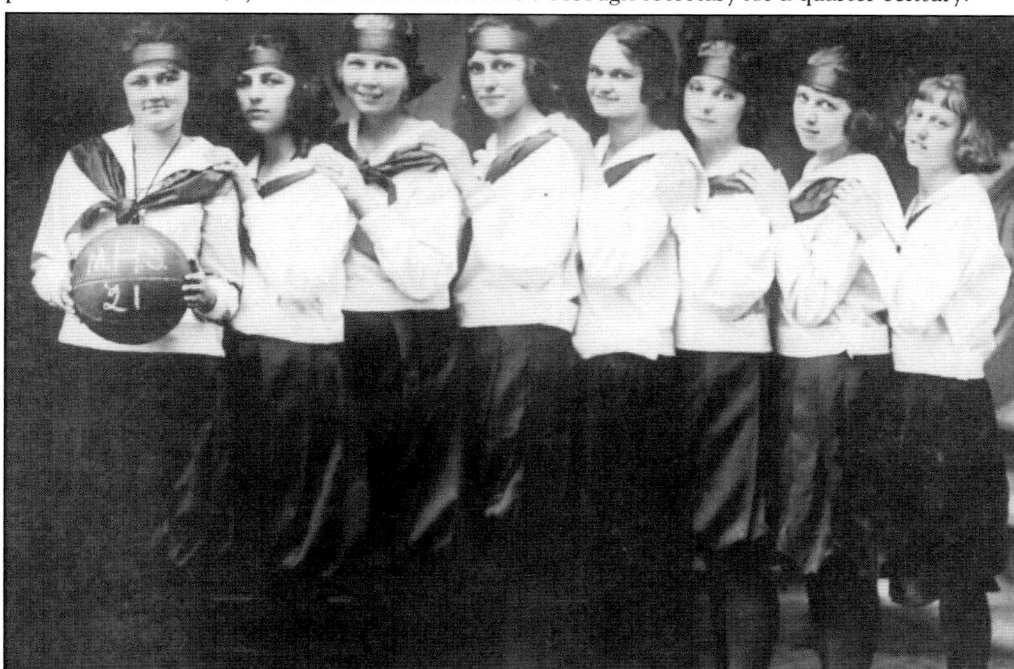

Morrisville High School's girls basketball team in 1921 included, from left, Rachel MacPherson, Madeline Smith, Lillian Rickey, Carolyn Gould, Lillian Mohr, Ruth Gunn, Adeline Coon, and Catherine Hunt.

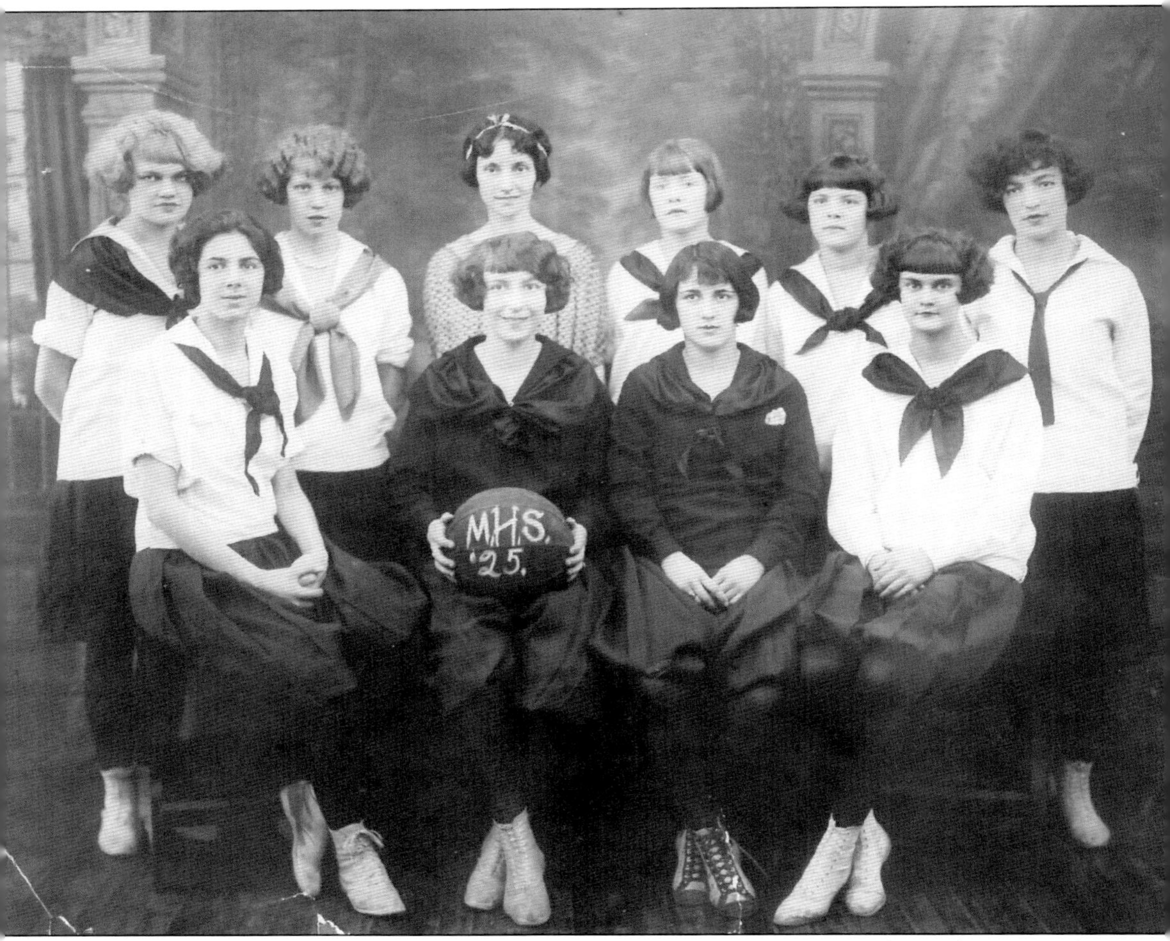

The girls basketball team of 1925 posed for this splendid photograph. Katherine Mohr is standing at left and Sylvia Naylor is seated at left, but unfortunately the rest of the players are not identified.

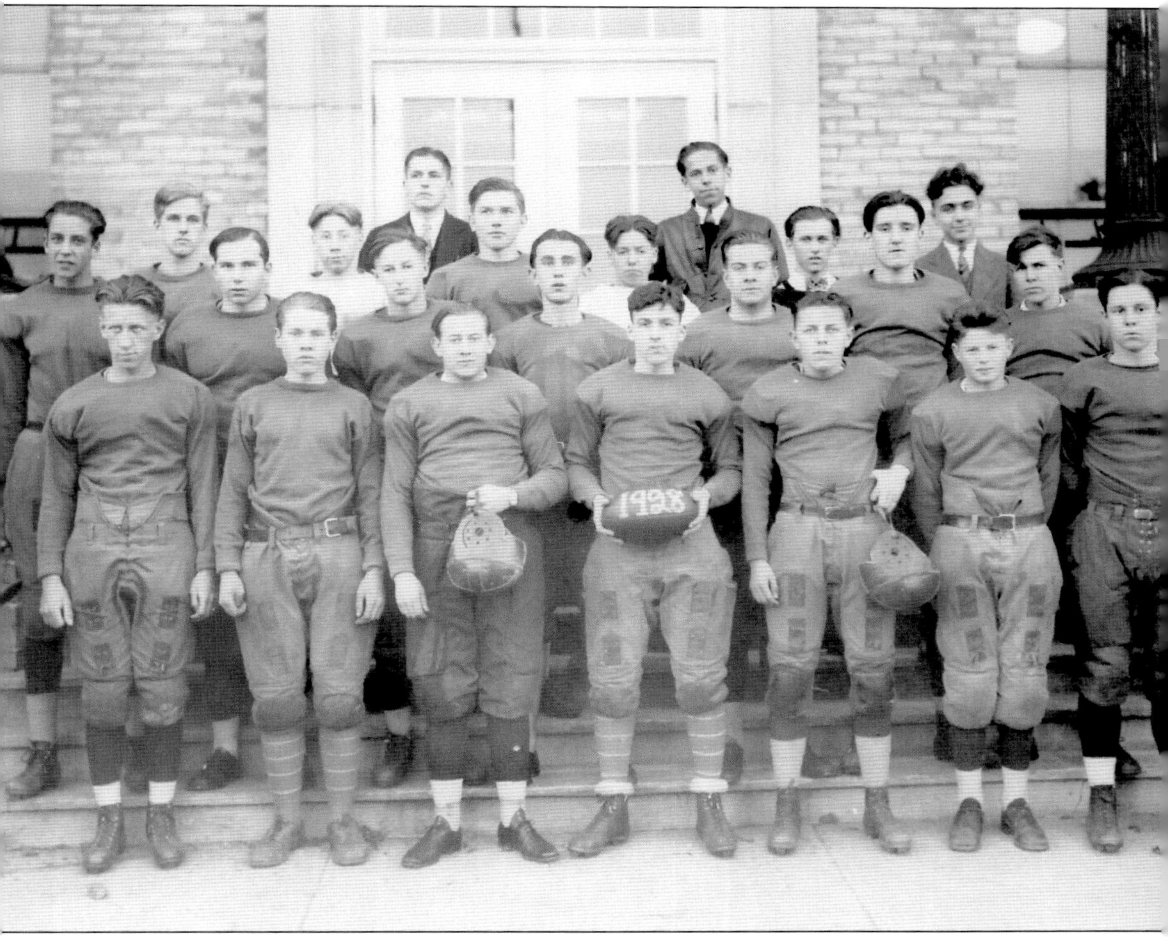

This is the Morrisville High School football squad of 1928, the second year the school fielded a team. From left, first row, are Ray Margerum, Charles Geanette, Frank Kirby, Martin "Brud" Wright, Aaron Young, Bill Burns, and Harper "Hip" Stockham. In the second row are Slim Hughes, Ira Gunn, and Bob White. Taylor Kirby is standing behind Brud Wright and Aaron Young, and John Foster is at right in the second row. In the third row are Bob Stockham, Fred Wright, Ed Wiley, and Clint Deitrick. In the top row are Lew Rupp, coach, and (wearing neckties) Mort Hensor and Emerson Levy. Not all of the young men pictured could be identified.

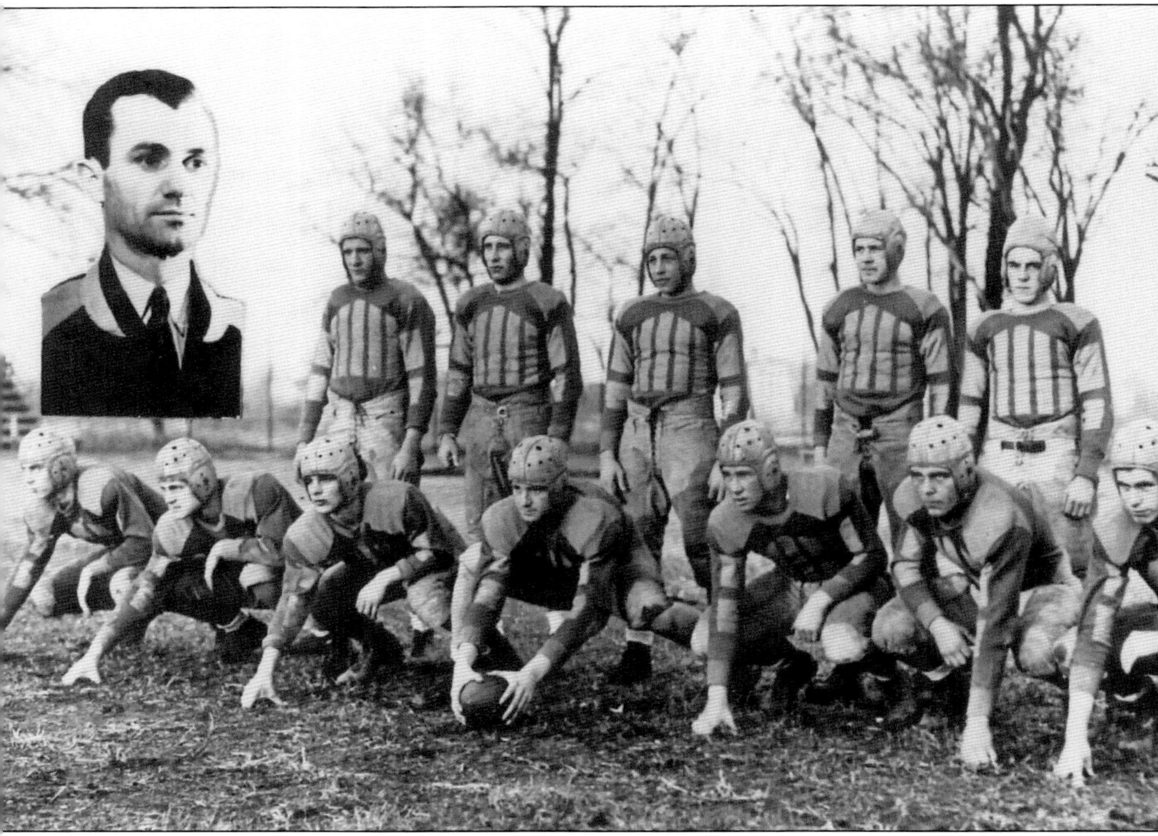

Morrisville High School's Lower Bucks County Champion football team of 1937 set a standard that later teams strove to match. They won eight games, tied one, and lost two, including a special post-season game with the much larger Trenton New Jersey High School. The linemen, from left to right, are Albie Johnson, Calvin Marsh, Frank Mattis, Ted Reitzle, Bill Wilson, Jack Margerum, and Robert "Bucky" Wallace. The backs, from left to right, are Art Baehr, Jim Pidcock, Jim Yeager, Andy Gavin, and Joe Hughes. The head coach, inset, is John Hoffman. The team was invited to play Olney High School, a suburban Philadelphia powerhouse that wanted a small school to beat while they dedicated a new stadium. The final score: Morrisville 21, Olney 6! Yeager went on to play football at Temple University and Reitzle played at Appalachian State. Calvin Marsh later was a baritone with the Metropolitan Opera Company.

Calvin Marsh played on a championship football team and sang in the Methodist Church choir, then served three years in the Air Force, Pacific Theatre, during World War II. After his discharge he studied at the Westminster Choir College and from 1954 to 1967 was a baritone soloist with the Metropolitan Opera Company. Later he entered into a full-time evangelistic concert ministry. He is pictured in the role of Count di Luna in Verdi's Il Trovatore at the Met. Calvin's older brother Howard, also a good high school football player, had a fine bass voice and they often sang together in church. Howard is a retired Army chaplain.

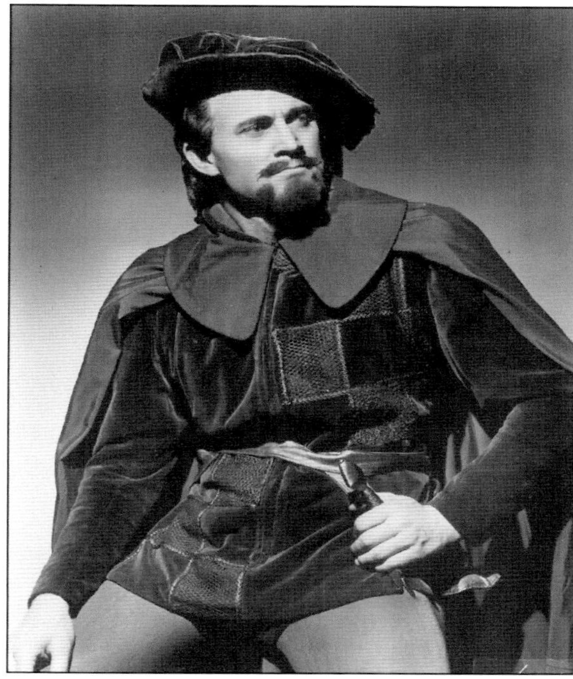

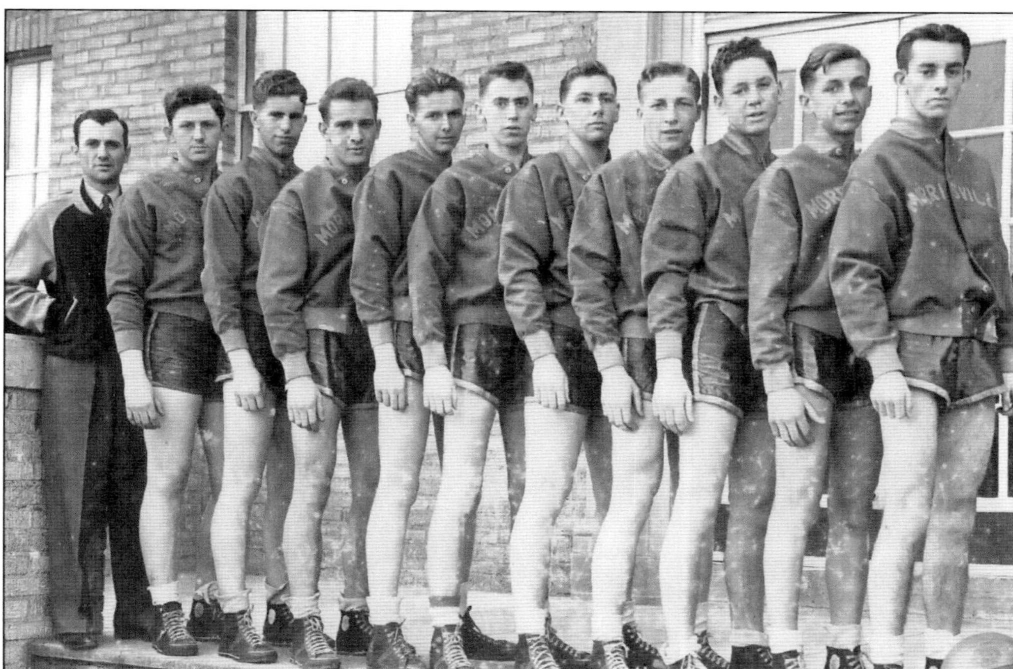

Many of the same athletes who played on Morrisville High's 1937 football champions were also members of the basketball team that won the Lower Bucks County Conference basketball championship in 1938. From left they are coach John Hoffman, Ted Reitzle, Bucky Wallace, Art Baehr, Charles Foster, Albie Johnson, Bill Wilson, Jim Yeager, Andy Gavin, Alex Rusecky, and William "John" Wilmot.

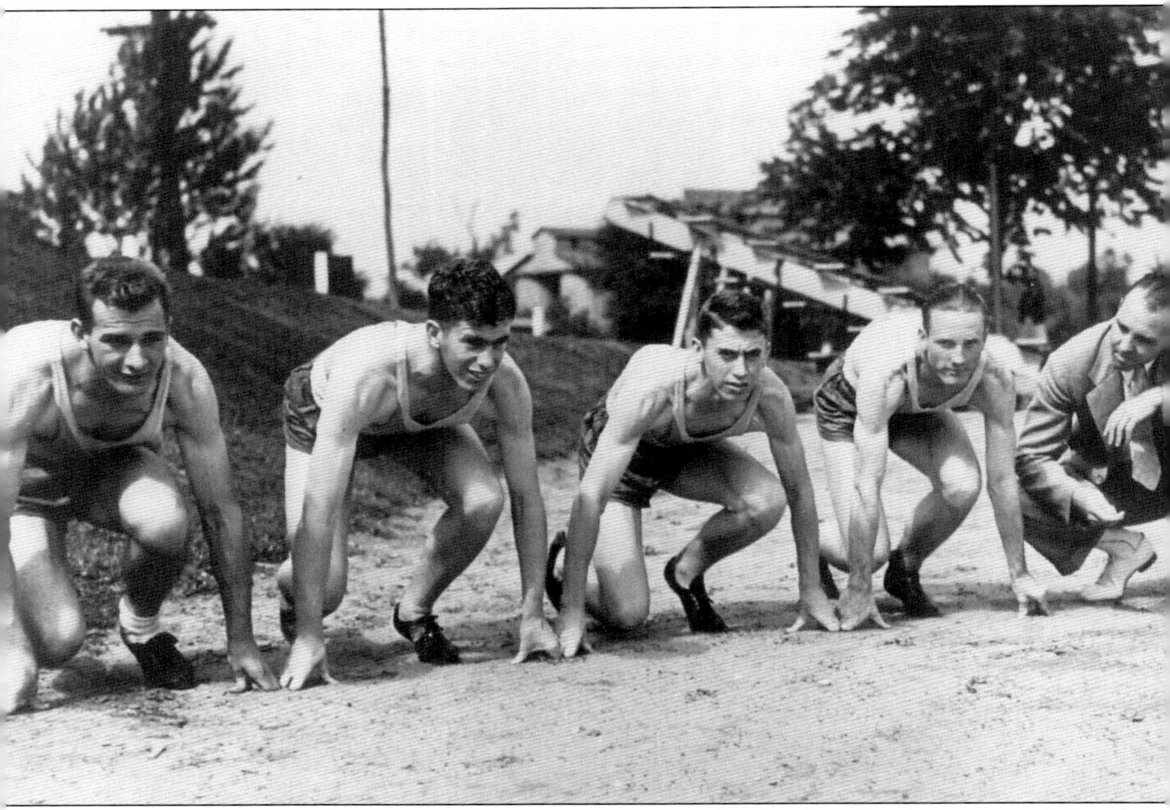

Local sports history was made in 1938 by Morrisville High School's mile relay team, undefeated in meets that included the Lower Bucks County and District One championships, the Bucks-Montgomery championship at the Penn Relays, and the Pennsylvania State Championship. The team's best time was 3:29.3. From left to right are Art Baehr, Bucky Wallace, Albie Johnson, Austin (Red) Beetle, and coach Floyd Kerr. Baehr also won the state 440 (quarter-mile) championship in the then-record time of 51 seconds flat. Johnson set a District One 880 (half-mile) record of 1:59.9 that stood for thirty-one years. Making their achievements especially noteworthy is the fact that the school had no track in 1938. They trained by running in the streets and occasionally visited Trenton High's quarter-mile track to learn to pass the baton. All the athletes served in World War II, Beetle later losing his life in Korea. Wallace was a prisoner of war in Germany late in the war, and Johnson was a marine who fought on Guam, Guadalcanal, and Iwo Jima.

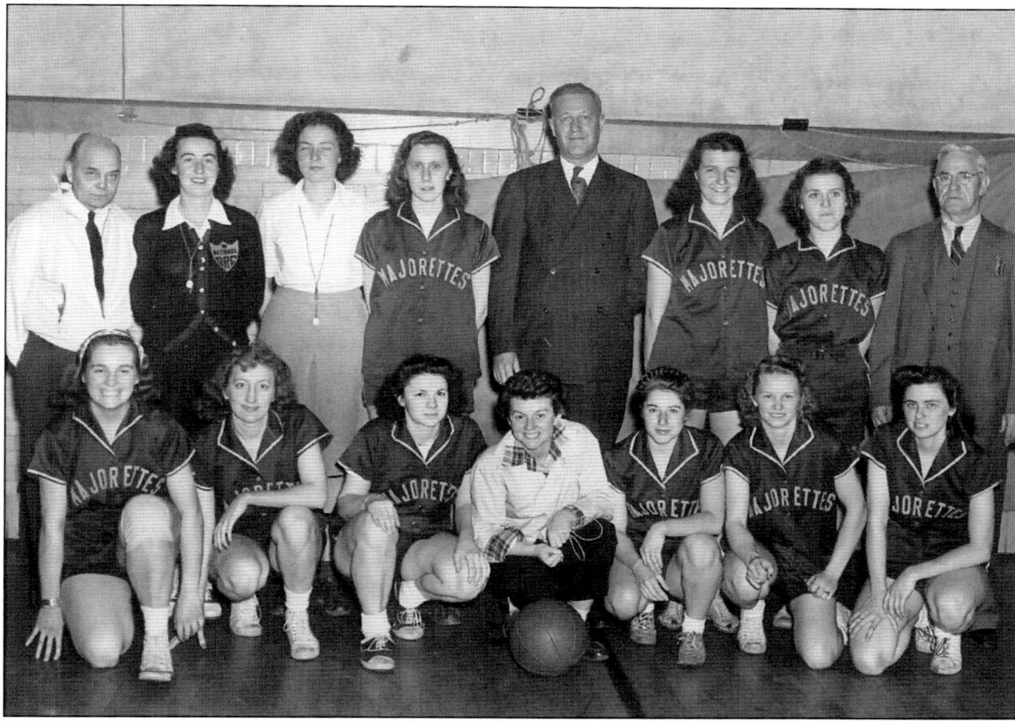

The Majorettes, winners of the Trenton, New Jersey, City Playground Girls League Basketball championship in 1945, included Morrisville's Jean Reitzle (third from left, kneeling) and Anne Parsons (kneeling at right), a teacher and coach at Morrisville High School.

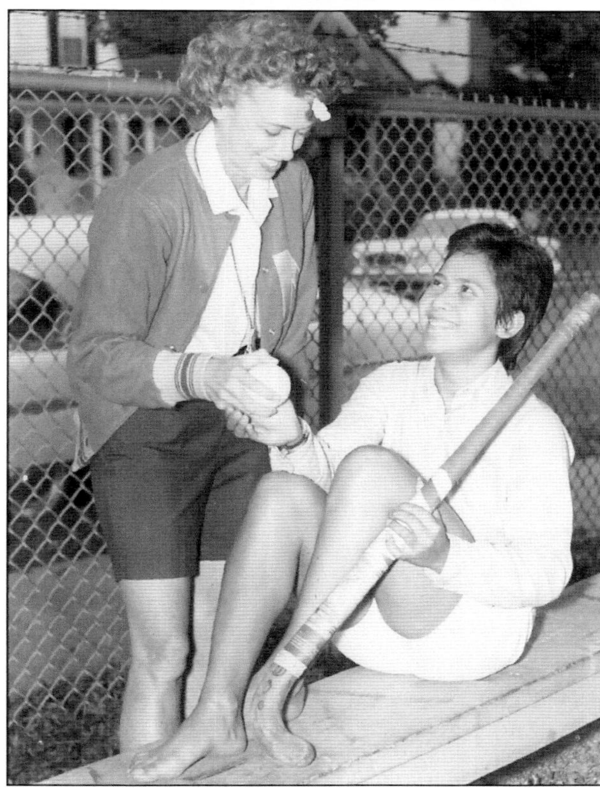

In 1963 Morrisville High School's field hockey team had an all-star who played barefoot! Torie Vanderlee, shown with coach Anne Parsons, led the league in scoring.

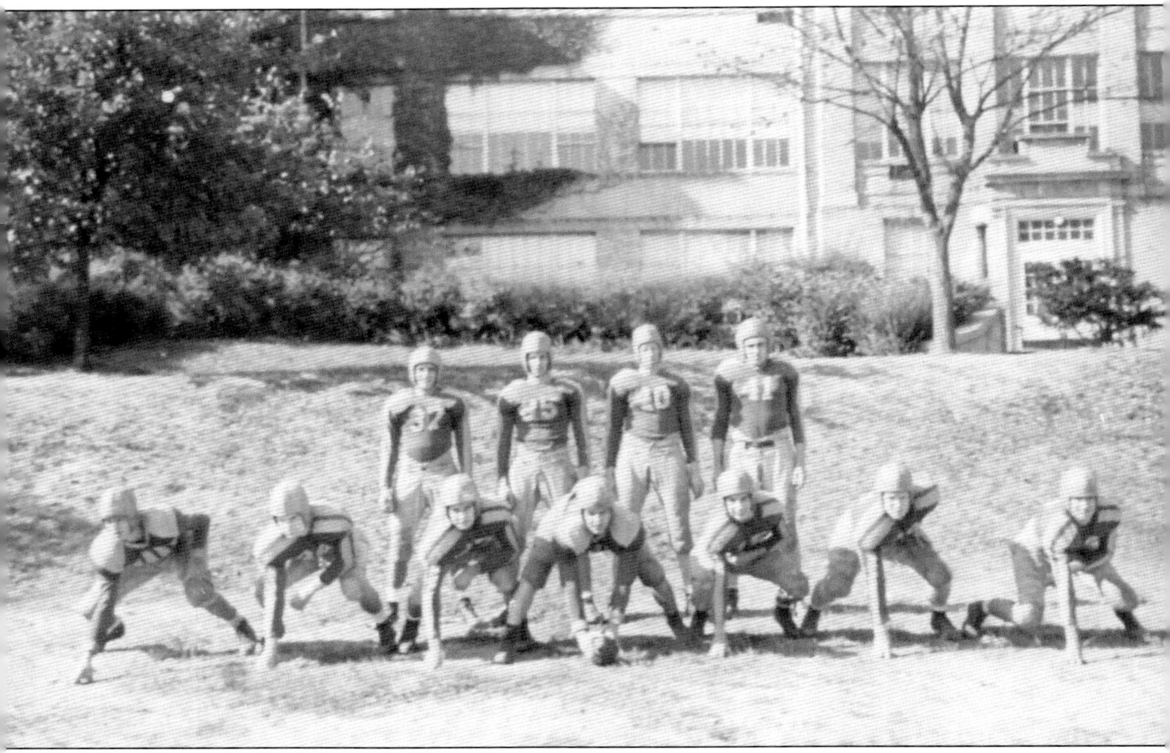

In 1943 Morrisville's football team won nine straight games after an opening 6–0 loss to Trenton High School (Morrisville graduated seventy students, Trenton more than one thousand) and was unbeaten in the conference for two years. The line, from left to right, are Ed "Scarhead" Burns, Jim Lorimer, Jim Campbell, Gordon May, Amby Summers, Jim Murray, and Dick Woolf. The backs, from left to right, are Reed Pratt, Bob Neeld, William "Mickey" Stradling, and Bill Hoernle. The coaches were John Hoffman and Al Lasky. This team scored 246 total points to its opponents' collective 32 and beat such New Jersey football powers as Trenton Catholic (33–7) and Bordentown Military Institute (18–0). Lorimer was a county 440 (quarter-mile) champion in track and Hoernle set a discus record. After World War II military service, Hoernle and Murray played football at Rutgers where Murray was the university's javelin thrower for three years.

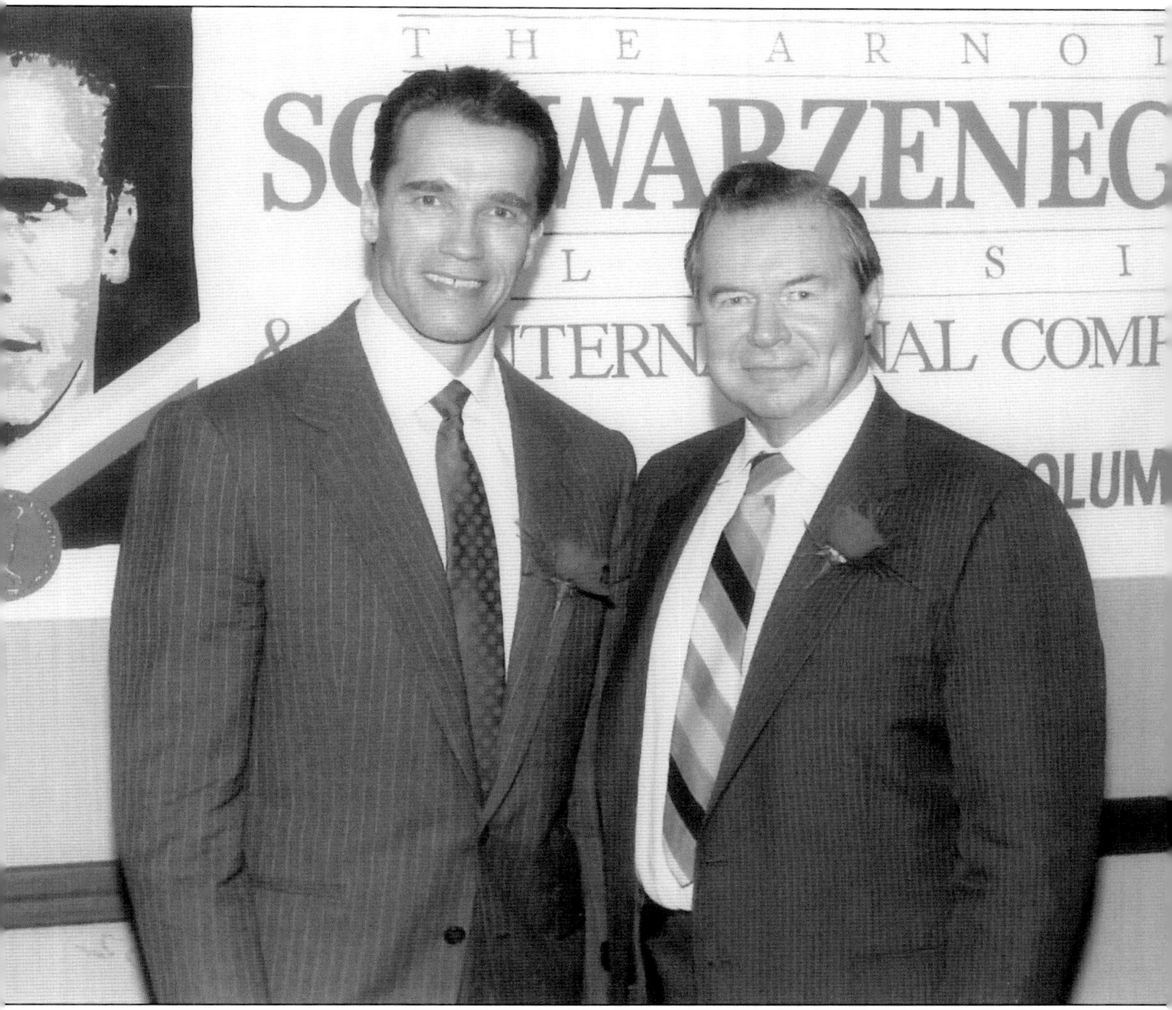

Jim Lorimer (right) was co-captain and right tackle on Morrisville's 1943 championship team. He and Jim Murray (co-captain; left tackle) had begun lifting weights in 1939 to build strength for football, though the activity was then frowned on. Continuing his weight training interest over the years, Lorimer became a partner of Arnold Schwarzenegger (left) in producing international best-built-man contests and major fitness expositions. Lorimer, an attorney and former vice-president of government affairs for Nationwide Insurance, was named with Schwarzenegger to the President's Fitness Council. Murray also remained active in weight training and authored seven books on the subject, published by A.S. Barnes & Company, Ronald Press, John Wiley & Son, Prentice-Hall, and Contemporary Books from 1954 to 1983.

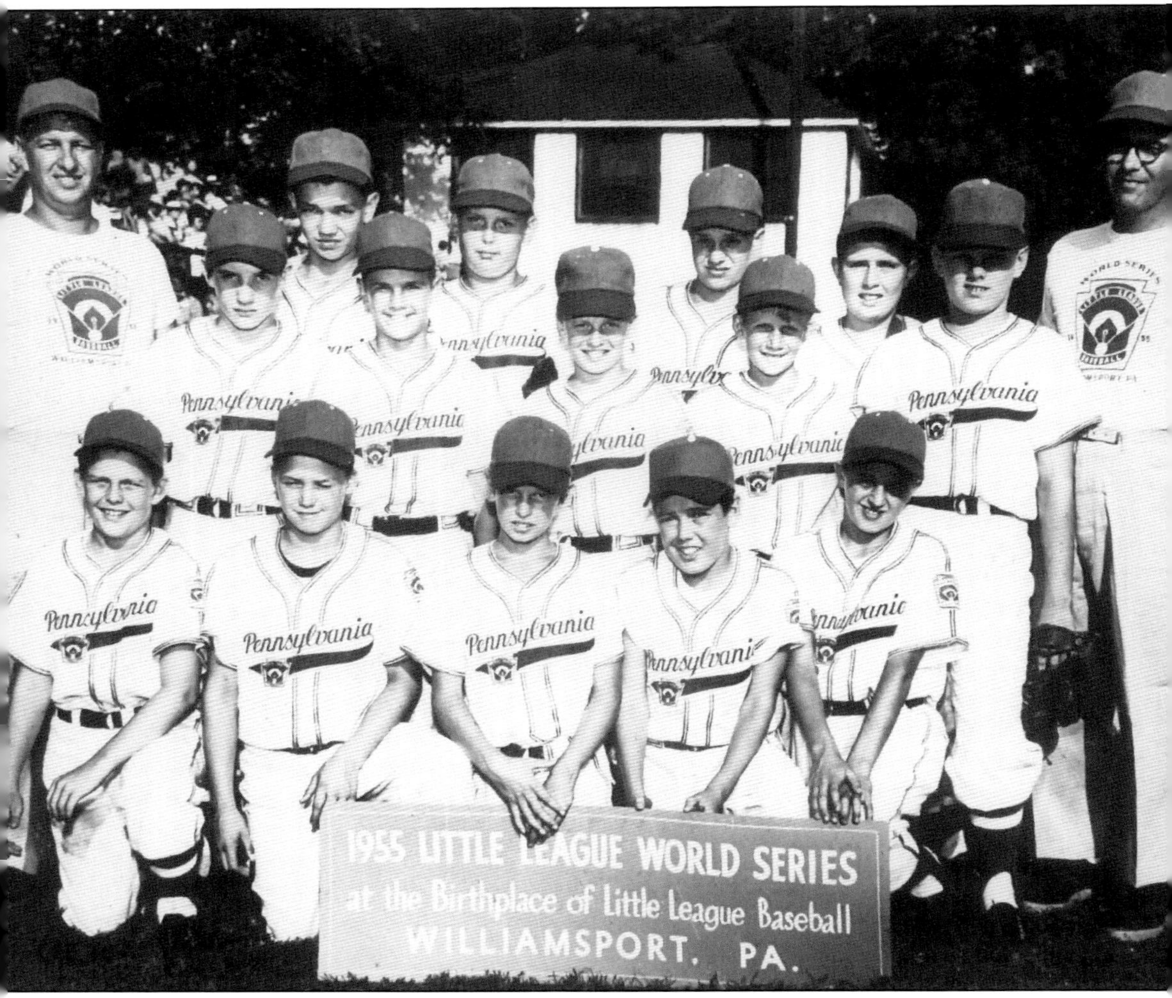

Morrisville's team won the 1955 Little League World Championship. From left to right are as follows: (front row) Skipper Foulke, Rich Cominsky, Denny Poland, Fran Valeriano, and Vince Sawyer; (middle row) Don Pidcock, Tony Cigarron, Jim Wiedenhaefer, Ed Fisher, and Leon Okurowski; (back row) coach Don Poland, Tom Kaczor, Vince Straszynski, Dick Hart, Carl Schell Jr., and coach Carl Schell Sr. Members of this team later were outstanding high school and college athletes, in baseball, basketball, football, and track and field.

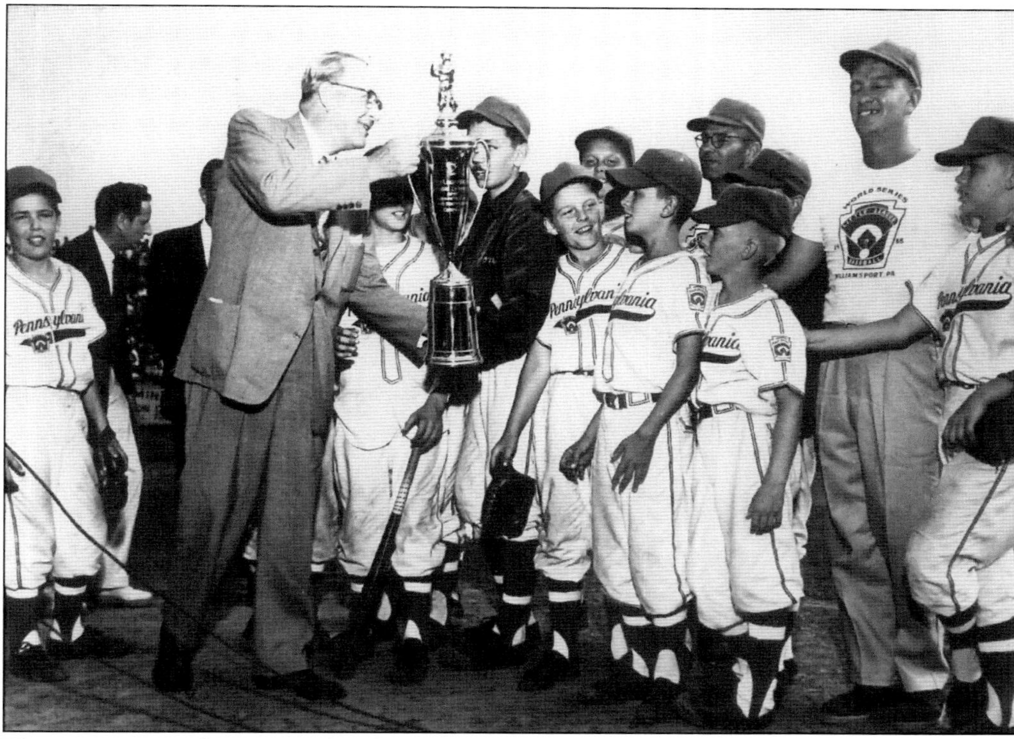

These pictures show an elated Morrisville Little League team receiving the world championship trophy and being honored with a triumphant parade upon their return home from Williamsport, Pennsylvania.

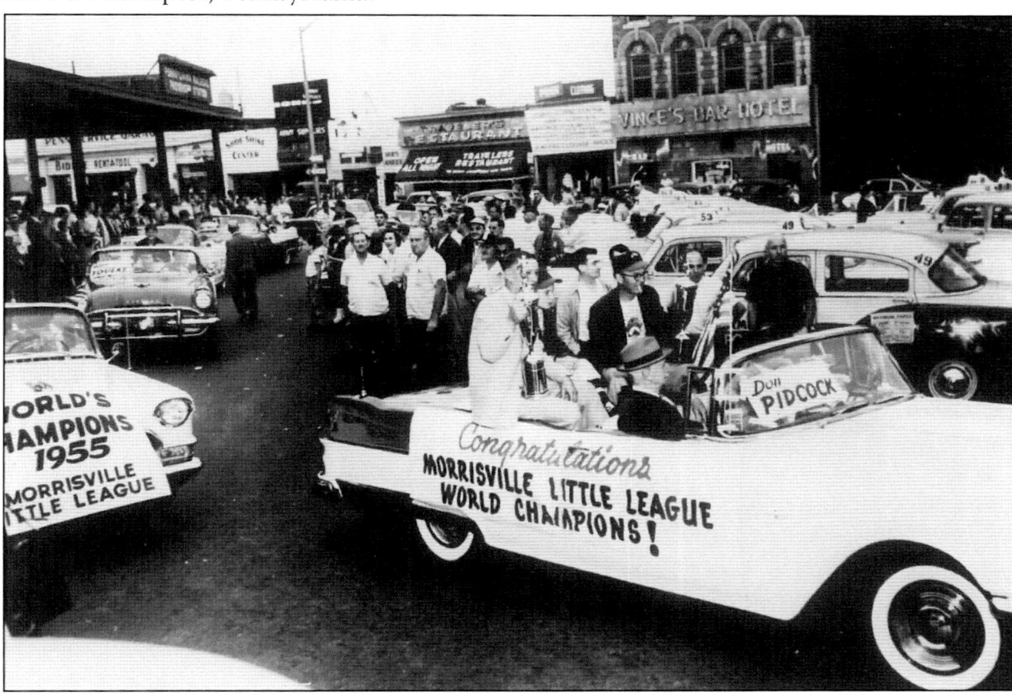

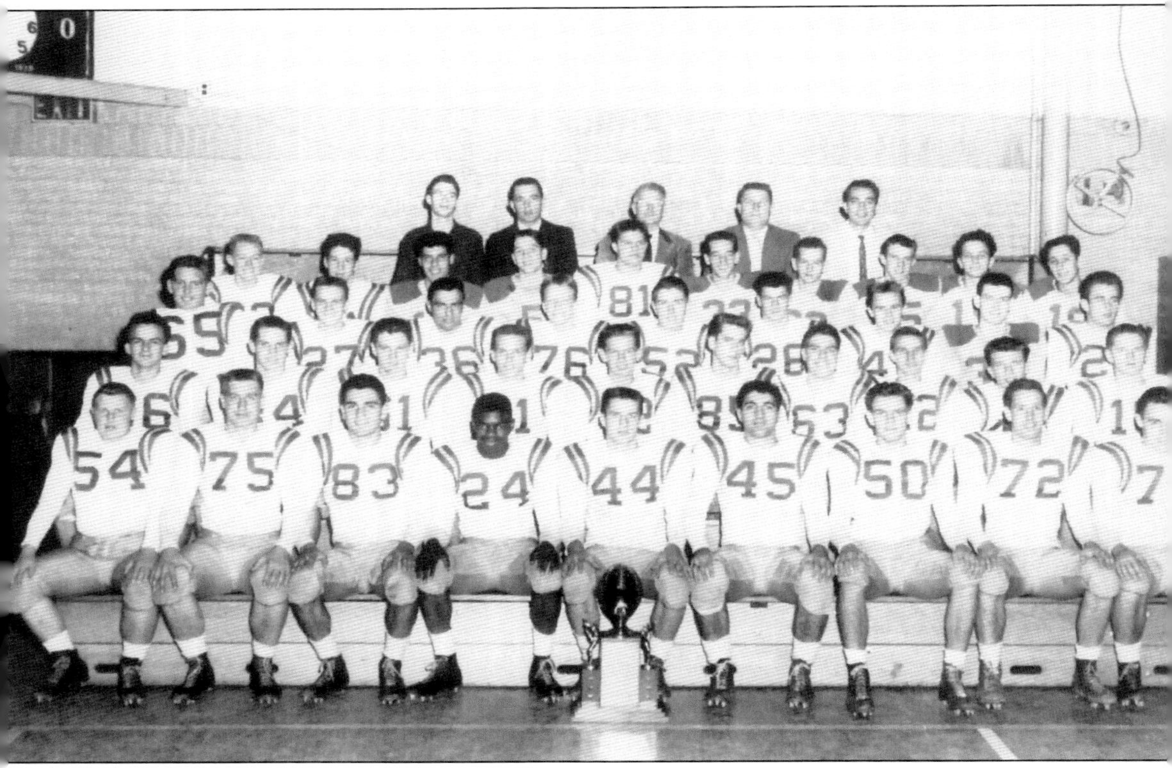

The last Morrisville High School football team to win a share of the Lower Bucks County League Championship against schools of all sizes, regardless of enrollment, was the 1958 squad. This team was undefeated in eight games, but tied Neshaminy, also unbeaten, for the championship. Two team members were also state shot put champions, senior Jim Tanzillo (83) in 1959 and sophomore Dick Hart (81, back row) in 1960 and 1961. Hart's county record of 64 feet, 2 inches was 2 feet better than his state record and still stood, thirty-six years later, as this book was published. Dan Napoleon (24) went on to success in professional baseball with the New York Mets. Jim Gafgen (third row, right) became a successful sculptor, and manager Ron Stockham (back row, left) is an attorney. The head coach was Gordon Davies (back row, center).

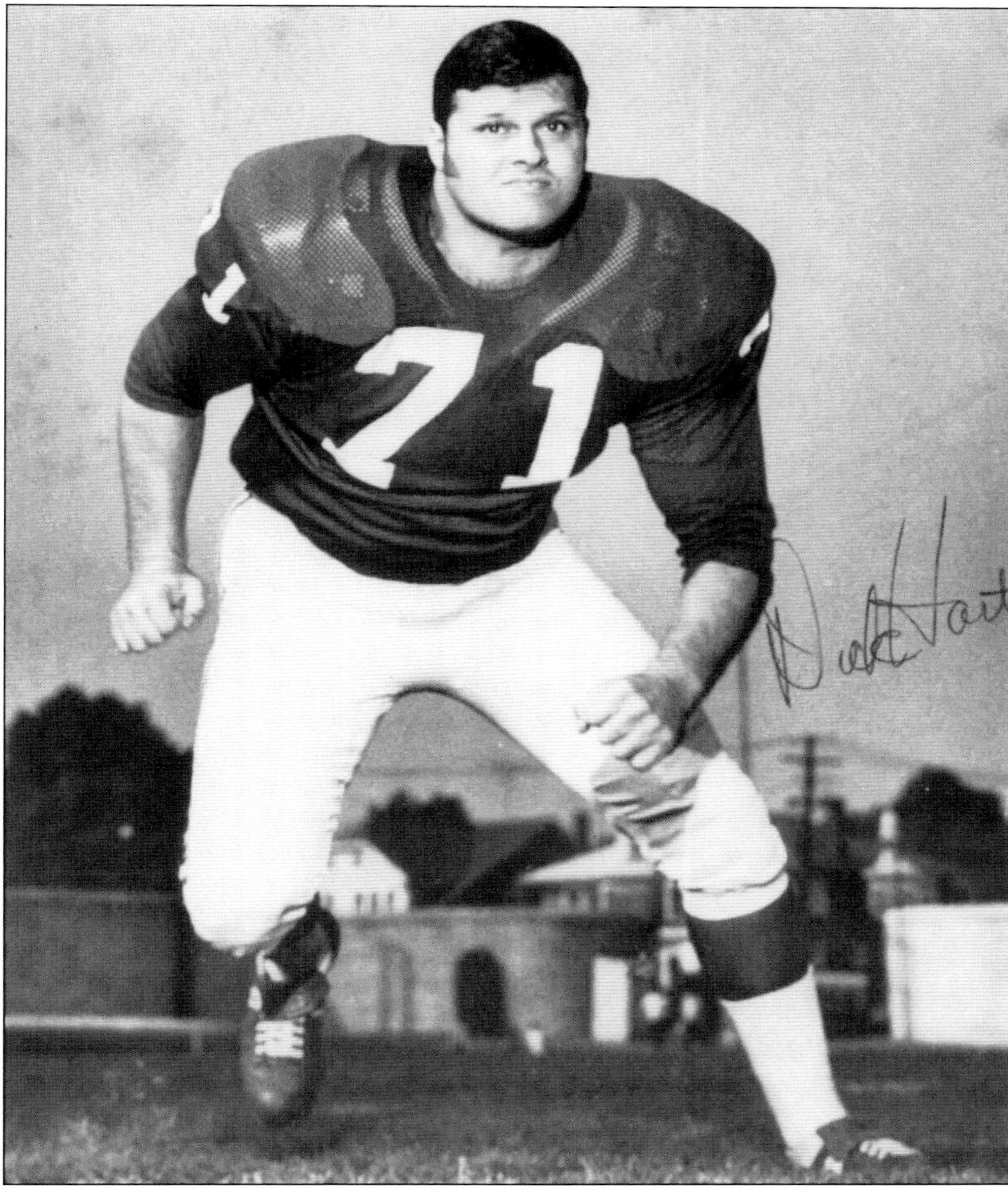

Dick Hart (81 in the high school team picture) set state shot put records and signed a professional baseball contract with the Braves, but was most successful in professional football, playing guard with the Philadelphia Eagles and later with the Buffalo Bills. He was named to the All-Rookie team his first year with the Eagles. Dick's brothers, Lew (named to Bucknell's all-time football team) and Bob (a guard at Penn State), were also outstanding shot putters and football players, Bob setting the state shot put record that Dick improved on.

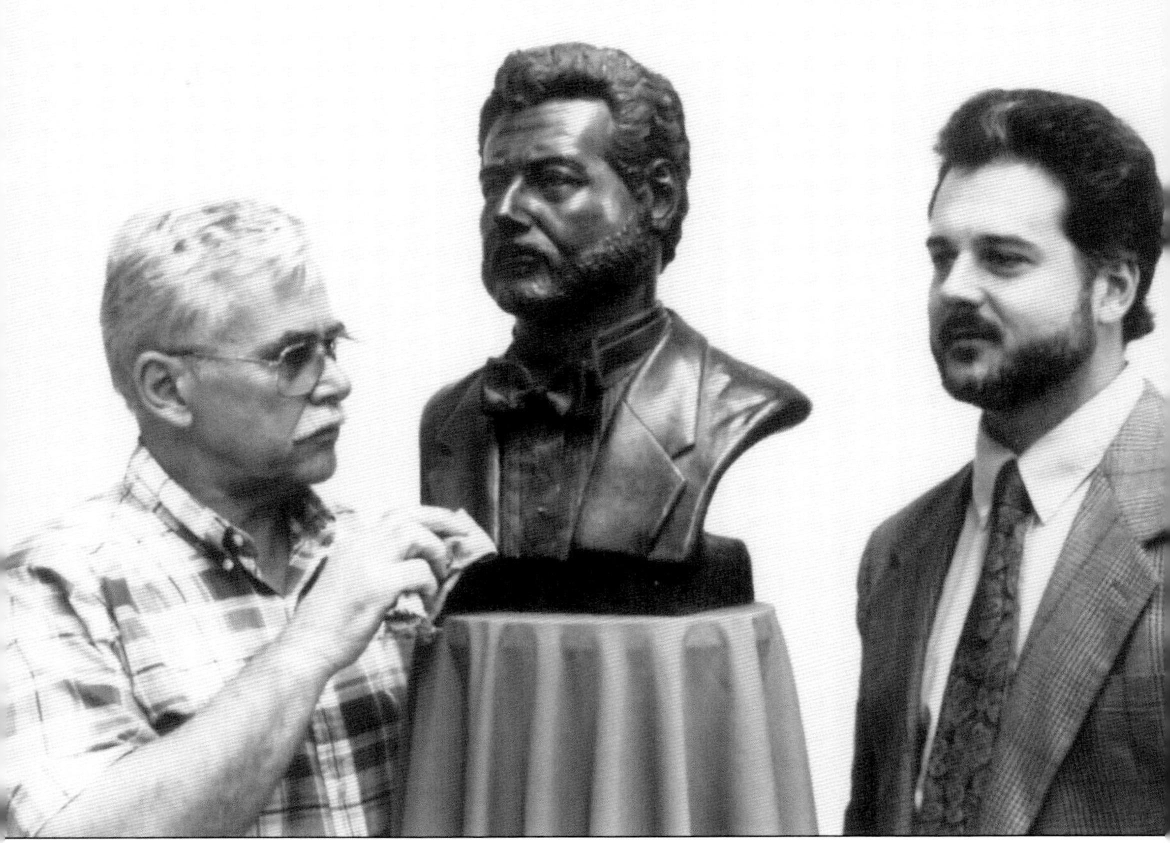

Jim Gafgen (right, third row, in the 1958 team picture), after retiring as a steelworker, turned a hobby into a successful career with the Johnson Atelier in Princeton. He is shown with a bust of his son, Jim Gafgen Jr., who set ground gaining records as a running back at Morrisville High and then went on to sing leading tenor roles with opera companies in New York, New Jersey, and Philadelphia.

Six

Views around Town

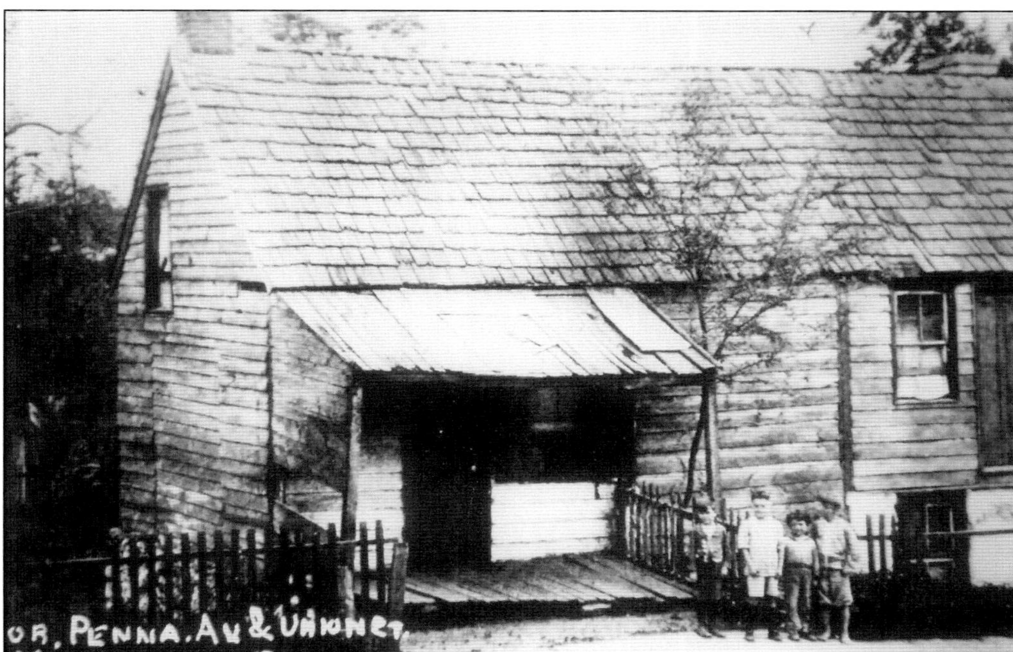

This old home, long gone, was located at the corner of Pennsylvania Avenue and Union Street, about where Burns' Pharmacy is today.

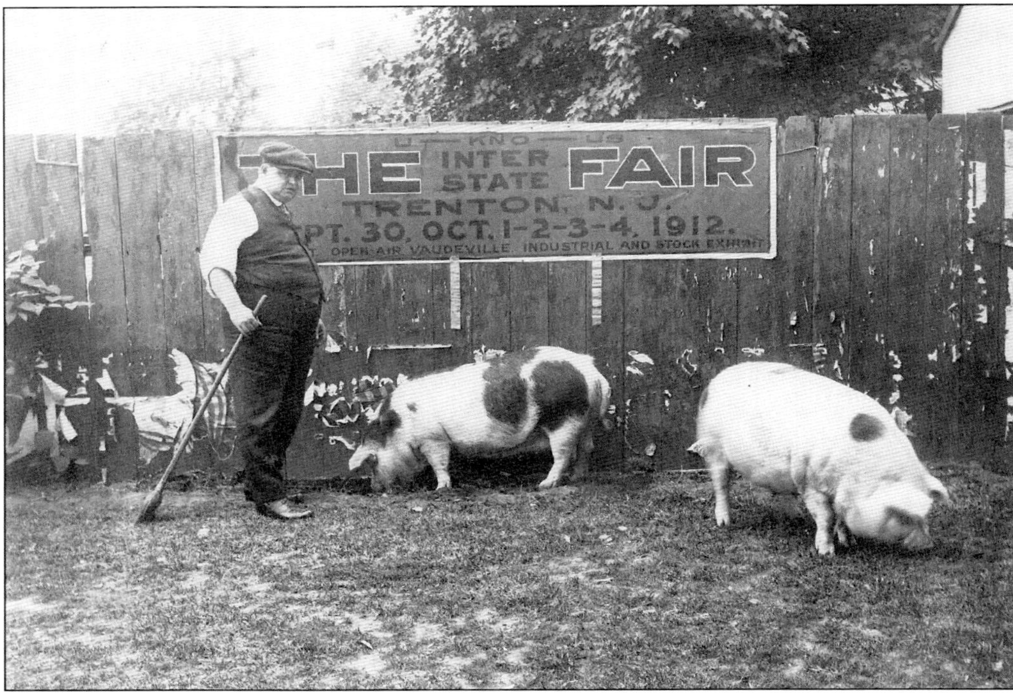

Believe it or not, this apparently rural scene was photographed in downtown Morrisville in 1904. The pigs were confined in a fenced area not far from the Robert Morris Hotel at the intersection of Bridge Street and Delmorr Avenue.

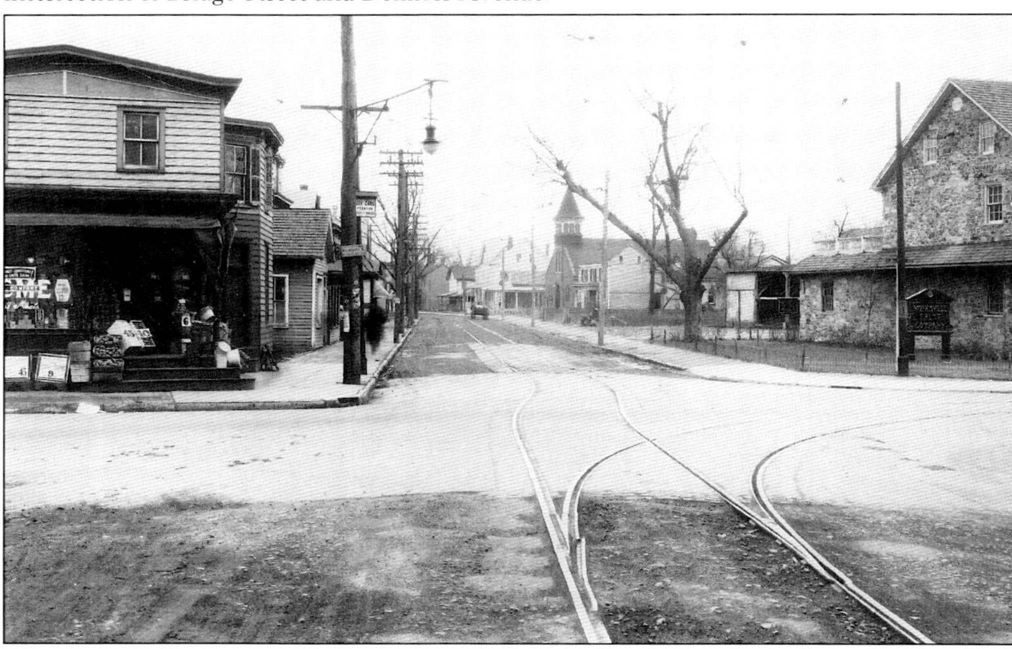

A view of North Pennsylvania Avenue in 1925 as it looked from the Bridge Street intersection shows the trolley tracks still very much in place. It was possible to travel by trolley east to Trenton, south to Bristol, and north to Newtown.

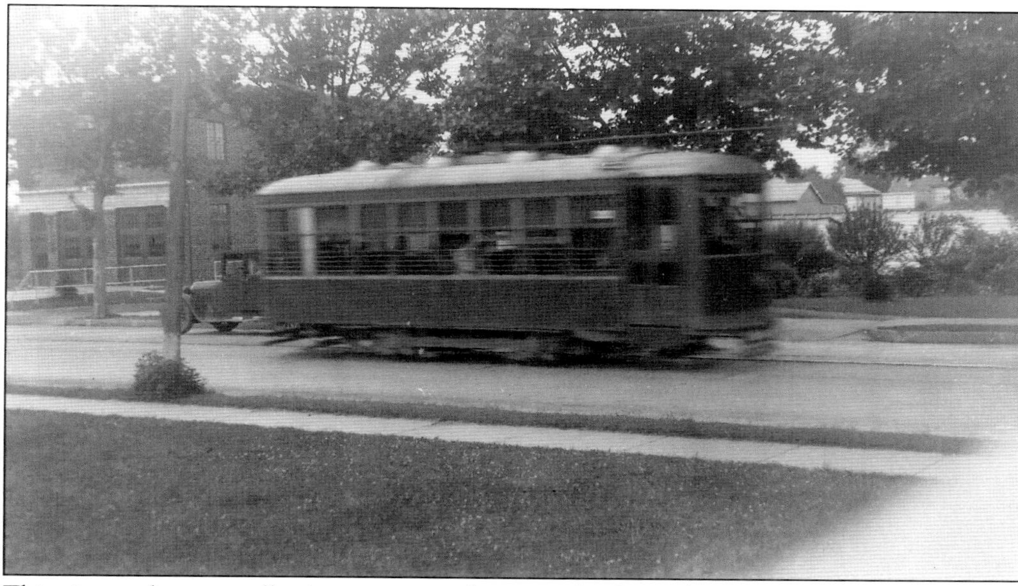

This picture shows a trolley in action, speeding past the Capitol View Fire Company on North Pennsylvania Avenue.

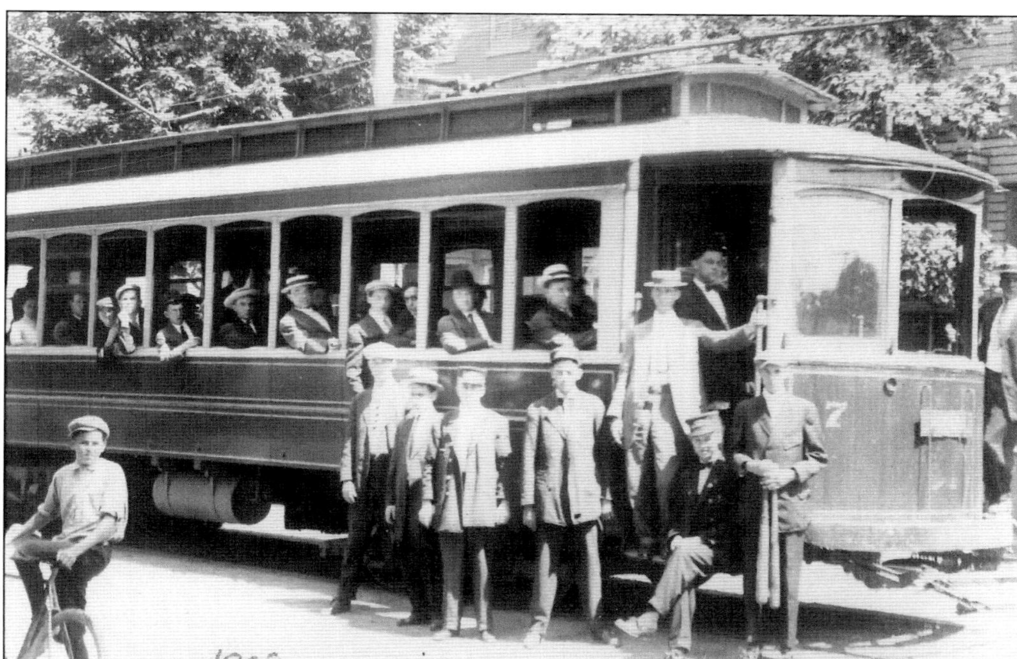

A trolley at rest appears fully loaded and ready to go, but the conductors are seated and standing near the entrance door. This appears to be the start of another trip by Morrisville's baseball team, judging by the bats held by the young man at right.

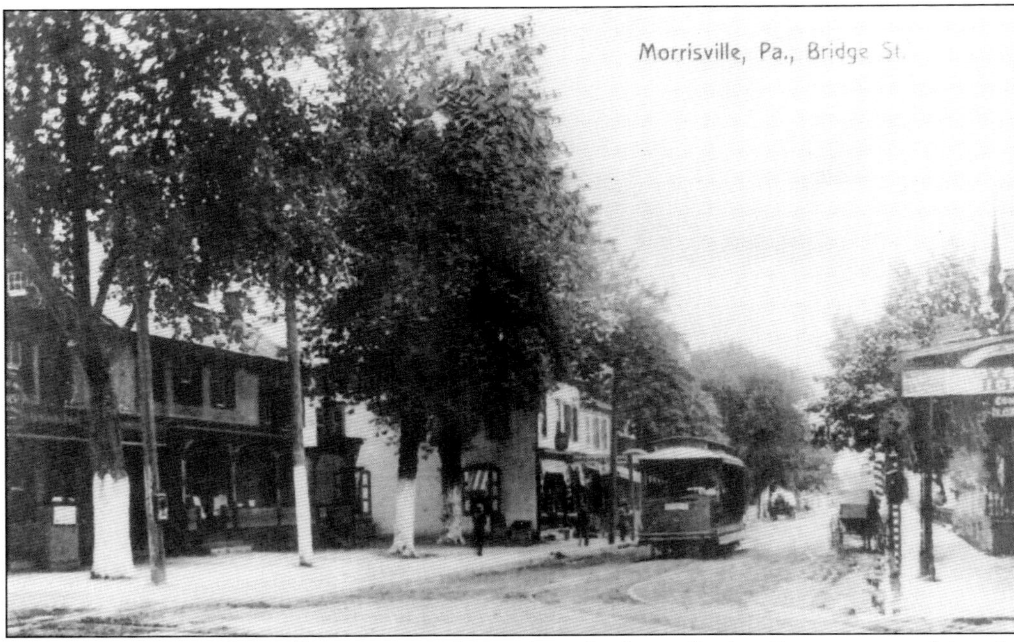

One more picture of a trolley in action shows the vehicle on Bridge Street, approaching the intersection with Pennsylvania Avenue.

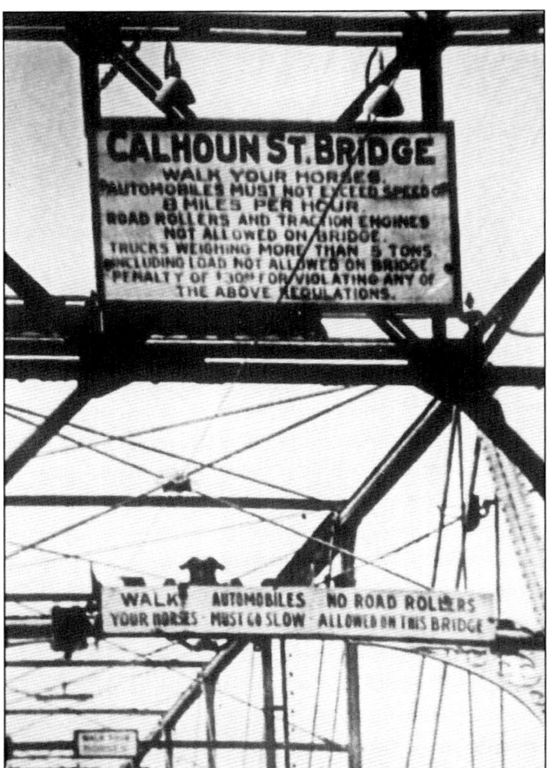

As a town of many bridges, Morrisville's entrance to the Calhoun Street Bridge once instructed travelers to "Walk your horses" and set a speed limit of 8 miles per hour for automobiles while en route across the river to Trenton. This bridge replaced an old covered bridge that had been built in 1861 and was destroyed by fire in 1884.

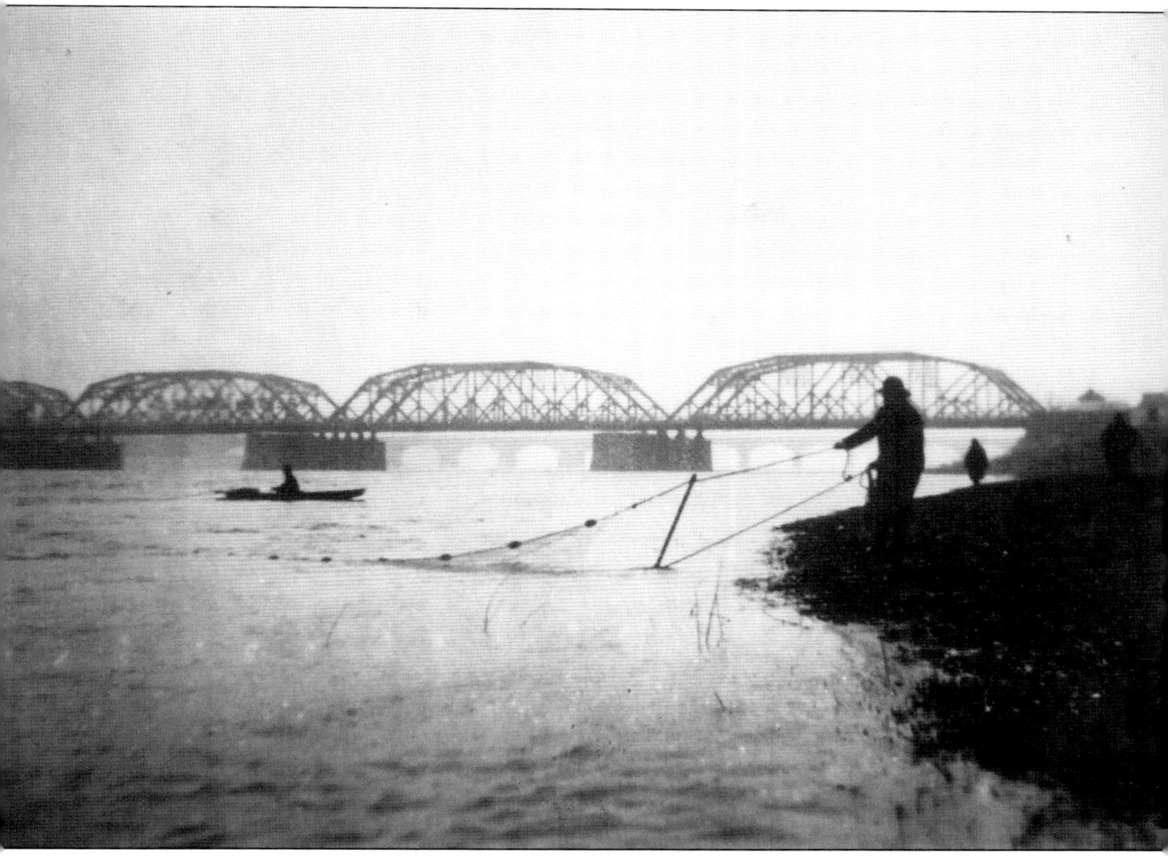

This photograph of Fred Reitzle netting shad provides a long view of the "Trenton Makes" bridge and the railroad bridge between Pennsylvania and New Jersey. The main highway between Philadelphia and New York City, U.S. Route 1, ran through the center of Morrisville to the Trenton Makes bridge. The railroad, which at one time shared the forerunner of the Trenton Makes bridge with pedestrians and carriages, has always been the main north-south rail link and has passed through Morrisville since rail travel was inaugurated.

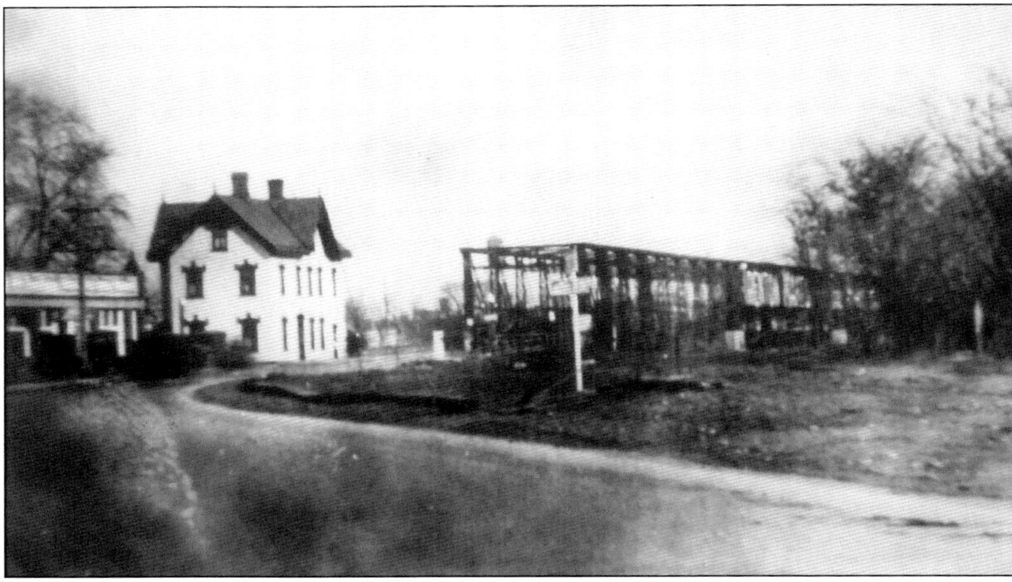

The first bridge was built across the Delaware River in 1804, the year that Morrisville officially became a borough. The photograph shows the long curving approach that required trains to slow down when the bridge was used for both rail and carriage crossing. When tracks were added, carriages were limited to using only one side of the bridge, so those wanting to cross had to wait if someone was coming from the opposite direction. The present railroad bridge was built in 1901.

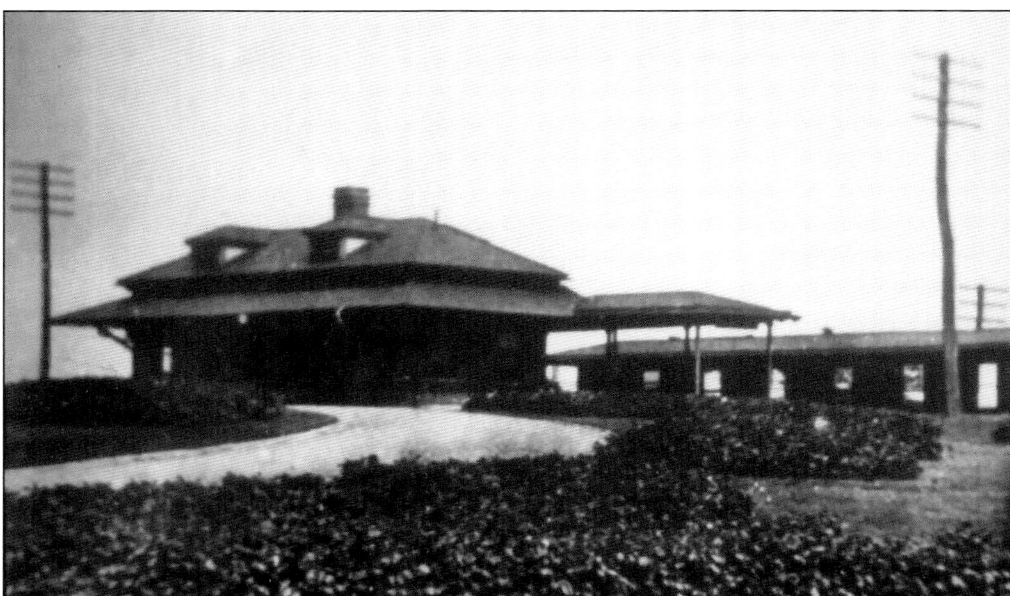

Morrisville once had its own railroad station, off Green Street for north-to-south travel and off Delaware Avenue for traveling south to north. The main station house was on the Green Street side, between Washington Street and South Pennsylvania Avenue, but there was a tunnel to the shelter on the Delaware Avenue side so people riding the trains did not have to walk across the tracks.

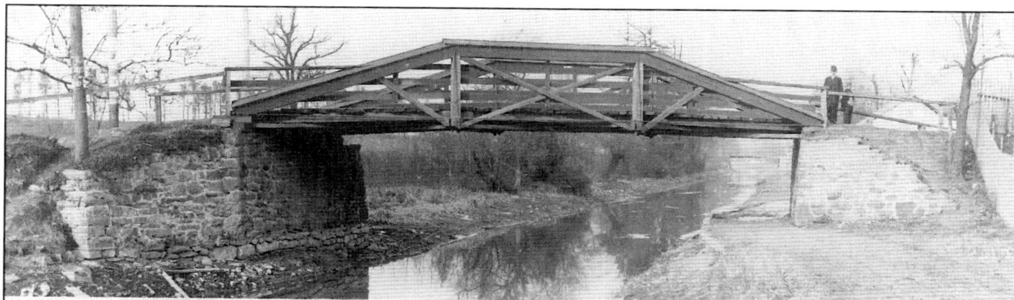

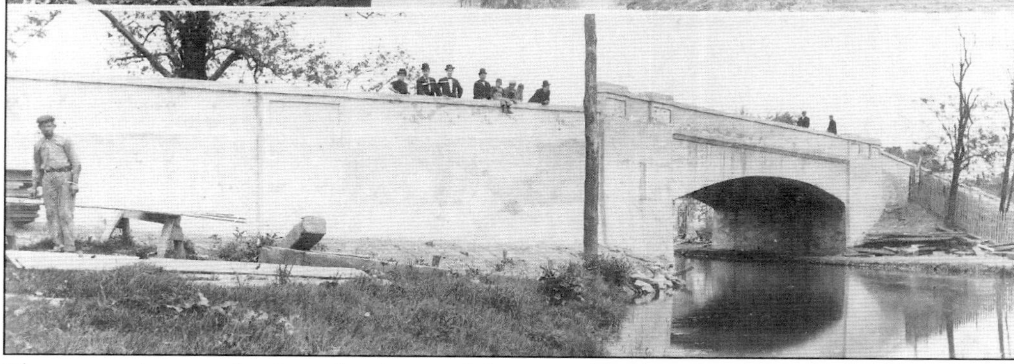

These two photographs show (top) one of the typical bridges that cross the Delaware Canal and the concrete bridge (bottom) that replaced it on Bridge Street in Morrisville. Subsequently the concrete "hump-backed" bridge was reduced in height to better accommodate the Route 1 traffic passing through the town before the present bypass toll bridge was constructed.

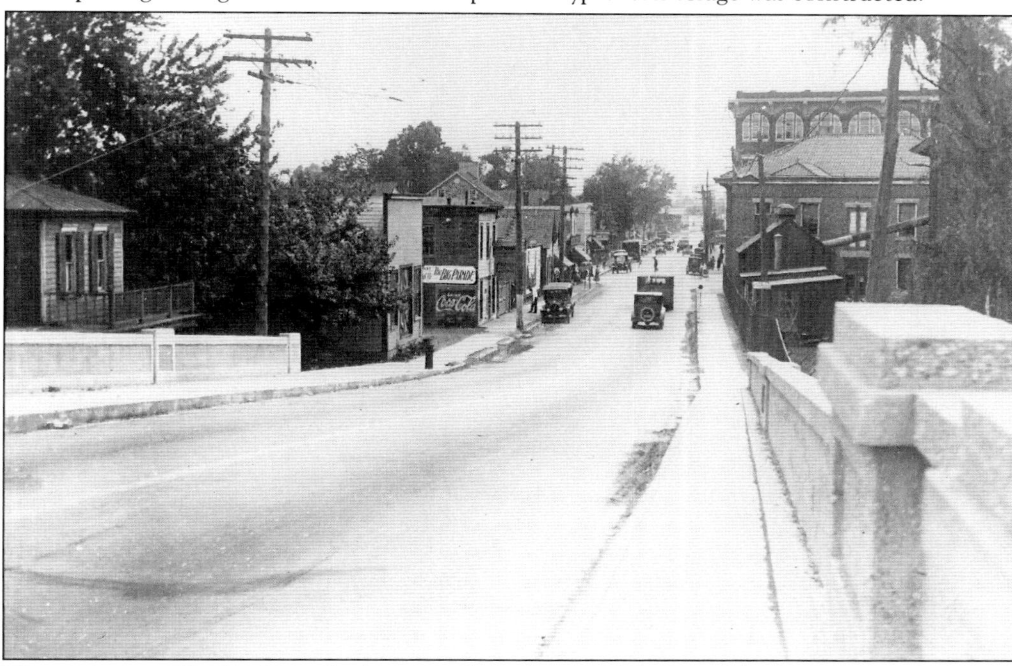

This is a view of Bridge Street looking east from the top of the hump-backed bridge that crossed the canal for many years. The Vulcanized Rubber Company is on the right at the intersection with Pennsylvania Avenue.

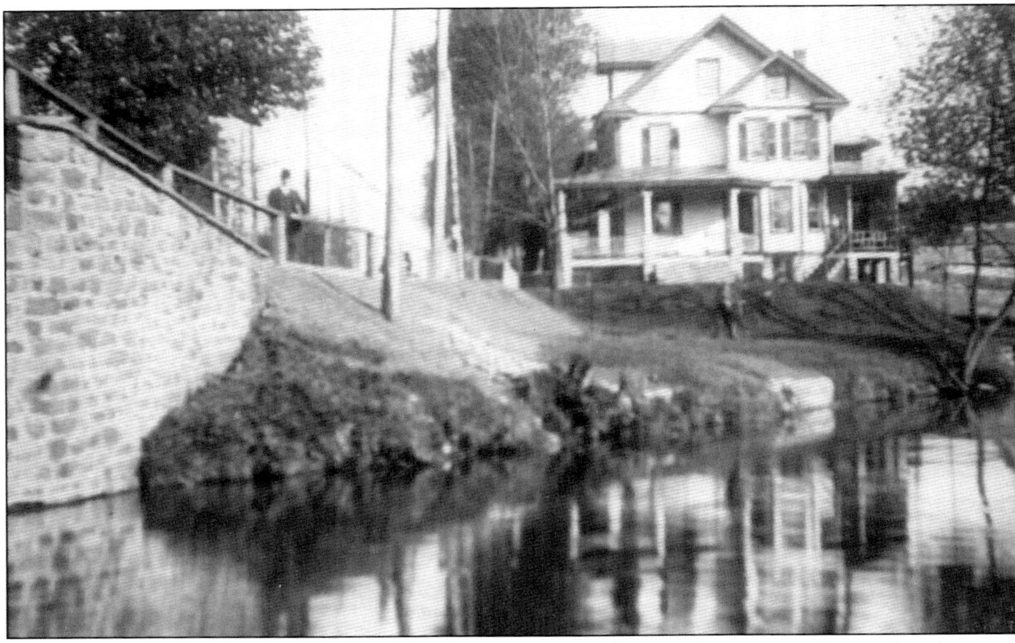

North of Bridge Street the canal passes under Pennsylvania Avenue with ample clearance at Union Street, opposite Hillcrest Avenue and the Morrisville Presbyterian senior citizens' high-rise apartments.

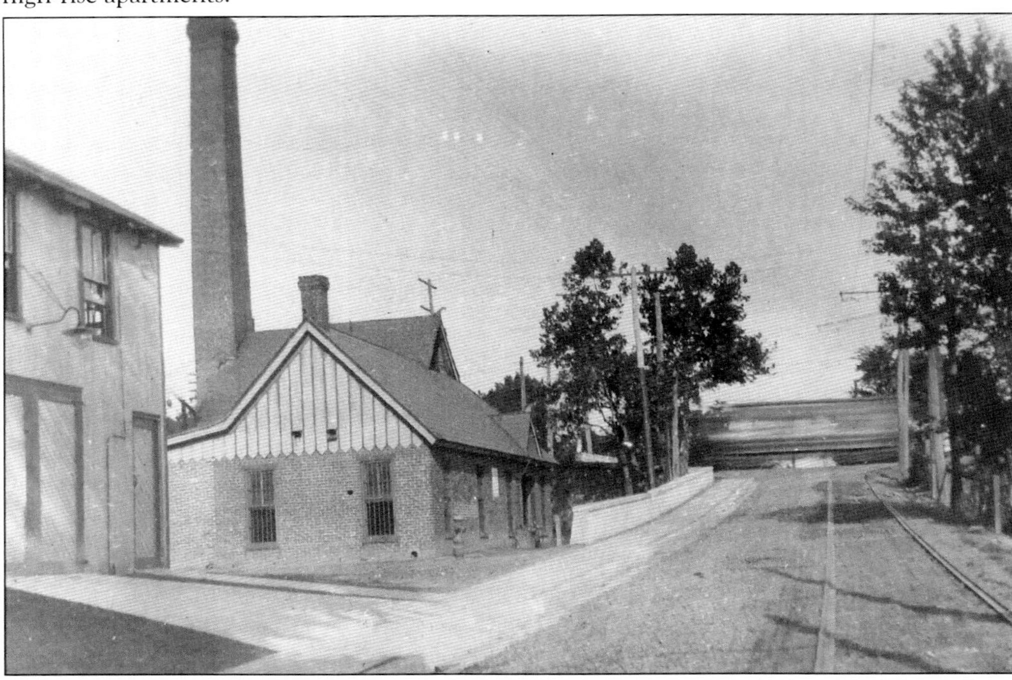

The uphill rise of Delmorr Avenue elevates the road along the river to the height of the Calhoun Street Bridge, to the right. The elevation also allows the Delaware Canal to pass under Trenton Avenue. The canal parallels Delmorr Avenue ("River Road") on the other side of the old water works, at left.

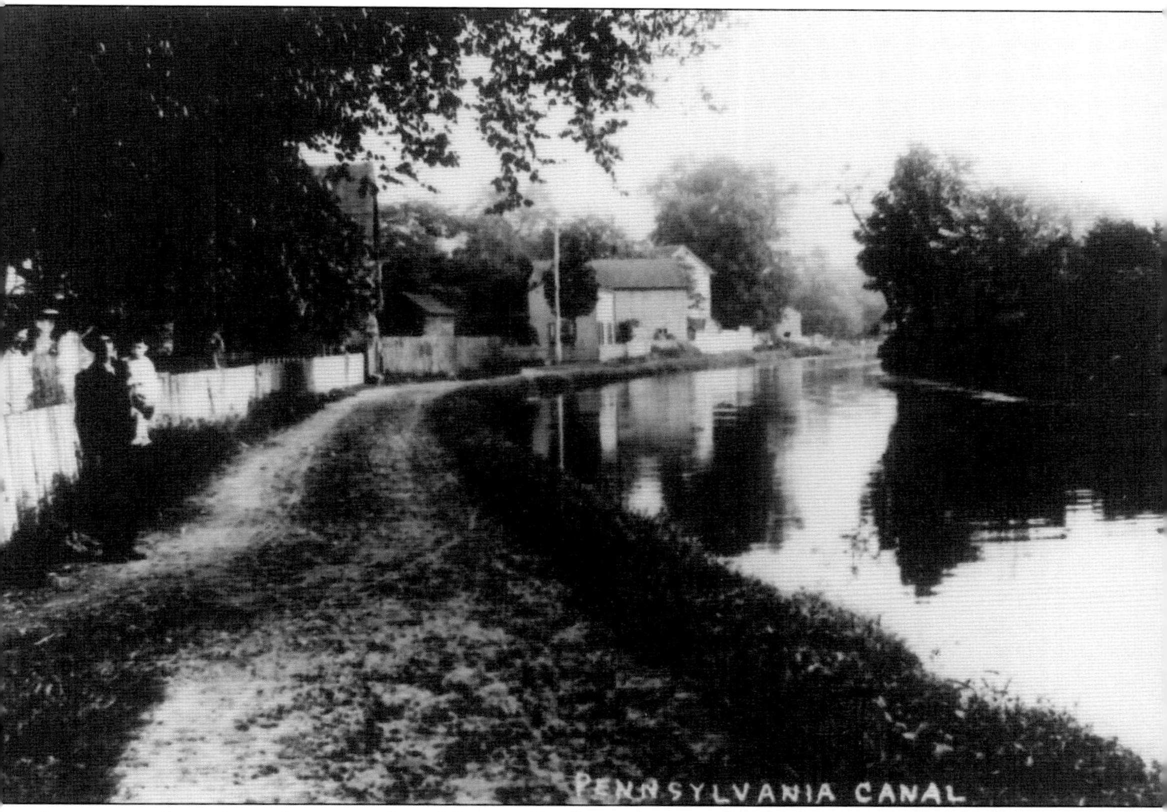

A picture taken along the towpath in Morrisville shows the canal full of water. As this book was published efforts were under way to clean and refill the canal, and to make the towpath more user-friendly for walkers and joggers.

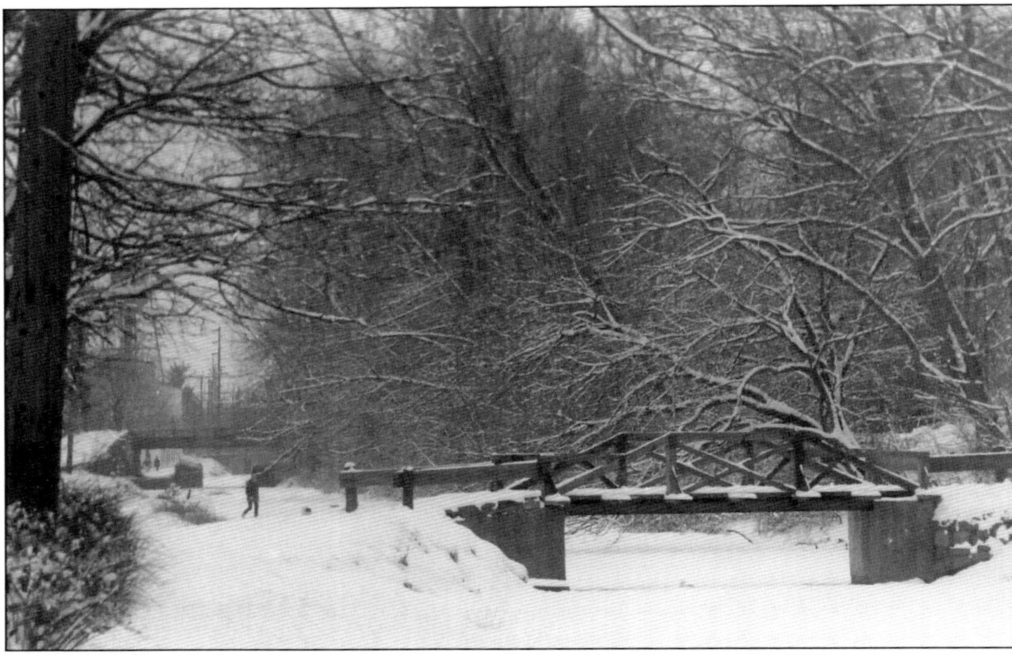

During the winter, the canal has attracted Morrisville's skaters for decades.

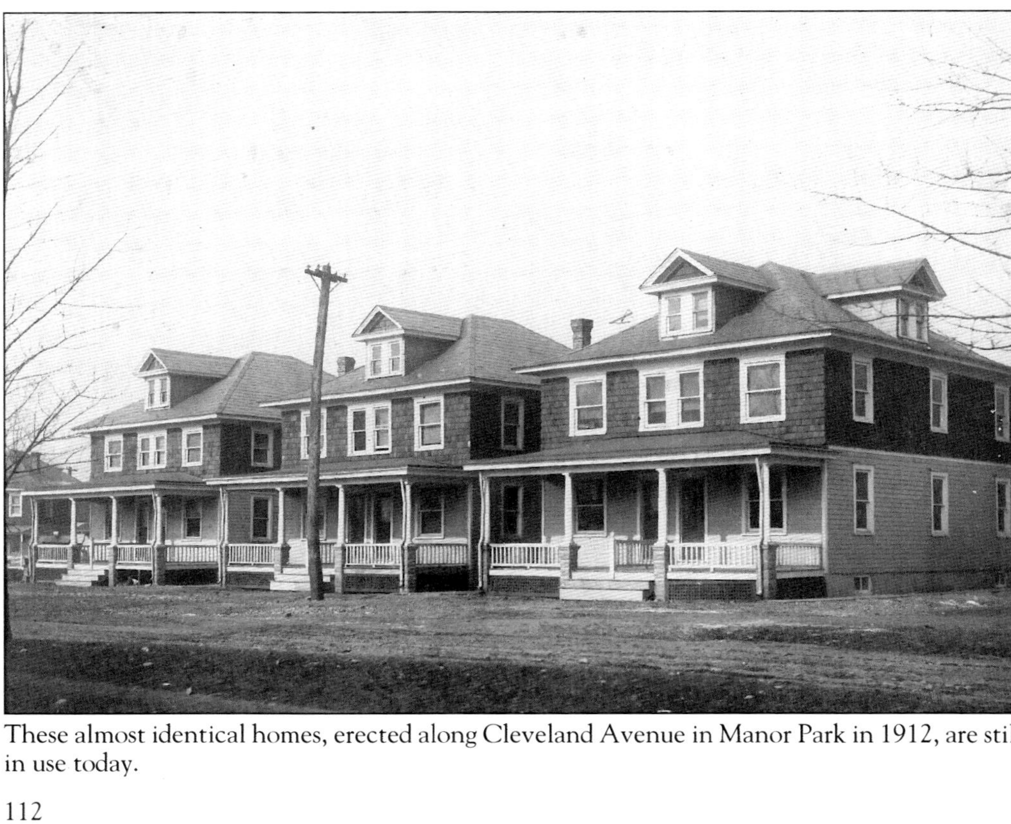

These almost identical homes, erected along Cleveland Avenue in Manor Park in 1912, are still in use today.

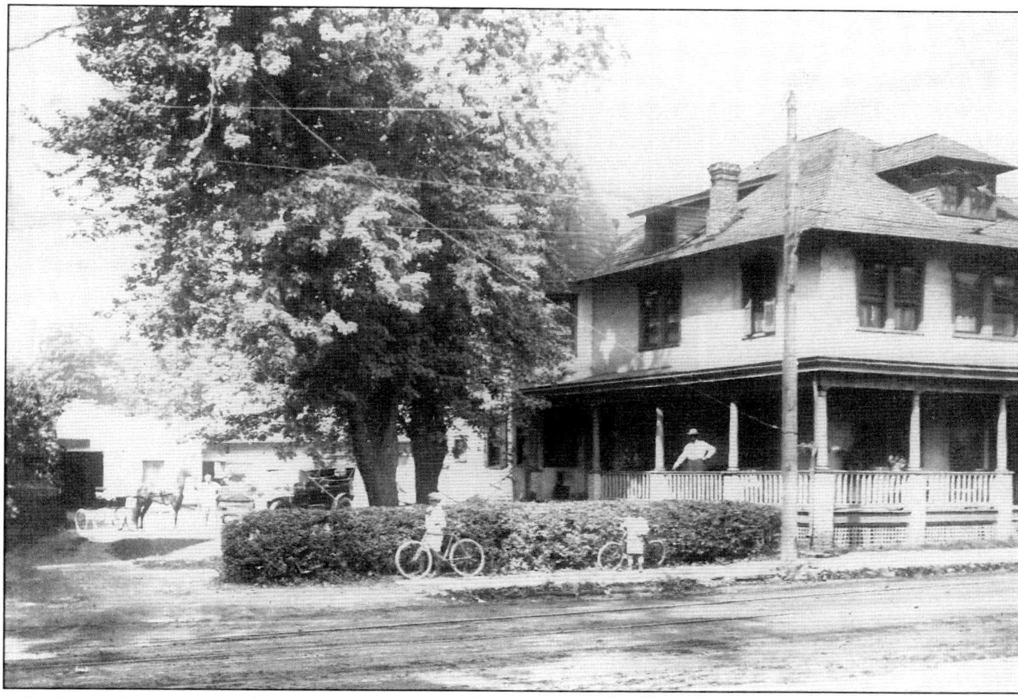

John Lewis's home on North Pennsylvania Avenue, not far from Bridge Street, is very similar in style to the Cleveland Avenue homes in Manor Park.

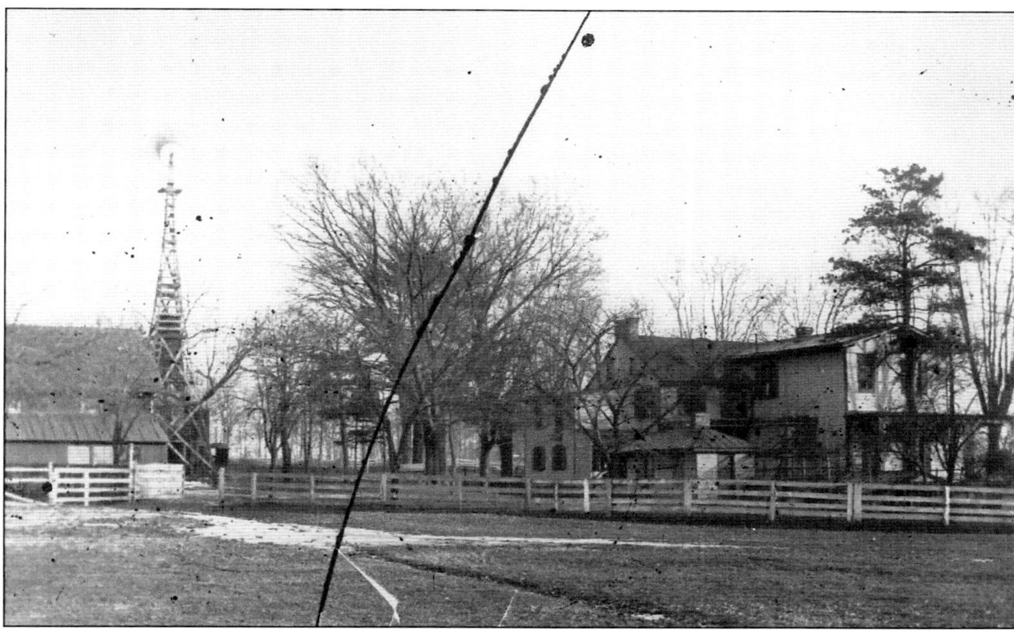

The Burgess farm appears to be in a very rural setting, but it was situated just off Trenton Avenue near North Pennsylvania Avenue and is the present site of the First Presbyterian Church. This picture was taken from what is now Lafayette Street where it intersects with Burgess Avenue.

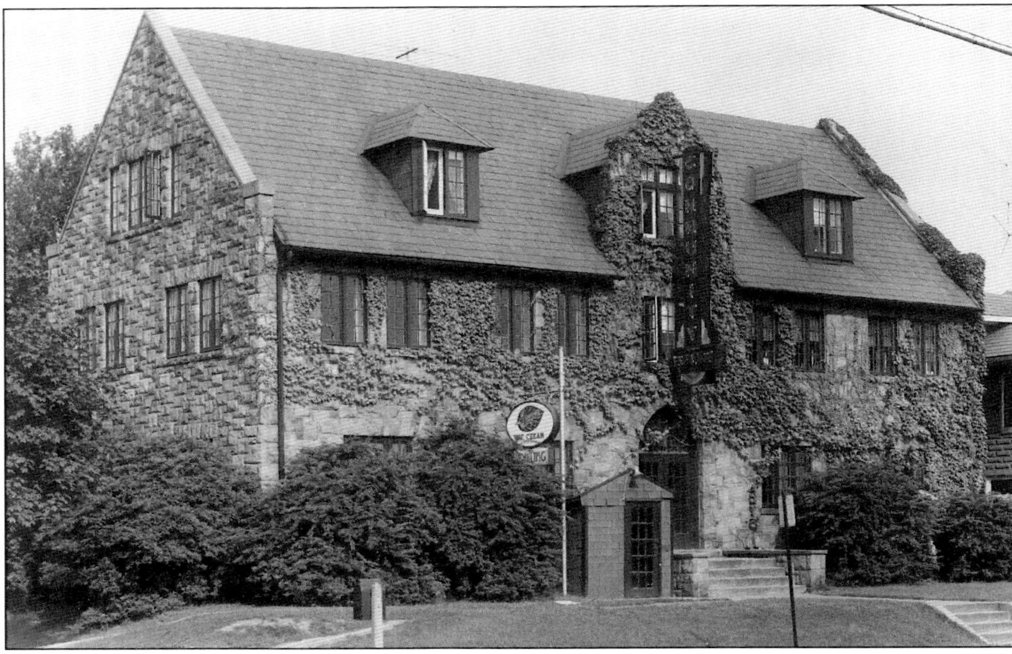

There are two buildings in Morrisville that have changed in use, but very little in appearance over the years. One was the Community House, now the Curtin & Heefner law firm. When this picture was taken it had a bowling alley in the basement, a large open area that had served first as a theater and later as a dance floor, and the Morrisville Library upstairs.

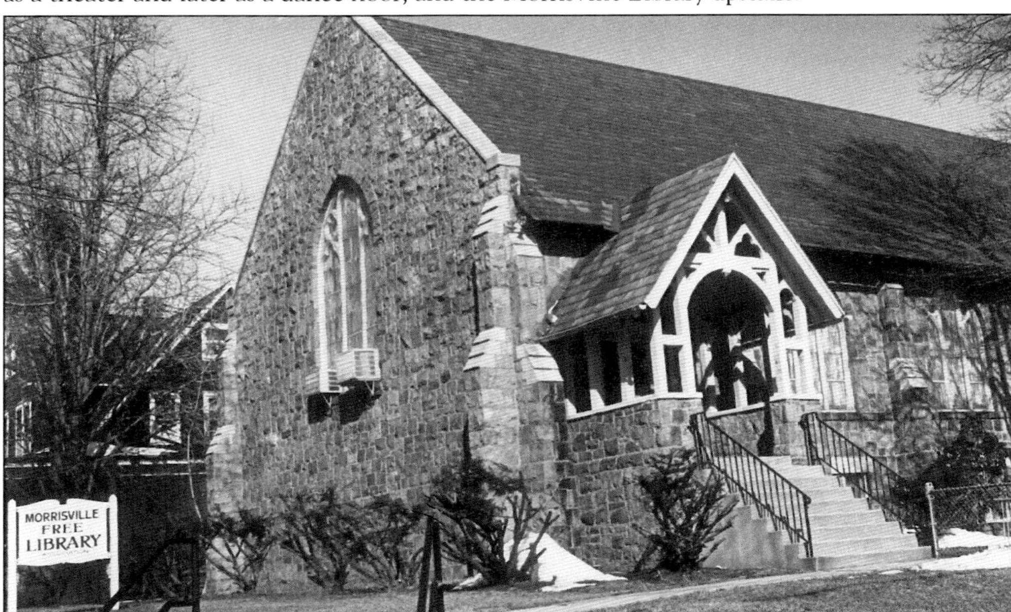

Another building little changed in appearance over the years was once the Episcopal Church but now houses the Morrisville Free Library. The library moved from the upstairs of the Community House to the basement of Summerseat before it finally became located in the former church building.

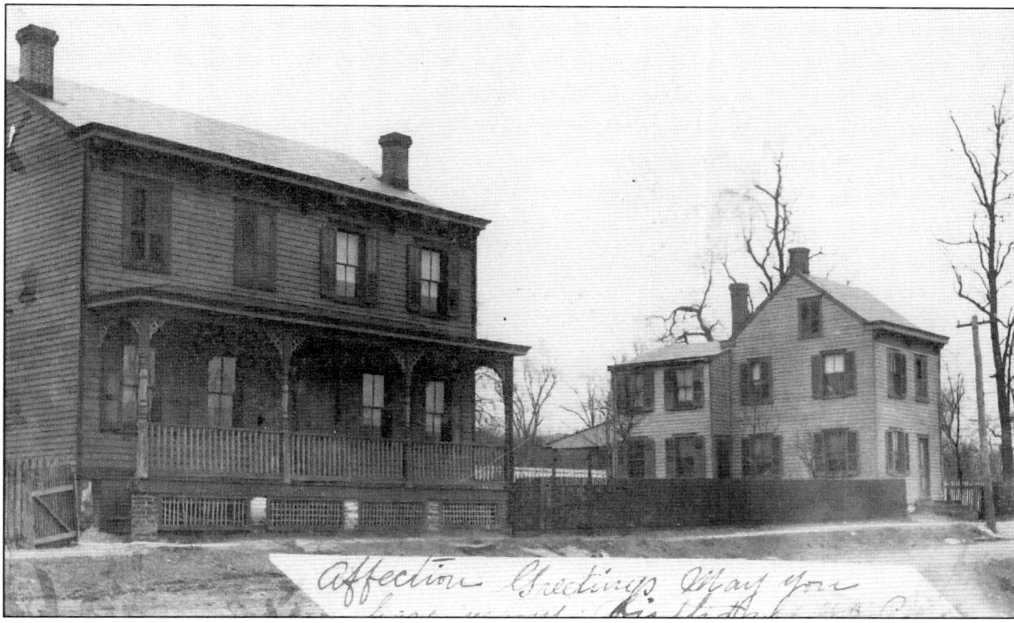

These homes on Delmorr Avenue looked much the same fifty years ago as they do in the 1990s but the spaces between them and beyond have changed greatly as many more houses have been built.

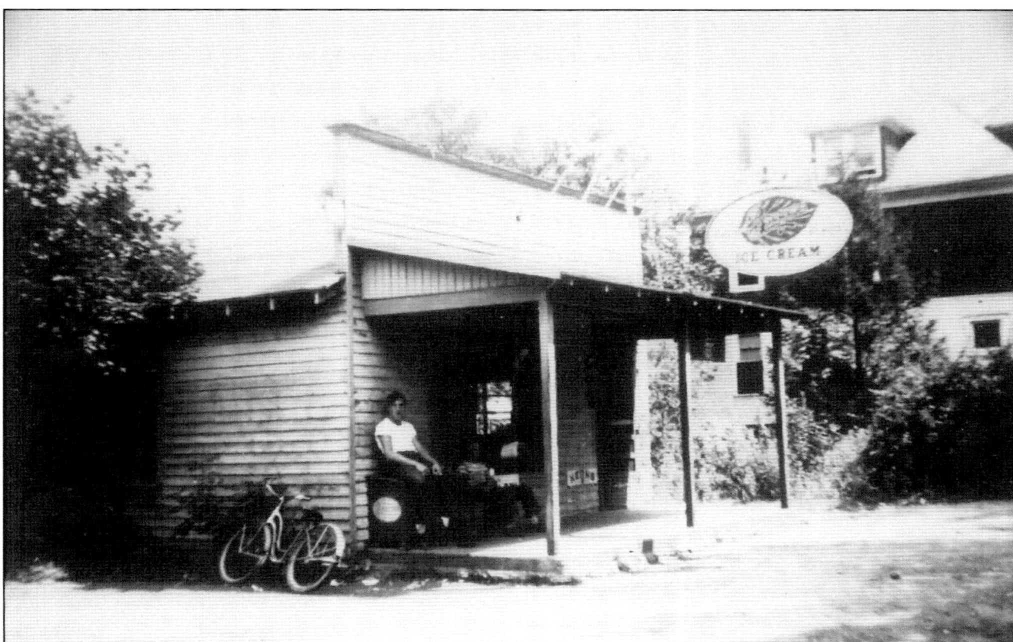

Morrisville men who were teenagers in the 1930s and '40s will recognize this building as Roy "Deacon" Lefler's store, a favorite hangout for the youth of Morrisville. It has given way to Cunningham's hardware store, just south of the Capitol View Fire Company on North Pennsylvania Avenue.

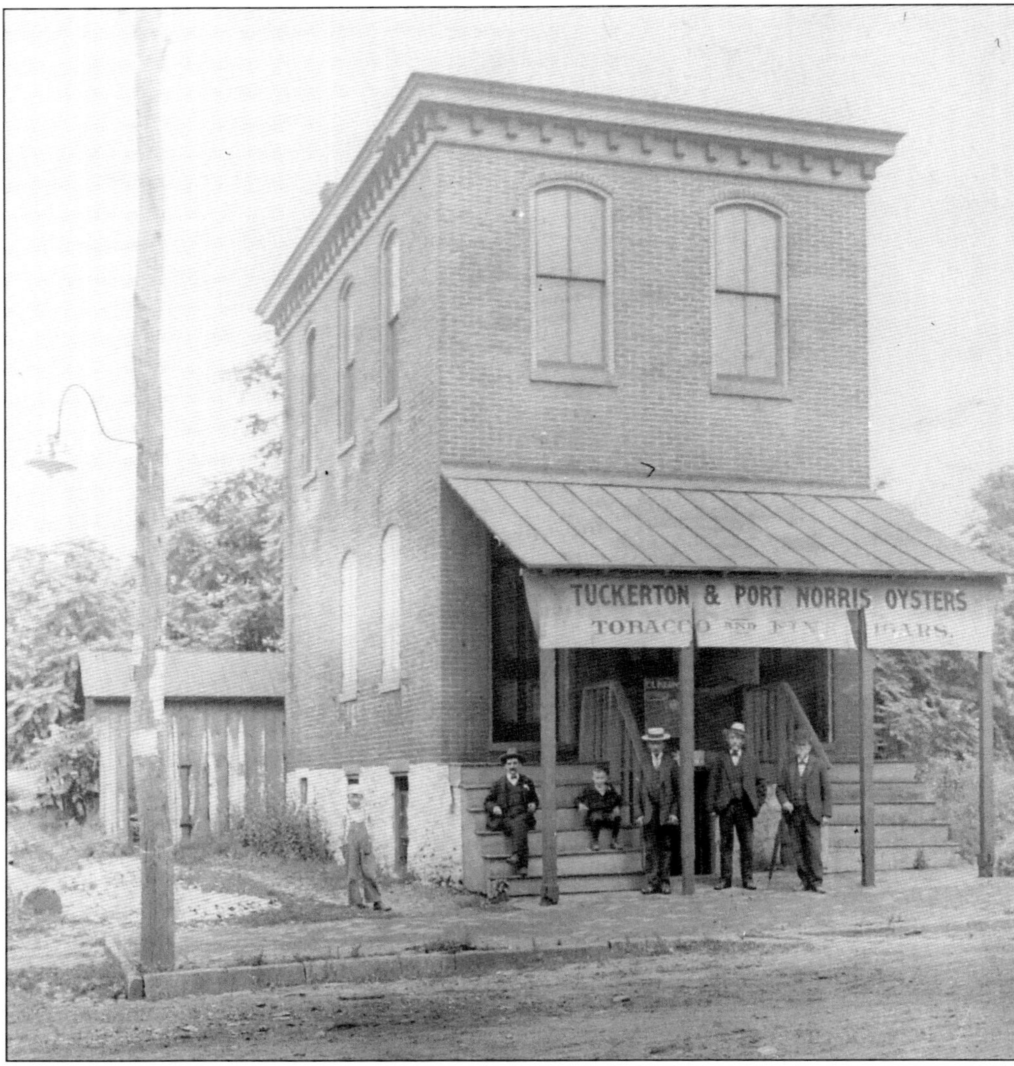

The building that later served as Morrisville's borough hall for years began as one of the ubiquitous oyster vending emporiums, this one on Washington Street a block south of the main business district.

Early in its incarnation as borough hall, the brick building on Washington Street was festooned with banners and flags, probably for a Fourth of July or Memorial Day celebration.

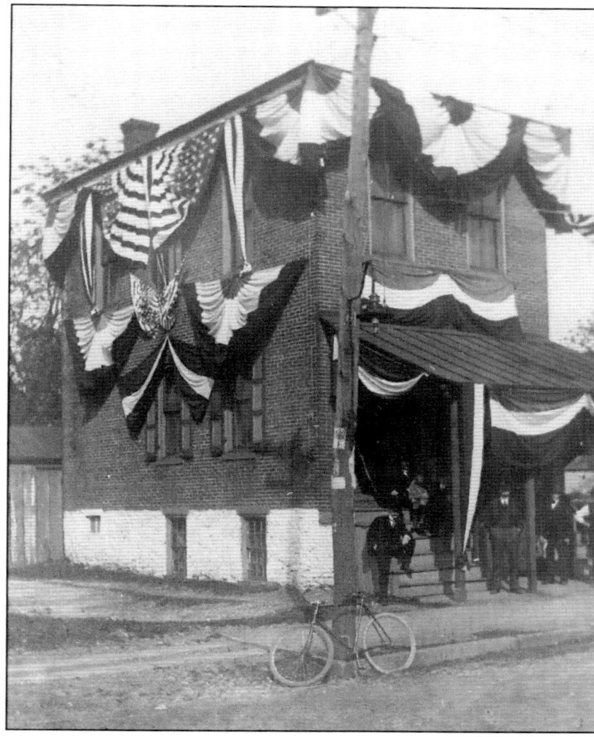

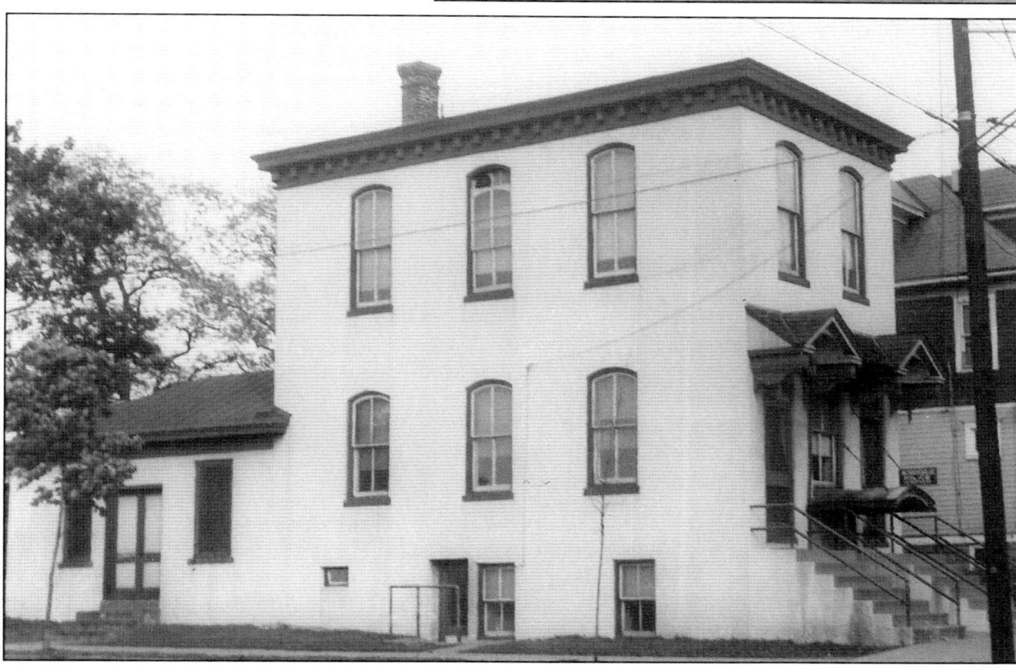

In the final stages of service as Morrisville's borough hall, before a modern new building was dedicated on Union Street in 1967, the old building had been given a gleaming coat of stucco. This was the office for Justice of the Peace Neal Nolan and there was a jail downstairs in the back.

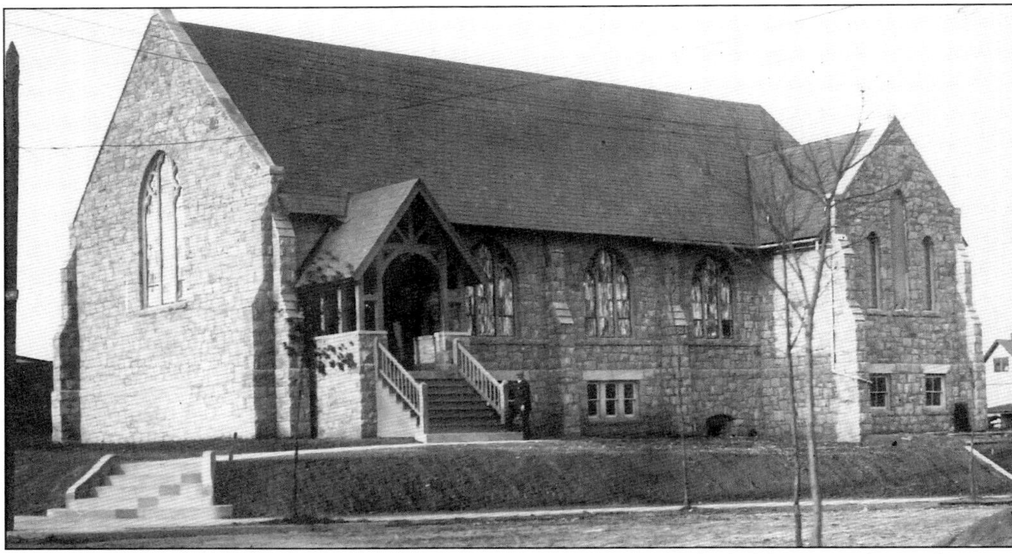

Before the congregation decided to move to Lower Makefield Township, this was Morrisville's Episcopal Church. The solid old stone building, built in 1912, is now the Morrisville Free Library.

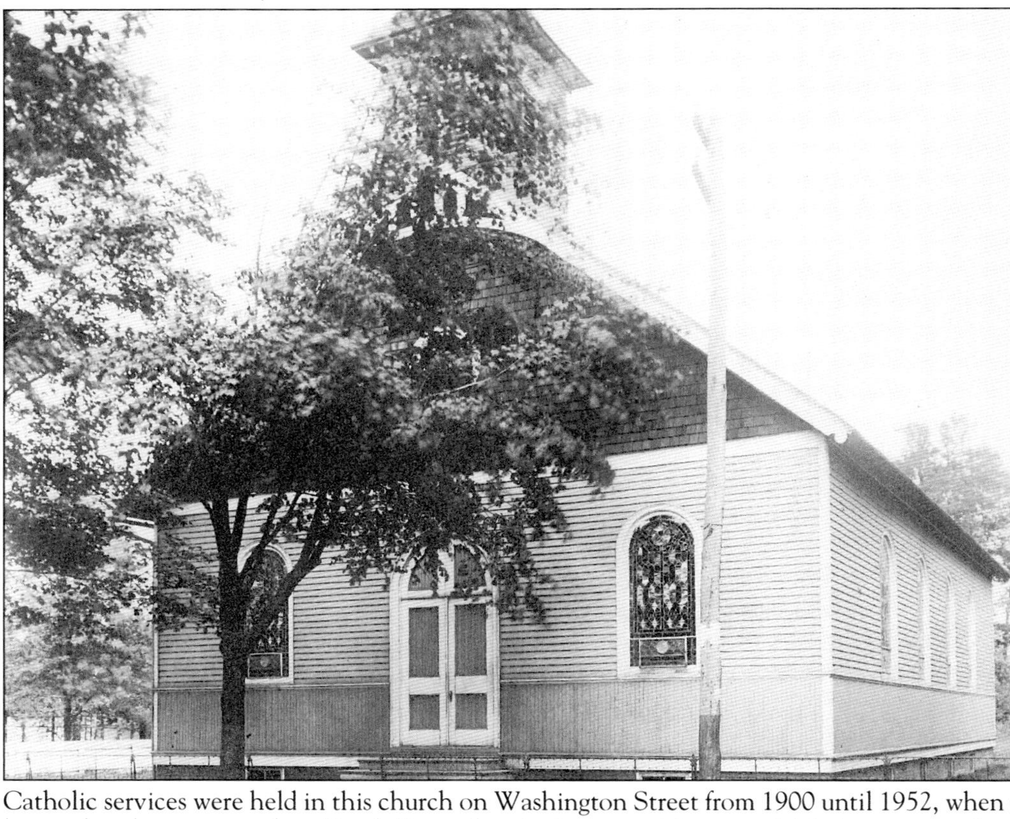

Catholic services were held in this church on Washington Street from 1900 until 1952, when a larger church was opened on North Pennsylvania Avenue with a parochial elementary school across the street.

Morrisville's Presbyterian Church on Union Street was built in 1869 and added to in 1891 and 1927. It was eventually outgrown by its congregation and a new, larger church building was built on North Pennsylvania Avenue on the site of the Burgess farm, holding services for the first time on Easter 1952.

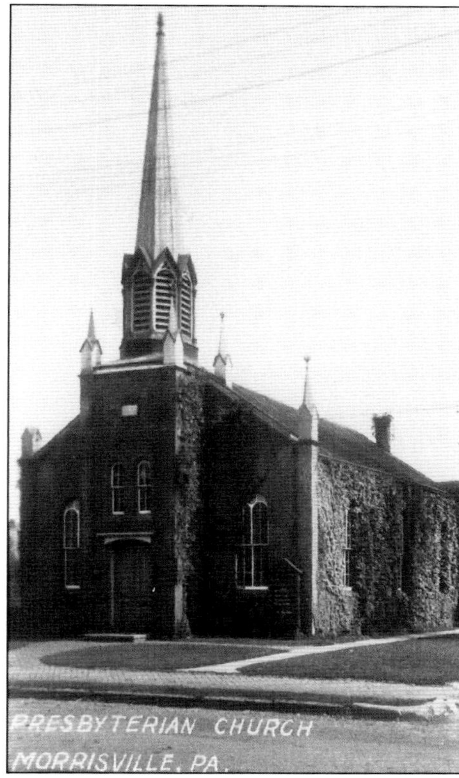

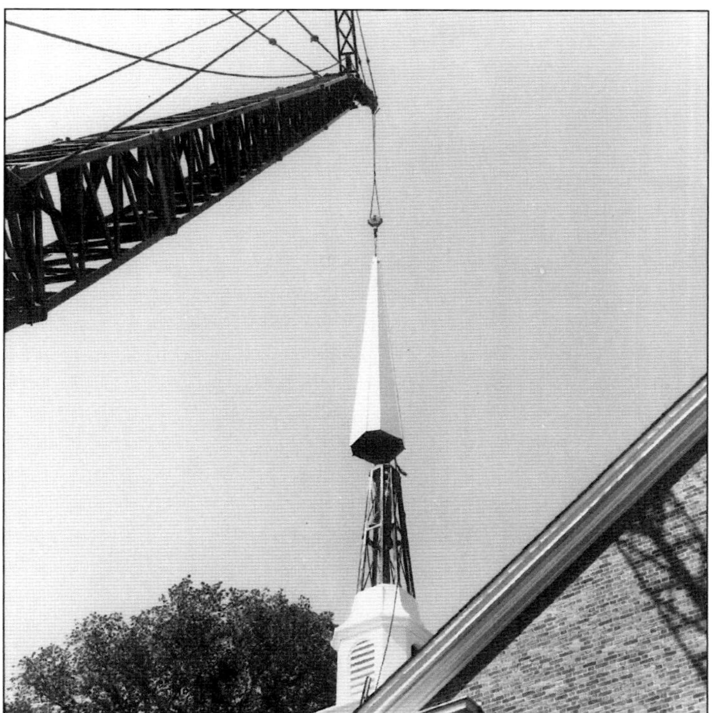

This photograph shows the final stages of construction on the new Presbyterian church on North Pennsylvania Avenue. The steeple is being lowered onto the framework that has supported it since 1952.

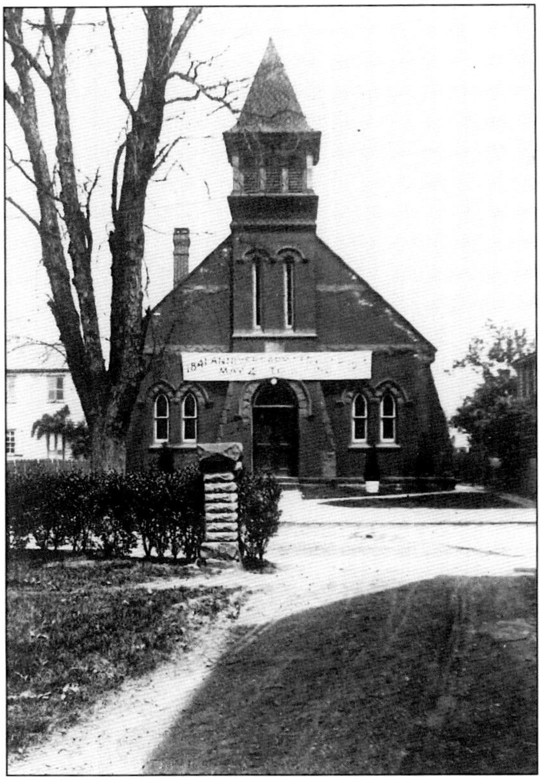

Built on Pennsylvania Avenue in 1854 as a Methodist church, this building was purchased by Morrisville's Baptist congregation in 1963 when the Methodists moved to a new, larger church at Taft and Maple Avenues.

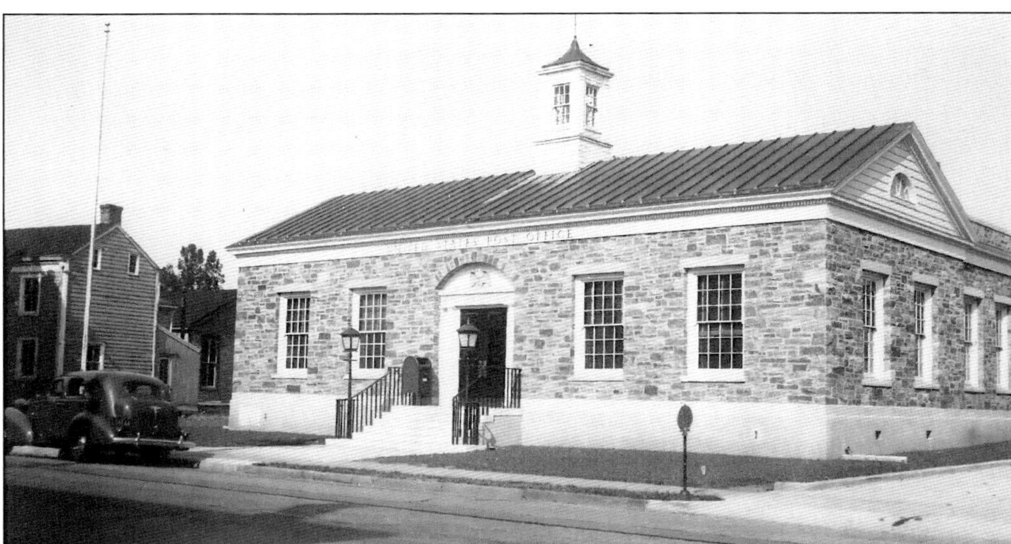

Morrisville's post office for years was situated on North Pennsylvania Avenue, a half block from the Bridge Street intersection. With a larger post office now in operation outside the borough on West Trenton Avenue, this building is now occupied by Garlits' printing business.

Seven

Water, Water Everywhere

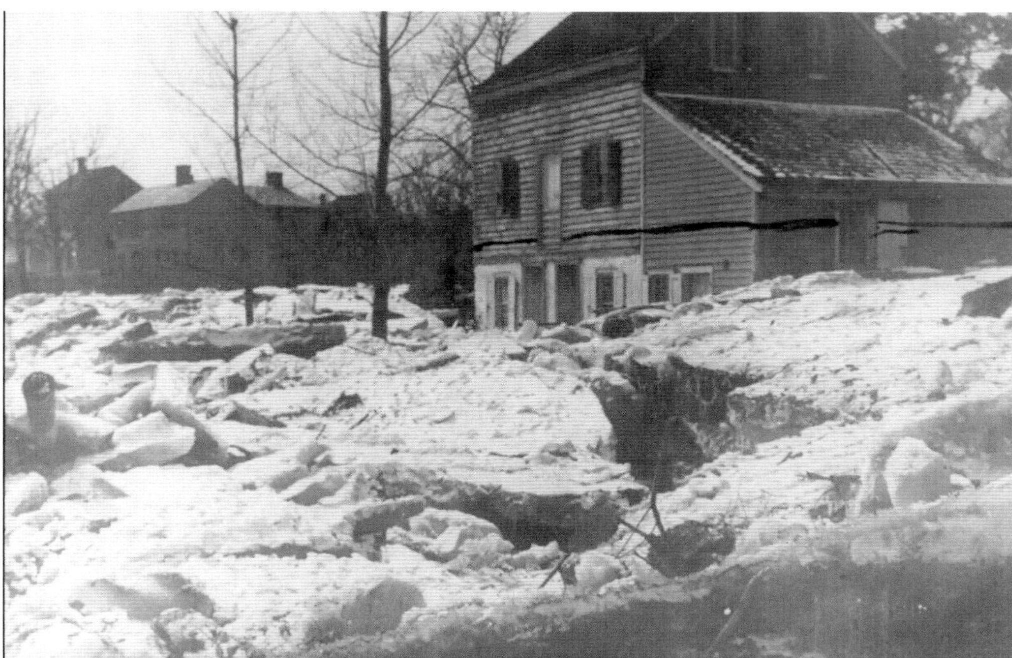

Starting with the flood in 1687 that carved out a fast-flowing stream used to provide water power for a series of mills, floods had major impacts on Morrisville in past years. During cold winters, ice would pile up in the Delaware and then, as it began to thaw, would be pushed with high water onto the land bordering the river. The picture shows the high water mark of a 1904 flood, with ice piled up to the home where Thomas Stockham was born in 1883.

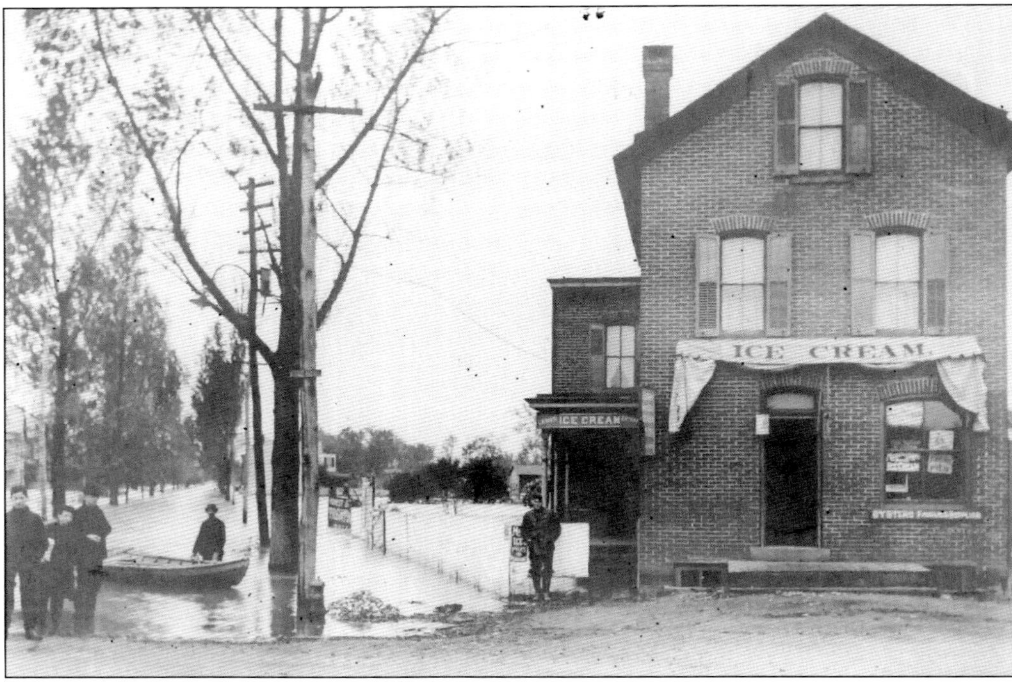

Morrisville's island—now protected by a dike—was flooded in 1903, boats being used as the only practical way to travel on Central Avenue.

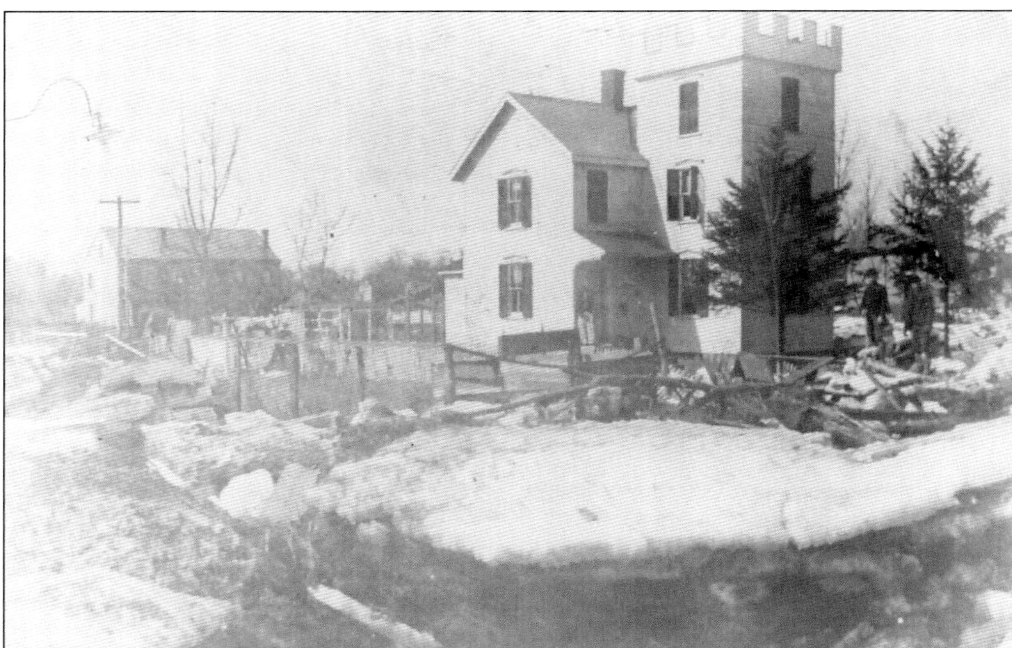

Another view of flooded Central Avenue shows water and ice encroaching on the home of Lillian Rickey Morris.

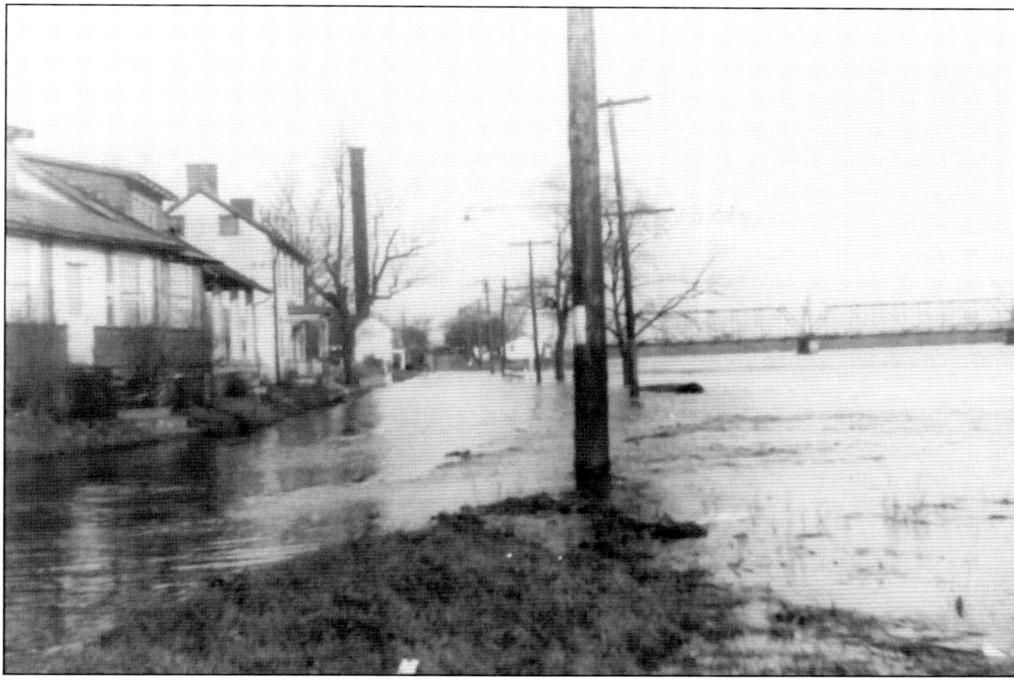

This picture was taken during a 1936 flood, looking north on Delmorr Avenue, toward the Calhoun Street Bridge. These homes are now protected by a dike that begins at the high point where Trenton Avenue approaches the bridge.

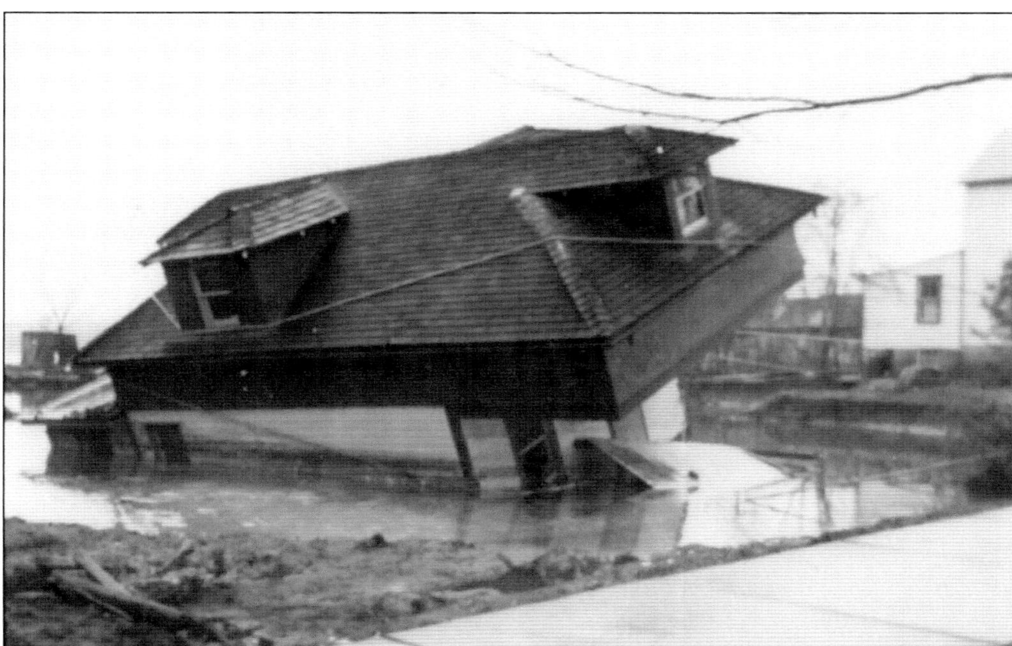

Flooding was severe on March 19, 1936—so severe that houses were lifted from their foundations.

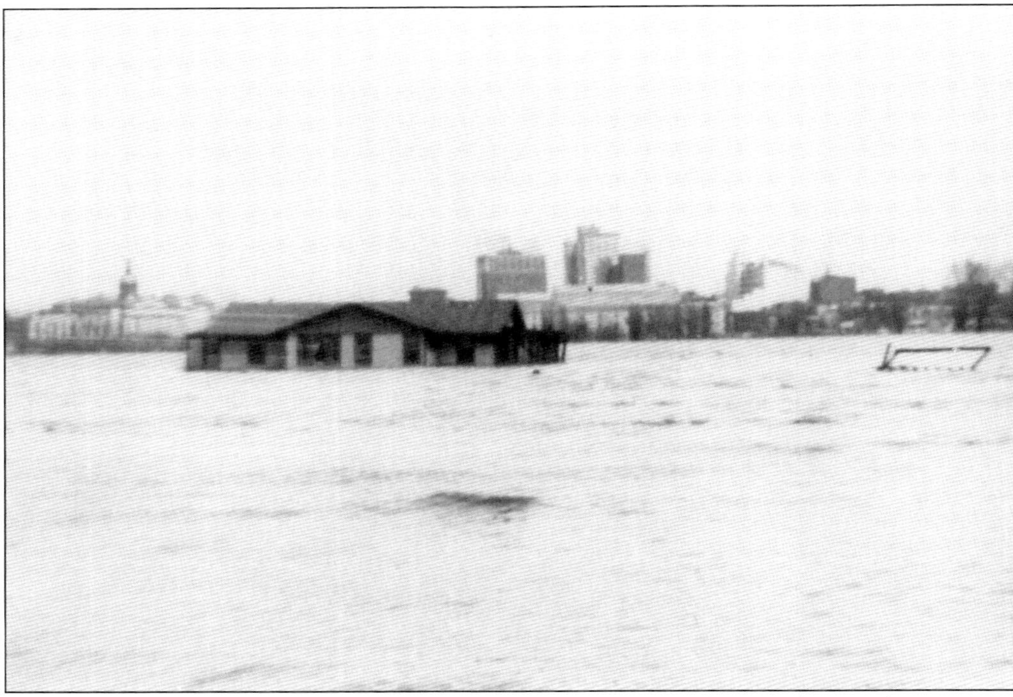

In the 1936 flood one home literally floated away from Morrisville, winding up downriver on the opposite side of the Delaware at Bordentown, New Jersey.

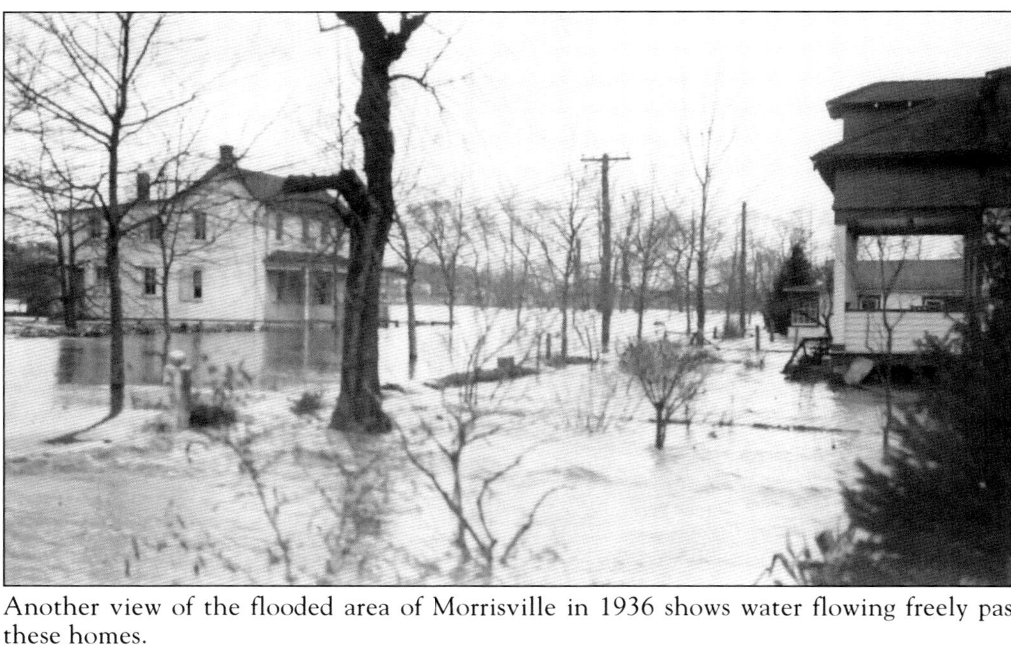

Another view of the flooded area of Morrisville in 1936 shows water flowing freely past these homes.

Eight

We Love a Parade

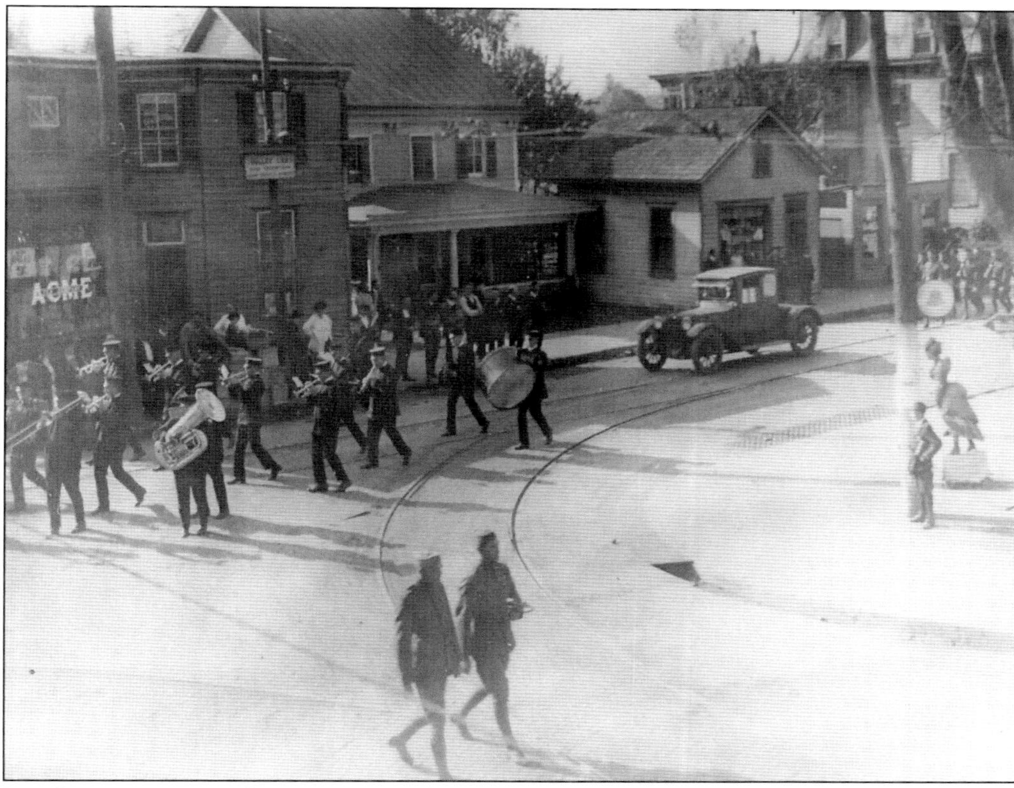

Parades in recent years have gotten smaller, but around the turn of the century and into the 1950s parades in Morrisville were events with a capital E. This photograph shows a parade making the turn from Pennsylvania Avenue to Bridge Street with the trolley tracks still in place.

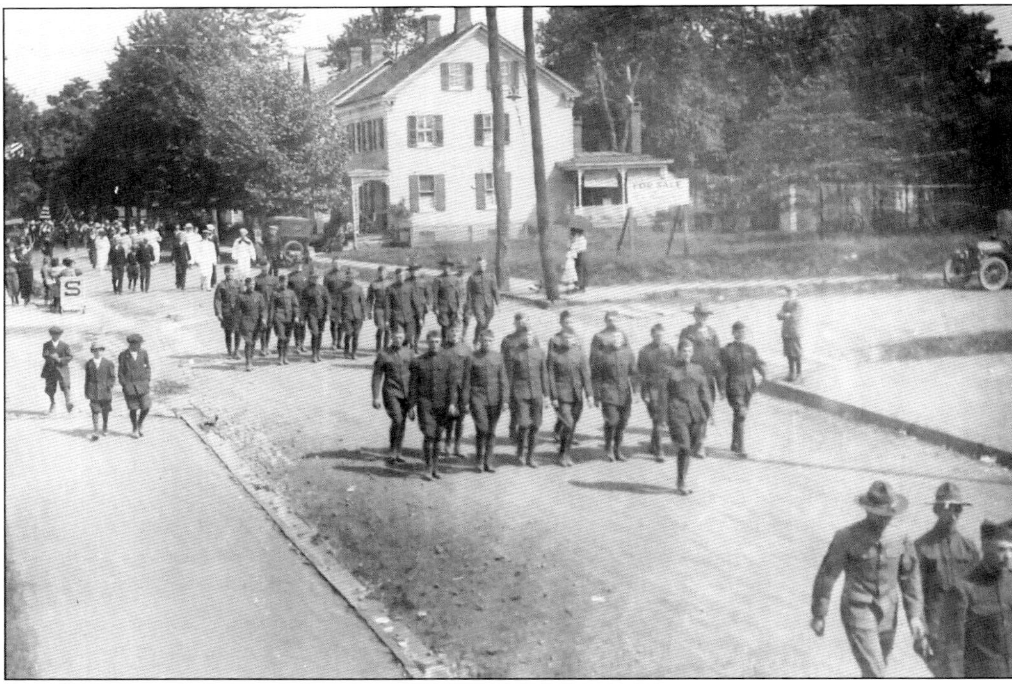

After World War I ex-servicemen proudly donned their uniforms and marched on Memorial Day. This group was photographed marching down Washington Street past Green Street and headed under the railroad bridge.

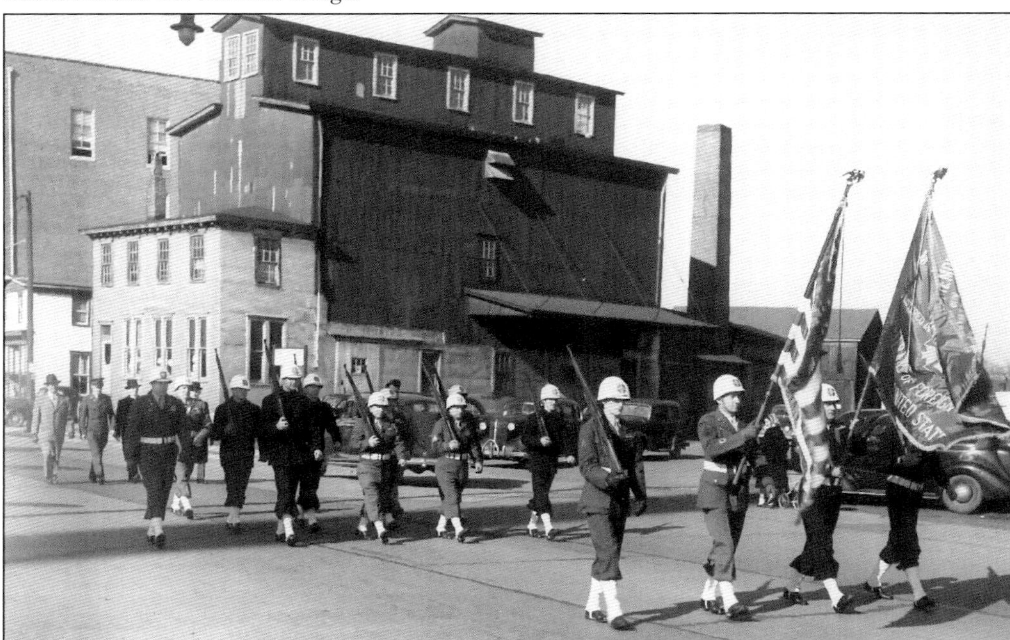

World War II soldiers and sailors are pictured marching as members of the Morrisville Veterans of Foreign Wars post in Morrisville. As the photograph was snapped they were on South Pennsylvania Avenue, passing the easily recognized Howell-Johnson feed mill.

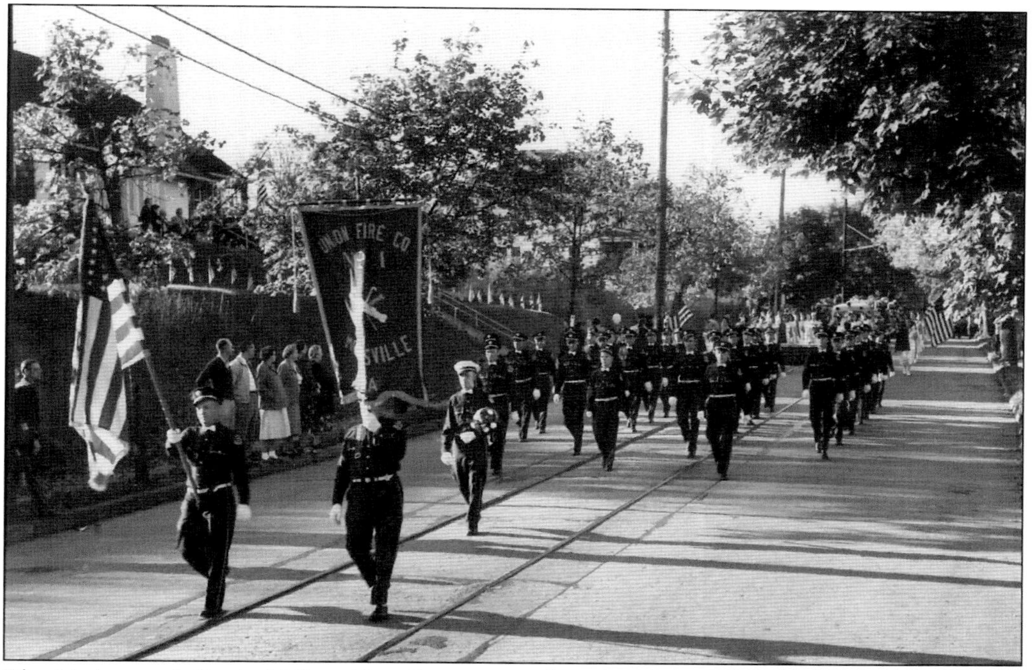

The Union and Capitol View Fire Companies always make a good showing in Morrisville parades. This is the Union Fire Company en route down North Pennsylvania Avenue.

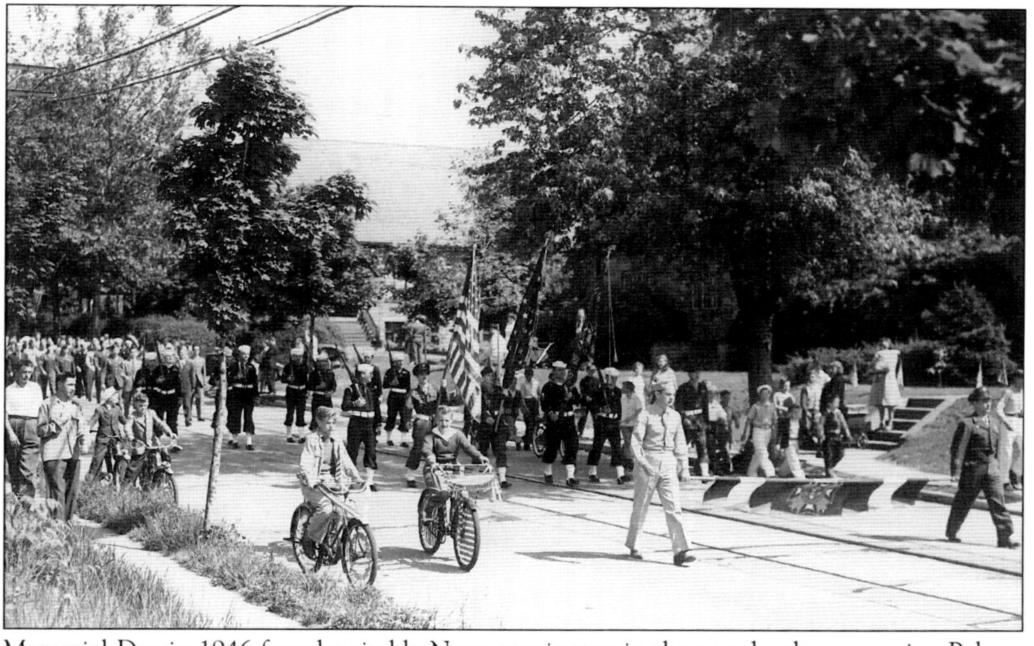

Memorial Day in 1946 found a sizable Navy contingent in the parade, shown passing Palmer Avenue on North Pennsylvania. The bicycles the boys are riding have the wheels decorated with red, white, and blue paper and also have streamers on the handlebars. Is anything more nostalgic than a Memorial Day parade on a bright, sunny day in a small Pennsylvania town at the end of World War II with most—but sadly not all—of the servicemen returning home?

Acknowledgments

Much of the information and most of the pictures in this book came from people who are no longer living. James E. Wood, history teacher, school administrator, and dedicated historian, turned over his voluminous files and collection of pictures to Historic Morrisville Society and I have used his material extensively. Mabel Whittaker, who shared her ninety-five-year memories of Morrisville with George Lebegern and me, turned over to Historic Morrisville Society the pictures of early Morrisville taken by her grandfather, William Pope. Millard Nice, the longtime Morrisville postman, kept detailed scrapbooks of every news item on Morrisville over a span of a half-century; his son Cliff turned over these fascinating local records to Historic Morrisville Society. Others, very much alive, who helped by lending pictures and providing information include Pat Brofman and Louisa Woodward, Jack Burgess, Dick Burns, Earl Davis, Al Johnson, Betty Lukens Sines, and Ron Stockham. George Lebegern, former head of the history department in the Pennsbury schools, and I have been sharing thoughts about history since first grade and we both were privileged to have Jim Wood as a teacher; George reviewed copy and pictures with me. My wife, Jane, pitched in and helped me wrap up the layout when I despaired of ever getting the book finished. I also appreciate the cooperation of Arthur E. Mayhew, publisher of the *Bucks County Courier Times*; Brian S. Malone, editor of *The Times*, Trenton, New Jersey; and Jeff Werner, editor of *The Yardley News*, who kindly granted permission to use photographs that had previously appeared in their newspapers. The picture of the Morris-Moreau home in Chapter One is adapted from a painting by Baroness Hyde de Neuville, a friend of General Moreau, that was reproduced in the M.& M. *Collection of American Water Colors & Drawings*, Museum of Fine Arts, Boston, 1962.

James A. Murray